BEHIND THE HEADLINES

"India Backs Red Proposals"

"New Arab-Israel Violence"

"Burma Spurns U.S. Loan"

——Amid these disturbing front-page symptoms of world unrest, this book by a leading foreign affairs expert gives timely insight into increasing tensions and anti-American sentiment by analyzing the beliefs and emotions ruling the hearts of Russians, Asians, Latin Americans, and other non-Western peoples.

Dr. Vera Micheles Dean, in colorful historical summaries of these nations' cultural and political developments, shows how such traditions as India's castes, Muslim infidel hatred, and oriental "face" obsessions pose vital problems for the whole world. She explains how long humiliation as a second-class power now helps Russia in claiming kinship with Asian problems. In dramatic contrasts, the book points up the huge modernizing task faced by many nations and examines technological ways to speed up the process. And with profound understanding, it strikes to the heart of East-West conflict—the new nationalism and "revolutions of rising expectations" in envious, poor, but fiercely proud countries.

Supplemented with two maps and valuable reading lists, this thorough, thought-provoking study is an essential to understanding the 1,500,000,000 human beings whose actions may decide the world's destiny.

THE NATURE OF
The Non-Western World

by

Vera Micheles Dean

A MENTOR BOOK
Published by THE NEW AMERICAN LIBRARY

Published as a MENTOR BOOK

FIRST PRINTING, MARCH, 1957

Cover photograph by Mark Riboud, Magnum Photos.

Library of Congress Catalog Card No. 57-8030

MENTOR BOOKS are published by
The New American Library of World Literature, Inc.
501 Madison Avenue, New York 22, New York

PRINTED IN THE UNITED STATES OF AMERICA

Acknowledgments

I am indebted to Warren S. Hunsberger, Haloid Professsor of International Economics at the University of Rochester, for the chapters on Japan and Latin America; to Harry J. Benda, Assistant Professor of History at that University, for the chapters on China and Southeast Asia; and to Vernon McKay, Professor of African Studies at The Johns Hopkins University, for the chapter on Africa.

I would also like to express my appreciation to *The New York Times Magazine* and *The Christian Century*, where I first presented several of the ideas developed in this book.

For the concept and execution of the book, and for such errors as it may contain, I am, of course, solely responsible.

Vera Micheles Dean

New York City,
February 1, 1957.

To President Cornelis W. de Kiewiet
and the faculty and students of
The University of Rochester
whose interest and cooperation
made this book possible

Contents

Introduction: The Land of Bandungia 13
1. Many Centuries in One 17
2. Russia: Non-Western Communism 26
3. Middle East: Islam versus Westernism
Turkey—Egypt—Israel 48
4. India and Pakistan: Anglo-Asian Synthesis 71
5. China: Confucius and the Commissars 92
6. Japan: Asian Westernism 113
7. Southeast Asia: Non-Western Pluralism in Transition 131
8. Africa: The Impact of the West 154
9. Latin America: Where Westernism Stopped 173
10. Telescoped Revolutions
Colonialism—Democracy—Communism Nationalism 193
11. Retooling for the Future 212
Political Problems—Economic Problems—Population and Food—Can Science Cancel Time?—Land versus Industry—Who Pays for What?
12. West and Non-West: The Heart of the Matter 254
Selected Readings 269
Index 277

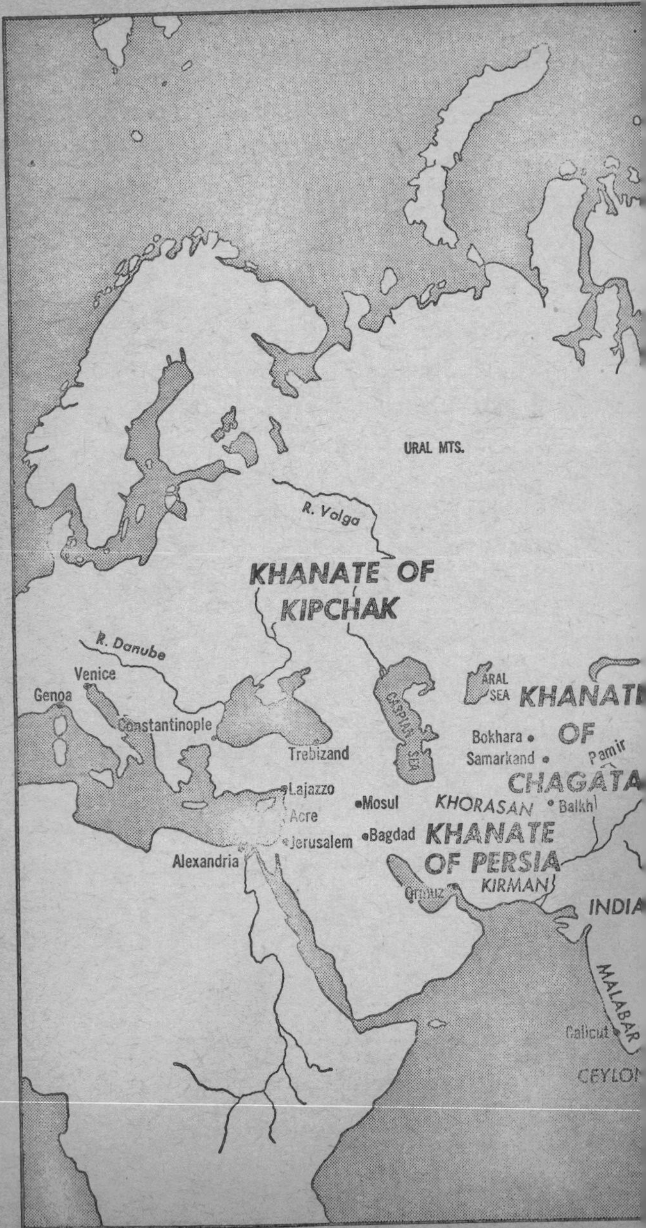
URAL MTS.
R. Volga
KHANATE OF KIPCHAK
R. Danube
Venice
Genoa
Constantinople
Trebizand
ARAL SEA
CASPIAN SEA
KHANAT
OF
CHAGATA
Bokhara
Samarkand
Pamir
Lajazzo
Acre
Jerusalem
Alexandria
Mosul
Bagdad
KHORASAN
Balkh
KHANATE OF PERSIA
KIRMAN
INDIA
MALABAR
Calicut
CEYLON

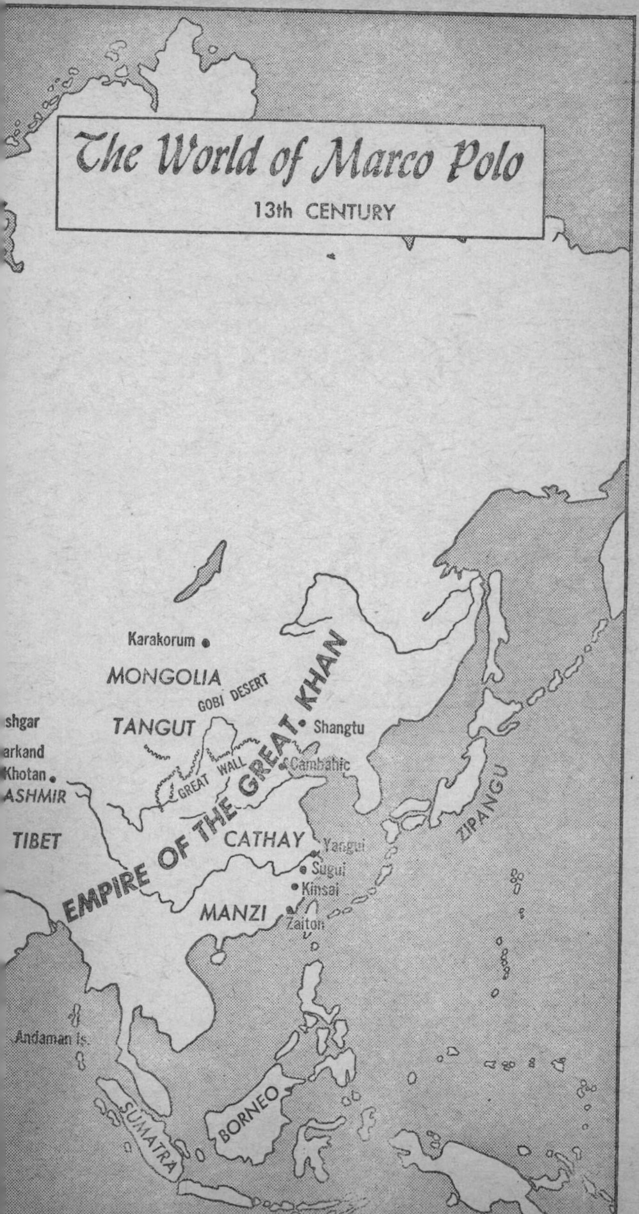
The World of Marco Polo
13th CENTURY
Karakorum
MONGOLIA
GOBI DESERT
TANGUT
EMPIRE OF THE GREAT KHAN
Shangtu
Cambaluc
GREAT WALL
shgar
arkand
Khotan
ASHMIR
TIBET
CATHAY
Yangui
Sugui
Kinsai
MANZI
Zaiton
ZIPANGU
Andaman Is.
SUMATRA
BORNEO

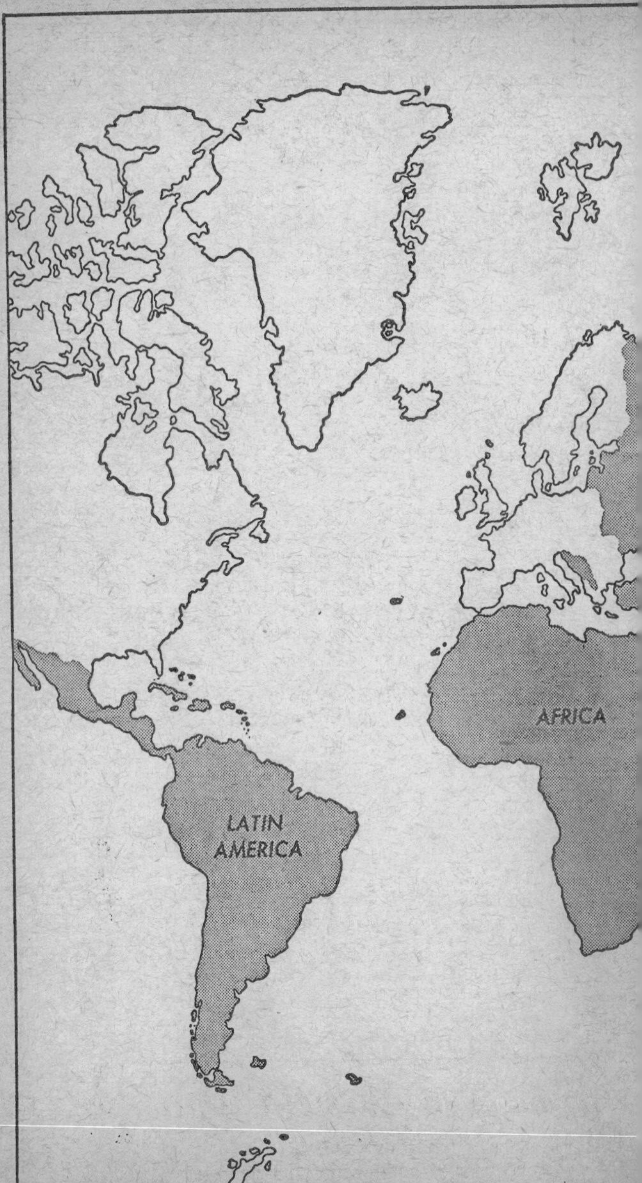
LATIN
AMERICA
AFRICA

U.S.S.R.
CHINA
JAPAN
INDIA
SOUTHEAST ASIA
The Non-Western World
20th CENTURY

Time present and time past
Are both perhaps present in time future,
And time future contained in time past.
If all time is eternally present
All time is unredeemable.

—T. S. Eliot, "Burnt Norton"

How could I span a gap of a thousand years—a millennium in a day? These people on the junk could be said to be living in the era between Charlemagne and William the Conqueror, in the time of serfs and villeins, before the Crusades, before Western printing and gunpowder, long, long before Chaucer and Giotto and Thomas Aquinas and Dante. And they were satisfied (or so I thought) to exist in Dark Ages, while I lived in a time of enlightenment and was not satisfied.

—John Hersey, *A Single Pebble*

INTRODUCTION

The Land of Bandungía

In the summer of 1954, Venice, celebrating the seven hundredth anniversary of the adventurous journeys of one of its most famous citizens, Messer Marco Polo, staged an exhibit of maps used in his times. The most striking feature of these maps, as might have been expected, was the contrast between the detailed contouring and nomenclature of the then known world of Europe, from the Atlantic to the Mediterranean, and the vast empty spaces, barely outlined and scantily annotated by mapmakers, stretching within the confines of Asia, the Middle East, Africa, and the Western Hemisphere. Here, for the most part, was *terra incognita*—lands yet to be discovered, demarcated, conquered, developed, brought within the range of knowledge and understanding of the West.

The scribe of *The Travels of Marco Polo*, a book brimming over with the thirteenth-century man's avid curiosity about the universe, adjures his readers: "Ye emperors, dukes, marquises, earls and knights, all other people desirous of knowing the diversities of races of mankind, as well as the diversities of kingdoms, provinces, and regions of all parts of the East, read through this book, and ye will find in it the greatest and most marvelous characteristics of the peoples especially of Armenia, Persia, India, and Turkey, as they are severally related in the present work by Marco Polo, a wise and learned citizen of Venice, who states distinctly what things he saw and what things he heard from others. For this book will be a truthful one. It must be known, then, that from the creation of Adam to the present day, no man, whether Pagan or Saracen, or Christian, or other, of whatever progeny or generation he may have been, ever saw or inquired into so many and such great things as Marco Polo above mentioned."

Since the great Venetian's day men and women of the West have journeyed far and wide through the spaces that were left blank or ill-defined on the maps of the thirteenth century. Military conquerors and benevolent administrators, merchants and missionaries, scholars and Point Four technicians have been enthralled by the marvels of non-Western civilizations, moved by the hardships of their multitudinous populations, and stirred to action in Asia, the Middle East, Africa, and Latin America either in the interests of their own homelands or in the interests of world-wide human welfare.

Yet in spite of the extensive and constantly growing first-hand knowledge accumulated by the West about the non-West, events in Jordan or Egypt, in Guatemala or Kenya, still frequently come as a surprise to Westerners. It is as if those of us who have been brought up within the orbit of Western civilization—from the Atlantic to the Mediterranean—much as we may know about politics and economics, geography and anthropology, have not yet discovered and explored the inner recesses of the non-Western mind, and are still groping for genuine understanding. We often think of the non-West as an undifferentiated bloc of masses of people. We do not always see the rich diversity of their many faiths, their diverse traditions, their contrasting cultures.

Here is the *terra incognita* of the twentieth century, which is yet to be carefully surveyed and properly mapped by the West. Here is the land of which we know so little—the land that we might call Bandungia, in honor of the first Afro-Asian conference in history held at Bandung, in Indonesia, in April, 1955. For this historic occasion, to which no white nations, including Russia, were invited, brought together twenty-nine nations of Asia and Africa with about 56 per cent of the world's population.

This land of Bandungia is peripatetic. It is found in Asia, in Africa, in the Middle East, in Latin America—and something like it existed in eastern Europe before 1939, and can still be seen in some parts of it today.

Its diverse people can look back to a long history, with distinctive traditions, culture, and way of life. Their early development, in many respects, was similar to that of the Western nations at a comparable stage: feudalism, primitive agriculture, little or no industry, authoritarian governments, powerful religious organizations wielding political influence, sharp cleavages between a small ruling group on top and a majority of the population at the bottom living in poverty on the land, often in thrall to landowners and moneylenders, and a tiny or nonexistent middle class of merchants, bankers, and professional men.

For a variety of reasons, recorded in history, this vast land stopped developing politically, economically, and socially around 1400, just about the time that the Western nations started on a period of extraordinary growth with the age of exploration and colonial expansion, the Renaissance, the Reformation, the English, French, and American revolutions, and the Industrial Revolution. As a result, Bandungia entered the twentieth century with institutions and practices not very different from those it had four or five centuries before.

Today Bandungia has either recently emerged from the colonial rule of a Western power or, if it had retained its independence in the period of colonialism, is trying to adjust itself to the nuclear age. Its government, even if there is a democratic constitution, is usually dominated by a strong leader who enjoys the confidence of his people and symbolizes their aspirations, having led either the independence movement against foreign domination or an internal revolution, or both. The majority of the people, sometimes up to 85 or 90 per cent, are illiterate; but, having become aware of technological, political, and social changes in the Western world, they are eager to embark on a "revolution of rising expectations," by peaceful means if possible. If, however, the expected change does not take place, minority extremist groups —most probably Communists, but possibly religious fanatics —may gain substantial influence.

The government of Bandungia, whatever its political philosophy, is aware of the need to carry out economic and social reforms, and prefers to expend the country's limited resources of money and technical skills on the tasks of developing the economy rather than on military defense. In the absence of a strong middle class which might devote its capital resources to the creation of private enterprise, the government usually finds it necessary to spark development programs through nationalization, state direction or control of the economy, and mobilization of internal resources for development purposes.

Since these resources are usually insufficient to effect the far-reaching changes necessary to bridge the gap of centuries, the government of Bandungia often seeks financial and technical assistance from more advanced nations, notably the United States, but recently also from the Soviet bloc. Because of its desire to maintain its new-found or traditional independence, Bandungia resists any conditions on the loan or grant of aid proposed by the advanced nations which might be regarded as a new form of imperialism. For the same reasons, Bandungia usually insists on adopting a position of noncommitment between the two great power blocs of the West and the Soviets, even if it favors the ideas and practices of democracy.

In its attempts to create a modern economy, Bandungia must at the same time try to solve the age-old problems of growing population, inadequate food resources, unemployment of the rising white-collar class, social and personal maladjustments brought about by the rapid transition of a society which must jump from the feudal age, or the eighteenth century, into the nuclear age. Above all, it must overcome the frustrations generated by the vacuum which develops when ancient faiths and ways of life disintegrate and have not yet been replaced by new forces of integration.

During this painful and dangerous transition period the people of Bandungia are apt to express what the West may regard as anti-Western views or act in a way that shocks the West—not because of hostility to one Western nation or another, or predilection for the Communist bloc, but because of envy and fear of the West mixed with a powerful desire to imitate the achievements which have made the West—and the U.S.S.R.—strong. This mixed feeling about the West makes Bandungia susceptible to Communist propaganda, but by no means indicates that it will accept communism at home if a workable alternative is made available.

The West must rediscover Bandungia—its spirit and ideas—as it once discovered its geography. And Bandungia must realize that it does not merely need to be developed technologically, but must also redevelop its ancient concepts and institutions for use in the modern world.

An enlightened Western policy toward Bandungia requires more than factual information. It requires sympathetic insight into the nature of the non-Western world—into the thoughts and feelings of the many peoples who constitute over half of the world's population, and whose decisions will profoundly affect the destiny of the West.

1

Many Centuries in One

Take a look at your newspaper any day in the year. It's a safe bet that you will run across some item reflecting what the King of Siam called "a puzzlement" about the pitiful inadequacies or sinister skulduggery of peoples who do not measure up to the standards of life or conduct of the United States midway in the twentieth century.

India, we are told, does not have enough protein in its diet. The Russians have far fewer television sets than the Americans. Turkey and Japan, which were believed to have acquired the habits of democracy, show signs of backsliding. The Latin American nations display a lamentable predilection for political dictatorship. Forced labor in Russia and *apartheid* —keeping black and white apart—in South Africa turn back the clock of modern humanitarianism. The slums of Calcutta shock the sensitive visitor. Women in Russia are allowed to do hard physical tasks. In a vast segment of the world, from New Delhi to Buenos Aires, private enterprise is, to use a British understatement, viewed with less than enthusiasm.

Anyone who has even glanced at elementary histories of western Europe and the United States must realize it was not magic, but centuries of travail and sacrifice, marked by a series of bloody wars and revolutions, that saw the peoples of the Atlantic community gradually move from the feudal society and manorial economy of the Middle Ages to industrialization, universal suffrage, separation of church and state (in the United States and France), scientific invention, enlightened social legislation, and the continuing expansion of intellectual inquiry.

But because by the clock and the calendar we are all living approximately at the same time around the globe, it is easy to assume that we are also all living in the same century. As a result, it is easy, and dangerous to make impossible demands on millions of our contemporaries by expecting those of them who now live in the neolithic age or in conditions of medieval feudalism, or in the pre-industrial era, to behave exactly like twentieth-century Western men and women. Then, when expectations fail to materialize, it is easier still to become disillusioned and to look around for scapegoats.

The harsh truth is that today—and this has been true since the beginning of industrialization—the inhabitants of the globe live in widely differing stages of development. Before the 1600's there were no divergences of a fundamental nature between the living standards, the cultural achievements, and the political theories of Henry VIII in England, Peter the Great in Russia, a wise Chinese emperor or, in India, the Hindu ruler Asoka or his Muslim counterpart Akbar. In fact, some of the nations of the East, now regarded as "backward," then seem to have displayed a greater spirit of tolerance than the "advanced" peoples of the West, and at least equal capacity for artistic creativeness as well as scientific inquiry and invention.

But with the coming of modern industry, the rapid development of science, the growth of towns, the rise of the middle class, and the emergence of the modern nation-state, the West forged rapidly into another era, while the rest of the world continued to live in an earlier time. The age of exploration opened new overseas horizons for the Western peoples and put within their reach the riches of the New World and of Asia.

As the ancient overland routes for commerce and ideas withered away, countries cut off from the experience of the peoples on the Atlantic seaboard suffered from arrested development. They either consciously sought isolation, like the Japanese in their island home or the Chinese behind their Great Wall, or found it impossible to escape colonial rule by Westerners who were far more interested—and at that time perhaps understandably so—in opportunities for trade and, later, for strategic advantage than in the welfare of native subjects.

It is not an accident that the areas of the world which have either proved highly susceptible to communism or have struggled to maintain a position of detachment between communism and Western democracy lie along the periphery of the Atlantic orbit—from Russia through the Middle East and Asia, from Africa to Latin America. For these areas remained largely untouched by the forces that shaped Western civilization as we know it today—the philosophy and drama of the Greek city states, the legal concepts of the Roman Empire, Catholic Christianity (as distinguished from that of Byzantium, which influenced Russia and the Balkan Slavs), the Reformation and the Renaissance, the Industrial Revolution, the French and American revolutions, and resulting changes that came with a torrential sweep in politics, in economics, in social progress, in science, in the arts, in the sum total of human relations.

How did these changes come about in the Western world? Can we learn something from the character of these changes that might help us to understand the twentieth-century problems of the non-Western peoples, and might provide them, as well as ourselves, with clues to future development? Is it possible to compare conditions of the West during the intensely creative five hundred years between 1450 and 1950 with those we see today in Asia, the Middle East, Africa, Latin America, and eastern Europe—or were some of these conditions peculiar to the Western peoples, and therefore impossible to duplicate in our own times? Or, from still another point of view, is it possible that new inventions, such as atomic energy and photosynthesis, aviation and desert cultivation, may enable the non-Western world to skip centuries and find undreamed-of answers to once unanswerable questions?

The transformation of the West over the past five hundred years was due to many interlocking factors. Of these the most significant, each of which affected all the others, were the decline of the manor economy, the growth of towns, the expansion of Europe overseas, the rise of national states, and the Industrial Revolution with its use of man-made energy to replace the energy of human muscles.

The decline of the manor economy, in which the manorial estate had provided a more or less self-sufficient subsistence for the serfs who were attached to the land and were obligated to serve their lord in pursuits of peace and war, was brought about by the development of commerce, which, in turn, accelerated the growth of towns. The increased use of money, resulting from trade between various parts of a given country, as well as between countries, broke down the self-sufficiency of the manor, which had rested on the use of products available within its confines, as well as the barter of its products with other manors. Land once developed by manorial lords was either gathered up into large estates, as in Britain or eastern

Germany, or else broken up into small holdings acquired by peasants who had once been serfs, as in western Germany and France.

At that time the populations of the Western nations were relatively small. In 1400 England had only 5 million people, and France 20 million. Under these conditions serfs who were forced off the land could find work in the growing industries of the towns, while the introduction of modern agricultural techniques made it possible to produce an increased amount of food with fewer hands.

This decline of the manor economy was delayed in the non-Western world for four to five hundred years. It was only in 1861 that Tsarist Russia proclaimed the emancipation of the serfs, who were promised the right to purchase land with the aid of the state; but by 1914 only one-third of the peasants had succeeded in acquiring land, and even then this was done largely through collective groups—known as *mir*—and not by individual proprietors, as in western Europe. Nor is the process of land redistribution completed today, as can be seen by the post–World War II concern with land reform from Indochina to Japan, from India to Guatemala, from Italy to Egypt. The harsh fact is that in contrast to the Western nations five hundred years ago, the non-Western countries today have vast populations—600 million in China, 200 million in Russia, 400 million in India, 23 million in Egypt. Work cannot be found rapidly for these millions in urban centers, where industry is still in its infancy; and at the same time, it is urgently necessary to keep on increasing food production so that the still growing populations can be fed even at marginal levels.

It is only in recent years that towns have begun to grow on a considerable scale in non-Western areas. In the West the peasants who flocked to the new industries found that they had exchanged one form of serfdom for another, that they had become enslaved to the machine instead of the feudal lord, and had to live under harsh conditions which have been grimly portrayed by novelists like Dickens and Hardy. Marx, when he studied them in England and Germany in mid-nineteenth century, said with Engels in *The Communist Manifesto* that "the workers have nothing to lose but their chains." Non-Western reformers, keenly aware that in our times such conditions foster unrest and revolt which can bring to power demagogues with a strong appeal to the proletariat—whether they are Communists who advocate the dictatorship of the proletariat, or Fascists who rally the *descamisados*—try to find a way of avoiding this particular phase of the West's development.

At the same time, in the West, the growth of towns brought with it the rise of the middle class of merchants, and bankers, and professional people. In contrast to the manor—or the village today in the non-Western world—with its limited number of handicraftsmen, the barber, tanner, shoemaker, tailor, maker of pots and pans—the towns fostered the rise of a social hierarchy, with the aristocracy and clergy at the top, the merchants, bankers, and professional people in the middle, and the factory workers at the bottom. As the middle class acquired position and influence, it encouraged creative ideas. From its ranks sprang men who were determined to destroy the restrictions of feudalism, and to take authority out of the hands of kings, aristocrats, and ecclesiastics. This they accomplished through revolutions in England and France, which cleared the way for the rise of modern democracy.

So far the middle class is still weak in most of the non-Western areas. It has not yet acquired the influence which would enable it to destroy the remnants of old regimes. The result is that when revolutions occur, they are often led either by military men—such as Perón in Argentina, Naguib and Nasser in Egypt—or by those who come from the ranks of the workers or make their fortunes by appealing to the workers over the heads of the aristocrats and the middle class. Because of the lack or meagerness of the middle class, which in the Western world served to cushion political and social shocks, changes in non-Western areas are more fierce, and involve prolonged struggles for power, often marked by great cruelty and efforts to stamp out opposing ideas.

It is not an accident that Russia has been more closely associated in this century with the peoples east of the Oder than with those of the West. Russia, too, for the most part, belongs historically to that sector of the world which has had only indirect, and often unhappy, contacts with the "advanced" nations. It is for this very reason, and not because of any peculiar spell that the Kremlin has been able to cast, that Russia has had an impact on what we call the underdeveloped or nonindustrialized areas. As it moved toward modernization, it would have had influence even without benefit of communism.

For it is not communism as an ideology, or the Russian system established by Stalin and his associates, that impressed people in Asia, Africa, Latin America, and the Middle East.

It was, instead, the fact, made manifest every day, that a nation which had lagged a hundred or more years behind the West has succeeded, haltingly and at great sacrifice of men and materials, in fulfilling Stalin's injunction that the U.S.S.R. must "catch up with" and, he added, overtake the "capitalist" world.

To a Westerner Russia's living standards and way of life understandably appear short not only on ordinary necessities but also on human values. The peasant of Afghanistan or Iran, on the other hand, although he does not want to have a dictatorship like that of Moscow, wonders why he cannot have electric lights such as he sees twinkling across the border in Russia. The Indian has no ambition to match the military power of the U.S.S.R., but he is interested to know that Russian scientists have mastered the secrets of atomic energy for peacetime development.

In short, peoples who are still living all the way along the arduous route from the age of bronze weapons to the nineteenth century wonder whether Russia's experience, so close in time to their own, may not offer them a short cut for the jump they feel they must make from their own age into the nuclear age. And if Communist China should succeed in effecting this historic transition within a relatively short period of time, its experience will have an even greater impact on the non-Western world.

Unlike Russia, which at least has geographic links with Europe and a white population that has been exposed over the centuries, however remotely, to Western ideas, China is non-Western. Other peoples outside the Atlantic orbit will say to themselves, "What the Chinese can do, we can do," and some may even say, as India does, "We can do it better, with no resort to force and violence."

Given the far-reaching impression created by Russia and, more recently, China, we should carefully weigh the value of preaching today to non-Western peoples the advantages of political democracy and private enterprise. Desirable as these assets may seem to them, and particularly to their small elites who have studied and lived in the West, our concepts and practices simply do not yet correspond to their actual experience and therefore must remain alien to them, at least until such time as they, in turn, achieve the conditions which produced Western democratic institutions and a competitive economy.

Universal suffrage would have sounded ludicrous to the

feudal barons and, later, the absolute monarchs of Western Europe. Louis XIV, *"L'état, c'est moi,"* is much closer to the current experience of Russia and China, of Egypt and Japan, than he is to Churchill or Eisenhower. The state-controlled or state-regulated economies of non-Western nations need not seem strange to those who are familiar with the mercantilist economy of Colbert. Working conditions in Calcutta should be understandable to anyone who has studied the horrors of the early Industrial Revolution in England's Lancashire mills.

Individualism and private enterprise have been regarded by the West as hallmarks of personal freedom, although in the twentieth century they have been reconciled, in a variety of ways, with the welfare and security requirements of the modern state. Yet in non-Western lands the individual, in the past, found his greatest fulfillment through family ties, and with his caste, or his religious community—this was particularly true of Islam. While he did not by any means always shun material advancement and even great wealth, his religion—Hinduism or Buddhism, Islam or Confucianism—taught him that the highest values of life were non-material, that ethical achievements were superior to the accumulation of power or riches, and that man is but a pilgrim on the road of worldly life, who must be ever ready to divest himself of mortal goods and aspirations.

Forced labor is reprehensible under any regime, but it may help to orient ourselves in the many centuries amid which we live to recall that child labor and slavery were not regarded as shocking until a century ago in Britain, then the most advanced nation of western Europe. Or that as late as this century the colonial powers, whose contributions to democratic thought and practice we rightly admire, thought it perfectly proper that colonial natives should work under conditions we now consider intolerable.

It is pertinent to ask, subversive as it may seem, whether the tragic fate of Cardinal Mindzenty or Archbishop Stepinac would have greatly disturbed nations and religious organizations we now consider advanced at the time they thought nothing of beheading Sir Thomas More or subjecting alleged infidels to the tortures of the Inquisition.

If the barrier between Western and non-Western peoples is to be broken down, both sides must perform an act of imagination. Instead of urging the neolithic man of Central Africa, or the fanatically religious nomad of Arab lands, or the pre-industrial Chinese or Latin-American to become like ourselves, Westerners must strive to see the contemporary world through his eyes.

Instead of pressing on him a tractor which may erode his soil already impoverished by centuries of hard use and which cannot be serviced for lack of parts and skilled mechanics, let us look at his plow, no matter how ancient, and discover whether it can be improved by slight alterations.

Instead of expecting him to be thoroughly versed in the ideas of Thomas Jefferson or Abraham Lincoln—a happy state not yet achieved by every literate American—let us inquire who among his people has uttered thoughts which he has found a source of inspiration over the ages.

We shall thereby strengthen the roots of his past, instead of tearing them out. What is more, we shall also enrich our own, hitherto parochial, outlook, which until recently tended to assume that all wisdom flowed from the West.

Instead of insisting that every people, irrespective of its historical experience, must adopt the institutions we define as democratic, or else be labeled totalitarian, let us study the political way of life of others. Let us seek to identify those elements in their history which may gradually bring about improvements in human relations, even if this has to be done in the first instance and perhaps over a long period of years by governments which may only gradually shed the characteristics of authoritarianism. After all, seven centuries elapsed between Magna Charta and the bipartisan cooperation of British Conservatives and Laborites.

Let us not bemoan what we consider the obsoleteness of nationalism in countries which but recently achieved national consciousness or even independence. Let us recall, instead, the powerful nationalist sentiment which welded the modern states of Europe and the New World and which even today promptly rises to the surface in the West at the first sign of external intervention, whether it be the threat of Nazi or Communist conquest, or an attempt to have the United Nations inquire into colonial problems such as Cyprus, Indochina, or West New Guinea.

There is something humbling, as well as inspiring, for Westerners and non-Westerners alike to discover that the irrigation systems of Arab lands in Africa, silted over by sand, can be put to immediate modern use as soon as they have been restored to their original condition; that there are sound reasons for the seemingly inefficient agricultural methods of India and Japan; that Buddhism and Hinduism, Confucianism and Islam, are as lofty in their conception of man and his relation to the universe as Judaism and Christianity; that the political ideas of ancient rulers of Asia are startlingly relevant to our own times; and that elaborate and effective systems of administration existed in China and India when the Western nations were still struggling to achieve organized form.

For Westerners this should be reassuring. For we need not spend astronomical sums of dollars over incalculable eons of time to remake every people in our own image. What we need to do is to share our technical knowledge, our skills, and our managerial capacity in such a way as to ease the transition of widely diverse peoples who have their own ideas of how they want to live, from whatever century they may find themselves in today into our own. And as we study the various non-Western areas we may come to realize that this need not be either the American century or the Communist century, but, given wisdom on our part, could be the century of Everyman.

2

Russia: Non-Western Communism

There has been much confusion in the West's judgments of the U.S.S.R. and communism because of the tendency to think of Russia as a Western nation which, under the rule of dictatorial Communists, abandoned the Western fold, selling out its birthright of political democracy and private enterprise for the mess of pottage represented by a totalitarian society and a state-controlled economy.

Of all the assumptions made about Russia in the nearly forty years that have elapsed since the Bolshevik revolution of November, 1917, none has proved more persistent than the conviction that the Russian people were molded by the same forces and inherited the same traditions as those which shaped Western civilization, and that the Russian Communists have betrayed their country's past.

Yet this interpretation is far from the actual facts of Russia's development during more than a thousand years of history. It is true that, geographically, Russia is a part of Europe, and in this sense also of the West, but this has not of itself made it a European, and even less a Western, country—far less than Germany, which, although clearly a part of Western Europe, did not, during the Nazi era, show itself imbued with the ideas and practices of Western civilization. Russia spans two continents, Europe and Asia, and inextricably forms part of both worlds—Western and non-Western. And not only does it geographically belong to two worlds, but its population, too, is a mixture of Europeans and Asians. Of its 200 million inhabitants in 1956, approximately 156 million were white Europeans—Great Russians, White Russians, and Little Russians or Ukrainians—who have been exposed in some degree to Western influence (although before 1917 this was true only of a tiny minority of the aristocracy and the newly emerging middle class); and 44 million were Asians—Tartars, Bashkirs, Uzbeks, and so on—who even today are as remote from Western traditions as the peoples of China or Indonesia.

This vast Eurasian empire stretching from the Vistula to the Pacific, from the Barents Sea to the borders of India and Afghanistan, "gathered" for the most part by the Tsars, has been developed since 1917 by Russian leaders—not by foreign conquerors. These leaders, however, were all inspired, in the first instance, by the ideas of two Western political and economic thinkers, Karl Marx and Friedrich Engels. In this sense, it can be said that the Russian Communists, who in the West are regarded as having betrayed Russia's presumed Western past and plunged it into reaction, were actually its most advanced, if also most ruthless, Westernizers. In the Marxist analysis of the process and effects of early industrialization in England and Germany during the 1860's the Russian Communists, coming on the scene thirty or more years later, found striking similarities with the situation they knew in Tsarist Russia, which was then reaching the stage of development of the Western nations of Marx's time or even earlier.

But the moment the Communists established their rule over Russia, they began to adapt Marxist ideas to the practical conditions of a backward agrarian country. Marx, who wrote about nations where the Industrial Revolution had been superimposed on a relatively developed agriculture, had offered no significant prescriptions. Thus the Russian Communists in effect created a non-Western form of communism, built within the framework of Russia's traditional political authoritarianism, which had persisted into the first decade of the twentieth century—an authoritarianism profoundly different from the bourgeois democracy Marx was familiar with in the western Europe of his day.

Both Russia's geographical position in Asia and its adaptation of Marxism to non-Western conditions have proved a great asset to the Russians in world affairs, giving them an insight into the processes of thought and the needs of Asians which are not readily available to the British, or French, or Americans. Since 1917 this insight has facilitated Moscow's plans for Communist propaganda and infiltration in the non-West. In the current era of "competitive coexistence" it may also facilitate the economic and technological cooperation of the Soviet bloc with non-Western nations. Moreover, the fact that Russia is an Asian as well as a European power creates a common denominator between Russians and Asians which serves to allay the doubts and anxieties the non-Communist leaders of Asia may feel about the concepts and tactics of Russian Communists. Asians and other non-Westerners find in Russia what might be called "association by familiarity." For example, when former Premier U Nu of Burma, on his visit to the U.S.S.R. in 1955, said that what he saw of Russian Central Asia reminded him of his own country, and of Asia in general, he mentioned the affinity which has made it possible for the Soviet government to present itself in Asia not as an enemy but as a partner of the Asians and as their champion in the struggle against remnants of Western colonialism.

It can be, and has been, convincingly argued that the Russians have no right to denounce the Western colonial powers when they themselves have dominated not only the once free nations of eastern Europe described as Russia's "satellites," but from Moscow rule millions of non-Russians in central Asia and the Far East. This argument, however, so far as it applies to the Asian peoples of the U.S.S.R., is blunted by the character of the Soviet Union. In that Union peoples who would otherwise be properly called "colonial" form an integral part of a federation of 200 million citizens—not only geographically, but politically and economically as well. It is as if the inhabitants, let us say, of Nigeria and Kenya lived side by side with the English, Welsh, and Scots in a single state, instead of being separated from the "mother country" by thousands of miles of sea and land and profound differences in political, economic, and social conditions.

Whether, if this were the case, the British would find it possible to apply their methods of advanced democracy to so mixed a population must remain one of history's interesting questions. We do know, however, that when the French in an effort to demonstrate that Algeria, with a population of 8,500,000 Arabs of Muslim faith and over a million French settlers, is an integral part of France and not a colony—attempted to integrate this territory of North Africa into the administrative structure of mainland France, leaders like Pierre Mendès-France and Guy Mollet soon recognized that the policy of integration was unworkable. For the French were not prepared to treat the Arabs on the same basis as Frenchmen, and feared that Algeria's parliamentary representation in Paris might make it possible for Arabs to decide the future of France itself. And Britain, too, has found it difficult to accept the prospect that inhabitants of crown colonies such as

Malta and Cyprus might be represented in London's "Mother of Parliaments."

It can, of course, be further argued that the peoples of central Asia are not free in the Western sense of the word. This is true. However—and this is a fact of great significance to present or former colonial peoples—they are for the most part treated on a basis of equality with other inhabitants of the Soviet Union. Ruthless and undemocratic as this treatment understandably looks to Westerners, the important point is that it is, by and large, the same treatment as that meted by the Soviet dictatorship to its non-Asian population.

Although the U.S.S.R. is a vast land empire, it does not enjoy the geographic and strategic advantages of the United States, a continent which fronts on two oceans and is not exposed to overland attack from its neighbors to north and south. By contrast the U.S.S.R. is a landlocked continent, barred from access to the high seas by its territorial configuration and its shortage of ice-free ports. Such warm-water ports as it possesses open on straits or gulfs or closed seas—the Gulf of Finland, the Black Sea—whose entrances and exits are controlled by other, and in the past often hostile, countries, as in the Baltic, where the Russians have on many occasions in their history fought Teutons, Swedes, and Poles, or in the Black Sea, where the Russians have fought thirteen wars with the Turks, backed in modern times by the British, for control of the Straits of the Dardanelles.

In this latter objective the Russians have thus far failed, in spite of the World War I pledge they obtained from their Western allies that control of the Dardanelles would be Tsarist Russia's reward for its wartime efforts—a pledge which the Allies, in 1919, considered to have been canceled by the rise to power of the Communists, who had taken Russia out of the war. In 1955 and 1956, however, it began to look as if Russia might outflank the Dardanelles by a bold move into the Middle East, where, through the Soviet bloc's arms aid to Egypt, it could obtain access to the Suez Canal and thus the exit it had sought for centuries into the eastern Mediterranean. Except for this development, the U.S.S.R., successor of the Tsarist Empire, remains bottled up both in Europe so far as direct outlets to the North and South Atlantic are concerned and in Asia, where it has only indirect access to warm waters.

Contained in Europe for two centuries by the British—"containment" of Russia, new to Americans, has long been practiced from London—the Russians turned eastward in the seventeenth century. But even on reaching the Pacific the Russians did not find any ice-free outlets, since their principal port in Asia, Vladivostók, was too far north to escape the grip of ice. Thus frustrated, the Russians moved southward down the Pacific coast. After the Sino-Japanese war of 1894-95 in which Japan defeated China, Tsarist Russia, in return for aid to the Chinese obtained a long-term lease on the ice-free harbors of Port Arthur and Dairen, which it lost a decade later to Japan as a result of its defeat in the Russo-Japanese war of 1904-5, but recovered from Nationalist China in 1945 and is now in the process of returning to Peiping. It also obtained a foothold in Korea, where it established a sphere of influence in the north while Japan obtained a sphere in the south, but surrendered its portion to the Japanese in 1910 in return for Tokyo's recognition of Russia's special right in Manchuria and Outer Mongolia.

In the past Russia has been strategically weak because it has no natural safeguards against invasion either from overland by Germany (and, in 1919, also by the Poles under Marshal Pilsudski) or from overseas by Japan. No mountains such as the Alps, Pyrenees, or Himalayas guard Russia in the west; and from the east, Russian territory has been invaded by the Tartars, who left a deep imprint on Russian history, and in our own times by the Japanese. Under the Tsars, as under the Commissars, Russia has tried to offset these disadvantages of nature by maintaining large land forces; by erecting buffer areas through four partitions of Poland between the eighteenth century and 1939 and, after 1945, through the creation of "friendly" satellites; and since the establishment of the German national state in 1871, by making security arrangements with the Germans, from the "reinsurance" treaties of the days of Bismarck to the Nazi-Soviet pact of 1939.

The development of modern weapons, however, is rapidly changing Russia's strategic outlook and its military calculations. Now that the U.S.S.R., like the United States, can produce A- and H-bombs, long-range planes, and intercontinental ballistic missiles, the importance of land forces has sharply declined. It therefore became possible for the Soviet government recently to proclaim demobilization of an estimated 1,200,000 men in its huge land force—which had remained practically intact after 1945, when the United States and the western European nations had promptly demobilized—and to use this much-needed manpower for the stepped-up development of industry and agriculture, particularly in climatically less attractive areas of the country, such as northern Siberia. The Russians are also on the point of overcoming their landlocked condition by building a fleet of submarines—estimated at 400—which Moscow may plan to use not so much out of Russian-controlled ports as by placing them at the disposal of nations which have access to open seas, notably Egypt.

At the same time the Russians have recognized that nuclear warfare would spell catastrophe for communism, as well as capitalism, and at the "summit" conference of July, 1955, in Geneva agreed with the Western powers on the necessity of avoiding such warfare. This historic decision, determined by the achievement of atomic parity between the West and the U.S.S.R., may lead to a nuclear weapons stalemate which, under favorable political circumstances, might deter both sides from large-scale war. Meanwhile, however, the U.S.S.R. remains opposed to detailed inspection of its armaments by other powers.

Adapting its strategic policy to changed military conditions, the U.S.S.R. has endeavored to avert the new danger it faces —attack by planes carrying A- or H-bombs and intercontinental ballistic missiles—from the Western, mostly American, bases established along its periphery since 1947 by calling for an end to all foreign bases. Since many of the American bases are located on the territory of non-Western nations—Saudi Arabia, Turkey, Japan, the Philippines, Libya, Morocco—all of which in the past have been sensitive about any attempt at Western pressure or control, Moscow's appeal may prove effective, particularly if Post-Geneva "neutralism" or nonalignment gains ground.

The greater sense of security Russia has achieved through industrialization, which has given it control of modern weapons equal, if not superior, to those of the West, may liberate it, in time, from the fear and suspicion of the West which have dominated its past history, and in the Communist period have been expressed in terms of anxiety about "capitalist encirclement." The anti-Westernism that Westerners find difficult to understand in the Middle East or Asia had been a marked characteristic of the Russians long before Karl Marx wrote *Das Kapital* or Lenin seized power through soviets of workers and peasants. The Russian people have been affected little or not at all by the ideas of ancient Greece and Rome in philosophy and law. Their concepts of religion and of the relationship of church and state were inherited from the Christianity not of Rome but of Byzantium. The close connection between the political *autokrat* and the religious leader—the patriarch—familiar in Byzantine experience, survived not only the downfall of Tsarism but even the anti-religious campaign of the Bolsheviks and their emphasis on rationalism and materialism. Today the Soviet government works closely with the Russian Orthodox Church, restored to a place in Soviet society and to some of its property and emoluments; and, like the Tsars, it uses the Church as an instrument of secular policy not only at home, but—most important of all—abroad, particularly in Middle Eastern countries which have Christian communities, notably Syria and Lebanon.

Nor was Russia affected by the Renaissance and the Reformation, which powerfully molded thought and action in the Western world. The English, French, and American revolutions were not a part of Russia's experience. Only distant echoes of these world-shaking events reached the Russians, as when Catherine the Great studied Voltaire and Montesquieu, or the young officers of Alexander I, after seeing Paris at the close of the Napoleonic wars and hearing about the ideas of liberty and equality generated by the French Revolution, fomented the abortive Decembrist revolt of 1825. And while Russia entered the early stages of the Industrial Revolution in the second half of the nineteenth century, it was still in 1917, nearly fifty years later, at the point now reached by most non-Western nations, which either started on the road to change after World War II or are still on the threshold of change.

In any confrontation with the Western world, Russia thus felt almost as much at a disadvantage as it had in the days when Peter the Great, after seeing at first hand the achievements of the Netherlands and England, went back to his capital of St. Petersburg determined to "raise Russia on its hind legs." To the Russians, throughout their history, the foreigner—given the generic name "German"—was either an actual or potential invader or else an example to be both admired and envied. The Russians, throughout modern history, have envied the West, have wished to imitate it, yet have also feared it and, therefore, resented it. Their actions toward the West thus ran the gamut of emotions with which we are familiar today in the underdeveloped areas, from Egypt to Indonesia, from Argentina to Japan.

In the past, Russia has swung, sometimes violently, between extremes of slavishly copying the West, as when administrators of German origin were brought to St. Petersburg by the Tsars to do a job the Russians were considered to be as yet ill-equipped to perform, and rejecting all things Western as inapplicable to Russian conditions or actually violating Russian traditions and religious beliefs. Peter the Great (1682-1725) was obsessed by the need to Westernize Russia and did not hesitate to tear off the beards of his boyars, or nobles, as symbols of orientalism. In the eighteenth century, as already mentioned, Catherine the Great, German in origin, studied French philosophers and sought to apply their ideas in reforms of justice and administration. In the 1900's, however, there was a sharp turn in the opposite direction. Dostoyevsky was strongly anti-Western and thought that Western "atheism" was undermining the concepts and role of "holy Mother Russia." He, in turn, was opposed by "Westerners" like Alexander Herzen, exiled in London, who believed that the political liberalism of the West would be of great benefit to Russia as it struggled to emerge from feudalism and Tsarist authoritarianism. This conflict of ideas was mirrored in the thinking of the new middle class which was gradually emerging as a result of nascent industrialization.

This middle class, at the outbreak of World War I was still numerically small, politically inexperienced, and unable to take the leadership in a country where the majority of the population were peasants, and the factory workers—who were as yet a tiny minority—lived in conditions comparable to the worst days of the Industrial Revolution in England. It was divided within itself. It yearned to become Westernized and yet, at the same time, felt itself a product of Russia's tradition, of the Russian Orthodox faith, of Russia's cultural achievements, and had a strong sense of nationalism. It was also a "conscience-stricken" group. It was keenly aware of the sufferings of Russian society in its transition from backward agriculture to modern industry, and was eager to alleviate these sufferings by "going out to the people," as Turgenev's hero-doctor Bazarov did in *Fathers and Sons*. But it was also fearful of the encroachments of ruthless merchants, crude and ill-educated by its standards, on the way of life to which it had been accustomed, like the family in *The Cherry Orchard*, which pitifully recognizes that it needs money yet is reluctant to sell the treasured family orchard to a "nouveau riche" who plans to cut down the trees to make room for new enterprise.

In Russia's history, too, one finds the prototype of the struggle between the ideal and the inevitable in a changing society, represented in India by Mahatma Gandhi. Russia's Gandhi admirer, Leo Tolstoy, whose aristocratic conscience was troubled by the evils he saw around him, and who in another age might have been a spokesman of revolution, ended up by relinquishing his wealth, and left home to trudge the roads like a humble peasant, in search of an answer to the question which also haunts the characters in *The Cherry Orchard*—"What shall we do about life?"—or, more precisely, about this new, unaccustomed, alien way of life.

What Tolstoy thought and said on his estate, Yasnaya Polyana, what Russian intellectuals discussed in St. Petersburg and Moscow at the turn of the century, was but a foretaste of what thoughtful and troubled men and women discuss in our times in Bombay or Jakarta, in Buenos Aires or Cairo.

Thus on the eve of the Bolshevik revolution of November, 1917, accelerated by the defeats and upheavals of World War I, Russia was in a period of far-reaching transition—political, economic, and social.

The autocracy of state and church headed by the Tsar, the "autocrat of all the Russians," had only begun to be modified by the revolution of 1905, a direct consequence of Russia's defeat in the Russo-Japanese war. At that time the liberal-minded middle class had forced the Tsar to accept the idea of parliamentary representation, in the hope of creating institutions like those of English democracy, with a limited monarch at the top, which it greatly admired. The English Revolution which had brought this system into being had taken place over two hundred years before, in 1688, and its roots can be traced as far back as the Magna Charta of 1215. Russia was thus from two hundred to seven hundred years behind the development of England, depending on which date is taken as the starting point of England's democratic growth.

The first parliament in Russian history, the *Duma*, might conceivably have developed with time into a genuine parliament, but it had been in existence a mere decade before World War I, and during that period had not become firmly established in Russian society. The transition from the authoritarianism of the Tsars to that of the Communists, therefore, was neither as unexpected nor as sharp as it seemed to the West.

Meanwhile the Russian economy, which until 1861 could

have been compared to the manorial economy in the West, had been stirred into change and development by the emancipation of the serfs in 1861. The freed serfs were given an opportunity to buy land from the landowners, and many of them did so with the financial assistance of the government. In most cases, however, they purchased land not as individuals, but as members of the *mir*, the traditional Russian peasant community which had marked aspects of collectivism. In the mir the peasants cultivated the land in common and shared its produce.

By 1914, however, when Russia was engulfed in World War I, only one-third of the Russian peasants had acquired ownership of land. The others, like the freed serfs of the West, left the land to seek employment in the cities, where industrialization was just getting under way. There, as in other countries at the early stages of industrialization, the peasants lived under harsh factory conditions at low wages, under conditions often far less favorable than those they had known on farms. Maxim Gorky vividly portrayed these conditions in his play, *The Lower Depths.*

These workers—as well as the peasants who, failing to acquire land, remained in the villages and hired themselves out to their more fortunate neighbors—became the proletariat of Tsarist Russia. It was to these people that Lenin and Trotsky, when they returned from exile abroad after 1903, addressed their revolutionary appeal. And in the turbulent decade which preceded the outbreak of World War II there had not been time to adopt measures of social improvement which in the more advanced nations of the West altered the raw, ruthless capitalism of the nineteenth century in a way Marx had not anticipated.

In that period of transition Russia, as we have seen, did not have a middle class sufficiently strong and experienced to take the leadership in improving political and economic conditions —a lack which we find today in most of the underdeveloped non-Western countries. Those who wanted to help the peasants and workers through reform lived and acted on the periphery of the industrial process. Most of the raw materials in Russia were being developed by foreigners—Belgians and French, English and Germans. The Russians themselves, when they had money, either plowed it back into the development of the land or used it to manufacture consumers' goods, notably textiles—as was done by the celebrated textile manufacturer

Morozov, who used his fortune to assemble one of the world's most distinguished collections of modern French art, now displayed in a Moscow museum.

Under these circumstances, when the revolution came in 1917, it was easy for the Bolsheviks to confiscate public utilities and raw material developments because anti-capitalism was, in essence, anti-foreignism—a sentiment which harmonized with the anti-Westernism of the Russian people. Similarly, in Argentina, for example, it proved easy for Colonel Juan Perón to attack British interests which owned the railways and American interests which owned the telephones. And when Perón shifted his ground and decided to let an American company explore for oil, he found himself opposed by the pro-democratic Radicals, who objected to having foreigners "exploit" national resources.

In this Russian society which was passing, with great travail, from feudalism and autocracy to industrialization and the beginnings of democracy, the numerically small but efficiently organized Communist party, in the closing days of a disastrous war, found it easy to seize power. There was no effective opposition, and the Communists made a strong appeal to groups of the population—poor peasants and factory workers—who seemingly had everything to gain by supporting Lenin and his associates.

The fact that communism came to office in one of the great nations of the world—although Russia was at that time a great world power potentially, rather than actually—gave communism a prestige and an influence outside the borders of Russia which it would not have gained had the Communists first seized power, let us say, in Spain or Bulgaria. Yet in countries much smaller and weaker than Russia communism has made headway only under conditions comparable to those which existed in Russia after 1947, and only when the promise of change by peaceful means was either long deferred, or seemingly hopeless.

Today, the Russian system sometimes defies description by the Communists themselves, as was indicated in 1955 during the controversy between Communist party theoreticians and then Foreign Minister Vyacheslav M. Molotov on the issue whether Russia had merely laid the foundations of socialism, as Molotov claimed, or had in fact achieved socialism and was on the way to communism. Actually Russia does not have a pure Communist system, for that would mean the practice of the principle, "from each according to his ability and to each according to his needs." Russia's system today, even after the downgrading of Stalin, is based on "from each according to his ability and to each according to his ability"—with relatively high salaries given to leading government officials, industrial managers, scientists, artists, and ballet dancers, and bonuses offered to factory workers who have shown initiative and special skills.

The actuality is far different from the ideal. Since 1917 Russia has been ruled by a political dictatorship controlled by a single party. This dictatorship governs a nation which comprises 180 different racial and national groups over an area spanning two continents. The question can well be asked whether it would be possible to hold so vast and varied a domain together except by an authoritarian form of government, and whether its removal might be the signal for the breakup of the multinational, multiracial empire.

Since Stalin's death in 1953, this all-embracing dictatorship has been modified by the principle of "collective leadership." If this principle endures—as foreshadowed by the case of Georgi M. Malenkov, who upon being removed as Premier in 1955, was appointed Minister of Electricity, a post which includes development of nuclear energy—Russia may begin to see, under a single party, the beginnings of a cabinet-type government, in which individual members may be demoted or dropped or transferred to other government posts without being purged.

At the start the old pattern seemed to be in operation when Stalin's successors executed Lavrenti Beria, head of the secret police, who knew too much about each of the members of the new "collective leadership" and, reportedly, aspired to succeed the old master himself. Since then, however, the secret police has been subordinated to the civilian authorities, a series of amnesties have brought about the release of political as well as ordinary criminals, the administration of justice has been decentralized, and labor camps are being disbanded. If this process continues, events may prove that the violent purges which for nearly forty years characterized Soviet rule may have come to a close. Some of the most shocking offenses against human rights and dignity may be on the decline—although, since Russia is ruled by an authoritarian system, the rulers could, when they chose, reverse the process.

It is important to note, however, that at no time since 1917 did Russia have a "monolithic" dictatorship comparable to that of Hitler. The purges revealed that even under Stalin's iron hand the top leaders, far from acquiescing in the *diktat* of a single autocrat, were engaged in a struggle for power as well as a struggle about ideas. Politically, the purges, which indicated the existence of something roughly approximating right and left wings and a center group within the Communist party, if not among the non-party majority of the people, were the bloody equivalent of elections. Economically, the government has faced a long and bitter struggle with the peasants over the collectivization of agriculture, which revealed that opposition, although expressed in ways different from those of the modern West—but not of the feudal West with its *jacqueries* and peasant rebellions—had not disappeared in Russia.

In spite of political changes, Russia even after Stalin continues to have a state-controlled, state-directed economy. The state, claiming to act on behalf and in the best interests of the people, owns all means of production—raw materials, land, industrial plants, financial resources. Through the State Planning Commission, it blueprints the entire economic development of the country under five-year plans launched in 1928, the sixth of which is now under way. With the exception of a small minority of self-employed artisans, all wage-earners are employees of the state, either in industry or on collective or state farms. As is well known, the existence of labor unions has not prevented the large-scale use of forced labor both as a punitive measure and to recruit manpower for unpopular tasks. Nor does it prevent the state from determining matters which in Western countries are the subject of collective bargaining—hours of work, rates of pay, and so on—although since Stalin's death some latitude of discussion has been encouraged among workers.

The state is also the source of investment in industry, transportation, and other enterprises. It is the state, not private individuals, which is concerned with the formation of capital necessary for the development of the nation's economy. The state derives a considerable part of this capital from various taxes, the most important of which is the turnover tax, charged every time an article of trade changes hands. In effect, the state sets aside national savings by withholding consumer goods and other amenities from the population. These savings, achieved at the expense of living standards—as was the case during Japan's industrialization in the 1860's—are then invested in the enterprises to which the government gives top priority.

The Soviet leaders have thus deliberately made a choice which faces every underdeveloped country. The choice is: What comes first? Satisfaction of the desire of the population for a better way of life, even if this means postponement, perhaps indefinitely, of attempts to create an effective base for the long-term development of the country's resources? Or a deliberate policy of austerity, ruthlessly enforced by a dictatorial government, with the object of creating such a base, irrespective of the wishes or resistance of the population? Faced with this decision, Japan in the Meiji era acted very much like Russia, sacrificing the comfort of its people to the rapid industrialization of the country—with this important difference: that the Japanese government used former landowners and warriors, turned into a new middle class upon being deprived of their feudal privileges, to perform on its behalf the process of national savings and investment. India has taken a different path, by first trying to assure a modicum of food, health, and social welfare for its vast millions under its first Five-Year Plan (1951-56) and then proceeding with industrialization under the second Five-Year Plan (1956-61) —but even then on a scale which would be regarded as modest in Japan and still more so in Russia. By contrast, Communist China has followed the development pattern set by Moscow, but with some important modifications which indicate that Peiping, profiting by Russia's experience, may prove more moderate in its demands on the Chinese people.

Unlike most of the other non-Western countries, Russia is rich in a wide variety of natural resources. This does not mean that the U.S.S.R. is economically self-sufficient. It lacks and must import natural rubber, tin, cocoa, coffee, and so on. Russia, however, unlike the United States, faces the same problem as other non-Western nations, where the demands of heavy industry, started at a stage of national development when the population is already large and still growing, compete with demands for consumer goods—both agricultural products and products of light industry.

The population of the U.S.S.R., estimated at 160 million in 1945, is increasing at the rate of 3 million a year, and has now reached 200 million despite World War II losses, estimated at between 20 and 30 million, both civilian and military. At the present time, Russia's known agricultural resources are not sufficient to provide its people with a living standard comparable to that of the United States, although it may soon approximate the level of several European countries, and already exceeds that of most of the non-Western areas. The food deficiency, as compared with the United States, is particularly striking in the case of meat, for Russia's never large quantity of livestock was sharply reduced by slaughter during the peasant resistance to collectivization in the 1930's, by war devastation in 1941-45, and by lack of proper attention to its development in the postwar years. Nor has the U.S.S.R. mechanized its agriculture as widely as the United States, with the result that far more manpower must be used on the Russian than on the American farm to produce the same quantity of food.

Great as is the need of Russia's new urban centers for food and fibers, the Soviet government has hitherto deliberately subordinated this need to its over-all development plans. Through its policy of harshly enforced saving and underconsumption the U.S.S.R. has succeeded in creating the internal capital it needs for investment in further and still further industrial production. Except for limited foreign credits obtained and repaid before World War II, and the large aid in the form of equipment which the West, and particularly the United States, provided during that war, the U.S.S.R. has relied primarily on its own resources for economic development. The result is that Russia, which in 1917 was a technologically backward country weakened by a disastrous war, and which then again experienced vast destruction in 1941-45, has expanded its production at a significant rate—the rate both of industrial growth and of expansion in gross national product (the total output of goods and services) being greater than that of the United States in almost all years since 1928, when the Stalin government launched the first of a series of five-year plans, and faster even than that of the United States during the period of its exceptionally rapid growth from 1860 to 1900. According to Professor Henry L. Roberts in *Russia and America: Dangers and Prospects*, "Most Western students of the Soviet Union would not, we believe, question the conclusion that the Soviet economy has expanded in postwar years at something like 1½ times the rate of our own."

This vast industrial development, which has transformed Russia in less than forty years from a backward, primarily agrarian country into a technologically modern power rated by Western experts as second only to the United States in several important respects, notably steel production, and as capable of outdistancing this country in another decade, may ultimately justify Stalin's formula that Russia should "catch up with and outstrip" the West—much as both the West and the Russian people may deplore the human and material sacrifices this development has entailed.

Eventually, however, consumer needs will have to be satisfied, at least in modest measure. Since the death of Stalin his successors have undertaken to do this by two methods: by opening up new lands to cultivation, with increased attention to crop diversification and the raising of livestock, utilizing American techniques, particularly in corn growing; and by using Russia's gold resources, second only to those of the Union of South Africa, as well as arms and manufactured goods produced in its own factories and those of the eastern European countries, for the purchase of raw materials and food, such as rice in Burma, cotton in Egypt, rubber in Ceylon, sugar in Cuba, coffee in Latin America. It has thus followed the pattern familiar to Western nations during their period of industrialization, when Britain and France, the Netherlands and Germany, obtained raw materials and food in colonial areas and, in return, provided manufactured goods and arms which those areas were as yet unable to produce at home. Russia's need for a wide range of foods, raw materials, and manufactured goods represents an important asset in the period of "competitive coexistence," when both the underdeveloped non-Western countries and the industrially advanced nations of the West prefer trade to aid.

While outwardly the U.S.S.R. has a monolithic economy, state-controlled and state-directed, actually it has had to accept a mixed system in agriculture, ranging all the way from the government-directed state farm (*sovhoz*), on which workers perform their daily stint on the same basis as if they were employed in factories, through the collective farm (*kolhoz*), where peasants pool their resources to cultivate state-owned land and share in the proceeds on the basis of their work contribution, to the limited but still significant individual farming which members of the *kolhoz* are permitted, and even encouraged, to do on their own small plots of land. In the collective farm the peasant works for the agricultural community, which sells the joint produce to the state at prices set by the government and then distributes the money received according to the work hours of each individual. On his own little plot of land the peasant can grow what he wants—fruit, vegetables, chickens, rabbits, pigs (but not cows or horses, which are collective property)—and sell his output in the free market at whatever price the traffic will bear.

The state-directed and state-controlled development of Russia's economy has produced uneven results to which both admirers and critics can point as evidence of their assertions that Russia is moving ahead with impressive speed or that it remains intolerably backward in spite, or because, of the Bolshevik revolution. On the one hand, we may point to primitive transportation by horse-drawn cart and to methods of production that can be classified anywhere from the fifteenth to the nineteenth century. But on the other hand, if we speak in terms of technological development, and of education for work in science, Russia has to be ranked in the vanguard of the mid-twentieth century, neck and neck with the world's most advanced nations.

Russia's experience under Communist rule shows that it is possible for an underdeveloped country to jump over centuries in scientific and economic development with marked success, even though this involves grave strain and stress for the human beings involved and infringements on individual rights as conceived in the West. But this experience also shows that it is far more difficult to jump over centuries of political and social development, which require the slow growth of new values, of new institutions, of new attitudes toward men's relations in society. Since Stalin's death it has become apparent that, in trying to catch up with themselves, the Russians may have in a sense to retrace their footsteps politically, in order to gain the experience of gradual, peaceful, non-dictatorial growth.

The "collective leadership" which replaced the personal rule of Stalin has shown its awareness of the need for far-reaching political and social changes commensurate with the technological changes Russia has undergone since 1917. While Stalin has been downgraded for his "cult of personality," no attempt has been made to denigrate or alter the industrialization of the country which took place under his aegis. Nor is such an attempt to be expected in the future. For the rulers of the post-Stalin period are themselves the product of the new society brought into being by Russia's industrial revolution.

The most basic and obvious political and social change, and one which no dictator, however powerful, could prevent has been the rise of a new generation. This new generation may turn out to be no more acceptable to the West than that of the Old Bolsheviks—and it would be wise to assume, until further notice, that it will be no less concerned with the interests of the country as they see them than the old. What is significant, however, is that this new generation was brought up in a climate very different from that of the period which witnessed the emergence of Lenin, Trotsky, and Stalin. True, conspiracy and dogmatism were still important elements of the conditions under which they grew to maturity, and it may take time before these elements are completely eradicated from Soviet society. But the new generation are not seeking to overthrow an existing order, as in the days of the Tsars; they *are* the existing order. They are not revolutionaries intent on tearing down a structure they regard as obsolete. They are or have been the builders of a structure which it is in their interest to preserve but also, if possible, to strengthen and improve. They are not fanatical prophets of a creed which promises Utopia. They are participants in political and economic operations for whose success or failure they are being held responsible, and their own livelihood—if not life itself—depends on their capacity to succeed.

They are not travelers to a Promised Land who are prepared to undergo any kind of hardship to reach their goal. They have, by their own assertion, reached the Promised Land and are now eager to enjoy some of its fruits. They may still be suspicious about the aims of the outside world, but to the extent that they master the once unfamiliar and often alarming environment of the twentieth century and reduce further the gap between Russia and the Western world through industrialization and scientific achievement, they will be less fearful of the West and more inclined to learn from it what they can by direct contact. And, meanwhile, as life becomes a little less strenuous than it has been since 1917, they may have more leisure to devote to literature, the arts, and pure science, where there has been a growing demand for individual freedom—a demand that may eventually affect political life as well.

This does not mean that we can expect a revolution that would overthrow the Soviet government, despite the 1956 uprisings in the satellite states. What we can expect is that Stalin's demise, by crystallizing tendencies which had been developing for a considerable period of time, may accelerate the transition of Soviet society in the direction of moderation, and thus bring about the gradual erosion of its authoritarian and dogmatic aspects.

Put in other words, what we see in Russia is the emergence,

in this new generation, of a middle class which before 1917 was still numerically insignificant. If Western experience is any guide, this group will not only want to maintain but to increase its material advantages and its influence, and could ultimately provide the initiative for political liberalization on a broad base which was not available in Tsarist Russia on the eve of World War I.

This new generation has at its disposal new political institutions and economic instruments created during the years of Stalin's rule. Some of these it may choose to discard or modify, as has already been indicated by the attitude of Stalin's successors toward the secret police, one-man dictatorship, and the need for reform of collective farms. Others it may choose to preserve and expand.

Whatever forms post-Stalin rule may take, it will have at its disposal a complex of basic industries; a pool of trained manpower for further industrial development; educational facilities which, by Western standards, are unduly permeated with propaganda but have been successfully used to make a largely illiterate population literate and to train them in the skills of a modern industrial society; and scientific achievement, which has made it possible for the U.S.S.R., primarily through its own efforts, to keep abreast of the West.

The key political question, from the point of view of the West, is whether the far-reaching internal changes that have occurred and may continue to occur in the U.S.S.R. have weakened or strengthened its position in world affairs. Answers to this question depend on one's definition of Russia's strength or weakness. Some Western observers believe that the downgrading of Stalin, by creating dismay and disillusionment in the ranks of Communists outside the U.S.S.R., will undermine the influence Moscow exercised in the past not only in a number of European countries but, most profoundly of all, among non-Western peoples. They also contend that the decision of the "collective leadership," headed by Premier Nikolai A. Bulganin and Communist party chief Nikita S. Khrushchev, to "go to Canossa" in Belgrade shortly after Stalin's death, and its subsequent efforts to conciliate Marshal Tito, the only Communist leader outside Russia who challenged Moscow's domination, is bound to have unfavorable results for the U.S.S.R. by loosening its hold over other Communist nations of Eastern Europe, which might adopt Titoism. And they think that, once the lid on the Soviet pot has been lifted ever so slightly, the Russian Communists will be unable to slam it back, and will sooner or later be blown up by the steam they have allowed to escape.

Viewed from another angle, however, the consequences of Russia's orderly transition from the personal and admittedly ruthless dictatorship of Stalin to a more moderate, open-ended regime—a transition which has surprised those Westerners who had expected an explosion of opposition forces once Stalin had passed from the scene—may prove a factor of new and increasing strength for the U.S.S.R. International communism was a useful weapon in Russia's armory during a period when it was internally weak and disorganized, when it faced hostility from many quarters, and when it needed supporters in other countries who could help communism, if not always Russia as a national state.

Today, when the U.S.S.R. has become one of the world's two great powers, militarily and industrially, it no longer needs so urgently the support of foreign Communists through a world organization with headquarters in Moscow. On the contrary, a close relationship with foreign Communists could prove a great liability, by closing doors to economic, scientific, and other exchanges with non-Communist nations, of non-West as well as West, which can redound to the benefit of Russia and other members of the Soviet bloc, including Communist China. By dissociating itself from Communist parties in other countries, Russia can straighten its international position in two ways. It can relegate to the past a relationship which has constituted the principal obstacle to closer contacts with nations which, while opposed to communism within their own borders, are ready to do business with the U.S.S.R. And it can help to clear the way to the eventual cooperation of Communists abroad with Socialist parties now active in the political life of their respective countries. Such cooperation, ultimately, could serve to achieve the goal Khrushchev stressed in his February, 1956, address at the twentieth Communist party congress when he said that revolution need not be brought about by force—that in some countries it could be brought about by parliamentary means.

The achievement of this goal could be greatly furthered by Moscow's reconciliation with Marshal Tito. This reconciliation was a dramatic demonstration that, in the opinion of Russia's new leaders, communism, once proclaimed as a monolithic doctrine from which no deviations would be permitted, is now ready to tolerate deviations within reason; and that Russia, a great power, intends to respect the independence of small countries like Yugoslavia. The enthusiastic reception accorded to Marshal Tito during his visit to the U.S.S.R. in June, 1956, symbolized, both for the Russian people and for the rest of the world, Khrushchev's assertion that there can be many roads to "socialism." While the Soviet leader's definition of "socialism" makes it appear to be synonymous with communism, the very fact that Yugoslavia, during the eight years when it was an outcast from the Communist fold, had remolded its communism in several important respects could be used as evidence that Moscow no longer expects even Communist-led countries to become carbon copies of Russia.

True, Yugoslavia, since 1948, has retained a one-party dictatorship, but it wears its Communist dictatorship with a difference. The new constitution it adopted in 1953, before Stalin's death, permitted some latitude for disagreement and discussion as compared with the 1945 constitution it replaced. While opponents of the Tito government, such as Milovan Djilas, have been barred from political activity, they have not been executed or exiled—although Djilas was imprisoned for questioning the survival of communism. The Yugoslavs have continued to emphasize the ultimate desirability of agricultural collectivization, but they have tolerated a situation where 80 per cent of the land is in the hands of individual farmers, have increasingly moderated their demands on the peasants, and have encouraged the expansion of farm cooperatives. Although they have not abandoned industrialization, they have slowed down the breakneck pace at which they had been starting new enterprises; have set for themselves more modest objectives; have accepted financial and technical aid from Western countries, notably the United States; have decentralized both administrative and economic institutions; through the Council of Producers have given "economic representation" supplementing political representation in Parliament; and through workers' councils have tried to democratize factories by granting workers a voice in decisions about industrial operations.

It is not mere coincidence that the Yugoslavs have called their system "democratic socialism," distinguishing it from the "dictatorship" of the U.S.S.R., which they regard as a "bureaucratic" perversion of socialism, or that after repudiating Stalin, who had insisted on Yugoslavia's expulsion from the Cominform, they asserted that Marx and Lenin, not Stalin, were the fountainheads of pure communism. In a sense that may assume increasing significance in the future, the course followed from 1948 to 1956 by Yugoslavia, which geographically and culturally has been closer to the West than Russia (particularly in Croatia, a part of the Austro-Hungarian Empire before 1919) foreshadowed the major developments that have occurred in Russia since 1953, as well as the more spectacular and far-reaching changes in Poland and Hungary in the autumn of 1956. Marshal Tito's "democratic socialism" might well become a model not only for other countries of eastern Europe, but also for Russia, and be used by Russia as a banner around which non-Communist Socialists of other lands—for example, India, Burma, and Egypt, all of which have expressed admiration for Yugoslavia— could eventually rally, to the advantage of the U.S.S.R.

In the future Moscow may find it useful to permit the gradual "withering away"—not of the state, but of communism as a rallying cry to unite the workers and peasants of the world. Now that Russia itself is moving, however slowly, in the direction of becoming a middle-class society, its appeal to other peoples may be couched in different terms. As can be seen already in the middle East, in Southeast Asia, in Africa, even in Latin America, the Russians are identifying communism with nationalism, the most powerful single force in the non-Western world of the twentieth century. Nasser and U Nu, Nehru and Sukarno and Nkrumah of the Gold Coast are no more interested than Marshal Tito in becoming puppets of Moscow or in being dominated by Russian Communists.

They believe, rightly or wrongly, that they can deal much more effectively with their own Communists once they have achieved national independence and discarded all remnants of Western intervention or control. But they are at the same time willing and eager to accept aid from whatever quarter it may come, irrespective of ideology, in the uphill task of developing their own economies at the highest possible speed. To the extent that the Russians support nationalist movements in non-Western countries, and back these countries' "socialist" systems with financial and technical aid, to that extent the U.S.S.R. may win an increasingly powerful role in world affairs without the necessity of relying on a world Communist movement. This is already clear from what Russia has done in the Middle East, where it has backed Islam's challenge to the West.

3

Middle East: Islam versus Westernism

TURKEY — EGYPT — ISRAEL

The key problem of the Middle East, ancient crossroads of many civilizations and goal of military strategists and oil prospectors, is the need to mesh Islam, which is a faith, a way of life, and a community with the thought processes and techniques of the modern world as developed by the West.

Nowhere in the non-Western world, with the exception of the U.S.S.R., is there such a profound feeling of anti-Westernism as in the Arab countries. Arab anti-Westernism is an explosive compound of still-vivid memories of Western colonial rule, desire to acquire the things which seem to make the West strong, both weapons and technology, fear that the adoption of Western techniques will destroy the ancient faith by which men have lived for centuries, and a passionate desire to achieve or maintain national independence. Unlike the anti-Westernism of other non-Western peoples, it is further compounded by Islam's rejection of the infidel, most graphically represented by the Westerner. This cluster of feelings, seemingly contradictory when seen through Western eyes, reflects the long-time struggle between Mohammedanism and the Christian West, from the Crusades and the Moorish invasion of Spain to Napoleon's bid for Eygpt and the post-World War I rule of France and Britain over areas of the Middle East which, on the breakup of the Ottoman Empire, had been assigned to the Western powers as League of Nations mandates.

When Western colonialism seemed on the decline, France had withdrawn from the Middle East and Britain had followed suit by terminating its 72-year-old control of Egypt and leaving the Suez Canal Zone in 1956, the Muslim lands of the Middle East found their principal target for anti-Western feeling in Israel. This small land, once peopled, when it was Palestine, by Arabs as well as Jews, has become a refuge—

in fulfillment of the ancient pledge of a "promised land"—for thousands of Jews from outside the Middle East: Jews who fled from the Fascist and Nazi rulers in Europe, from Yemen, and more recently from French North Africa, where they were threatened by disorders resulting from nationalist attacks on France in Tunisia, Morocco, and Algeria, and from Egypt.

Because of this influx of Western settlers, whose creation of the new state of Israel through the partition of Palestine in 1948 has been financed in large part by private as well as governmental funds—principally from the United States—the Arabs consider Israel not as an integral part of the Middle East but as an intruder who must be destroyed or, at the very least, so weakened by economic boycott that it will crumble and disappear from the map, leaving the entire area in the hands of the Arabs. Yet responsible Arab leaders recognize that the mere destruction of Israel would not of itself solve their basic problem. This basic problem is the modernization of a political and economic society which, in the nuclear age, is still living by principles and under institutions inherited from feudal times.

The determined quest of the Arabs for a new pattern that would retain the spiritual values of Islam yet raise the living standards of the Middle East to the levels achieved by the Western world has focused attention on the experience of Turkey, a Muslim country which since 1920 has emerged into a modern, Western way of life.

In comparing Turkey with Egypt, we must bear in mind that Islam is a four-fold phenomenon. It is a faith, and like Judaism and Christianity a strongly monotheistic faith. It is a religion organized as a community on a political basis—with the state, under Islam, based on the sacred book of the Muslims, the Koran. It is a way of life, with every activity down to the smallest detail regulated by Koranic prescriptions. And it is an interpretation of history which depicts Islam as having achieved temporal glory through militant application of its faith before its decline in the thirteenth century. This complete integration of religion, political system, way of life, and interpretation of history makes it extremely difficult to alter the institutions of the Muslim countries unless the priests, or *ulema*, who interpret the Koran, are favorable to proposed changes. If they oppose change, they may resort to fanatical resistance, up to and including the assassination of would-be reformers, as has happened in the case of the Muslim Brotherhood in Iran and Egypt.

Not that Islam has a well-organized religious hierarchy like the priesthoods of the Catholic and Greek Orthodox churches. The strength of the *ulema* is due not to hierarchical authority but to their authority as acknowledged interpreters of the Koran—that is, the word of God. If a strong political ruler decides to take the initiative and defy the *ulema*, he can do so, and succeed politically—as Kemal Ataturk did in Turkey in the 1920's, when he abolished the institution of the Caliphate and separated the state from the church, and Colonel Gamal Abdel Nasser, premier of Egypt, did by outlawing the Muslim Brotherhood in 1954 and depriving it of the powerful influence it had once wielded over political life. But while the men who interpret the Koran may be pushed into the background by political leaders bent on modernization, it is more difficult to suppress their ideas and attitudes, as Turkey discovered in the post-World War II decade after it broadened the base of the dictatorial regime through which Kemal Ataturk had cut down the power of the Islamic clergy.

The Muslim dilemma today stems from the fact that Islam achieved its intellectual peak in the thirteenth century, at a time when western Europe was just emerging from the Dark Ages. The Muslims then had philosophers, men of science, fine libraries, a rich and varied culture. But after this flowering the Muslim world "went to sleep" under the rule of the Ottoman Empire, run by Turkish military leaders and administrators who had originally come from central Asia. Islam did not awaken until the nineteenth century, when the empire began to disintegrate as it came into contact with the West, which, meanwhile, had leaped from the Middle Ages to the era of nationalism, industrialization, and democratization. Today, as we go through the frightening slums of Cairo, when we see the poverty, disease, filth, and ignorance of Arab lands, we see, as in a mirror, the reflection of what our European forebears were like in the Middle Ages.

The Muslim countries are now engaged in a struggle that will determine whether the rigid authoritarianism of Islam can be adapted to modern life—and adapted without the bloodshed of revolution—or make the attempt, favored by some Muslim leaders, to return to its glorious but now vanished past. Islam has never experienced a process of intellectual change comparable to the Reformation in Europe. It must go through such a reformation in our time if it is not to be rejected by the younger elements of Arab countries who want modernization. And rejection holds the danger that the Arabs, uprooted from their ancient faith, might feel disoriented and seek new roots in other political movements which combine a way of life with a faith, notably communism. This possibility should make us careful not to assert out of hand that Islam is in and of itself a safeguard against Communist ideas. On the contrary, the inherent authoritarianism of Islam may make it far more susceptible to the authoritarian ideas of communism than is true, for example, of a many-faceted, tolerant, absorptive religion like Hinduism. And by this token during a transition period communism may seem less likely to destroy the accepted Muslim way of life than the impact of the West, with its emphasis on non-authoritarian political and economic institutions.

Because of the complexities of adapting a Muslim society to modern life, Turkey is closely watched in the Middle East as a possible example for other Muslim nations. The Turks, the most militant people within the Ottoman Empire, which at its peak stretched from the Balkans to the Red Sea, gradually lost their grip on that empire with the rise of nationalism. Forced to yield to the pressure of Tsarist Russia, which in the nineteenth century proclaimed itself the defender of the South Slavs—who in 1919 created Yugoslavia—Turkey eventually became known as "the sick man of Europe." Following its disastrous participation in World War I at the side of Germany and Austria-Hungary, Turkey was ousted from what it still held in Europe as well as from its possessions in the Middle East and confined to the geographic boundaries in Asia within which it lives today. Yet out of military defeat came victory. Mustafa Kemal Ataturk, a military leader, spurred rather than dismayed by Turkey's setbacks, sparked a revolution, for the most part bloodless, which set Turkey, in three decades, on the road to becoming a modern state. He made Turkey, a country of Muslims into a republic built on Turkish nationalism. He separated church and state without destroying the religion of Islam. He introduced government ownership or control of the principal means of transportation, industries, mines, and public utilities. The fact that this revolution was staged by a military man, and not by a civilian, is a significant aspect of the situation not only in the Middle East but also in other non-Western areas which have not as yet developed a responsible reform-minded middle class. The same trend can be seen in Egypt and the countries of Latin

America, where changes are often initiated by military rulers.

Why does this happen? It happens because the military leaders have the weapons to stage revolutions. They have at least a modicum of education. And since they are concerned with the security and prestige of their countries, they often have the vision to see that military strength must be underpinned by economic and social strength. This, in turn, requires political changes and the capacity to challenge established authority, whether it be that of King Farouk, or the Muslim Brotherhood in Egypt, or the industrial group, or, in some of the Latin American nations, the Catholic Church.

One of Ataturk's first steps was to abolish the Caliphate. He thereby effected the separation of state and church which has been a fundamental feature of political modernization in advanced countries like France and the United States. He abolished other symbols of the past, notably the wearing of the fez by Turkish men, just as Peter the Great had tried to get rid of a symbol of the past by ordering the Russian nobles, the *boyars*, to shave off their beards.

Ataturk was a dictator, and his was a revolution from the top, not from below, as were some of the most influential revolutions of western Europe. He made Turkey not only a secular state—and this was a far-reaching revolution for a Muslim country—but also a national state, a state of Turks and of Muslims, with only a few insignificant non-Muslim minorities—a process aided by the exchange of populations with Greece successfully carried out in the 1920's. Thus under his rule Turkey rapidly went through two of the important phases which marked the development of western countries—secularization and nationalism.

Ataturk also carried out economic reforms. He introduced a planned economy, and started industrialization by establishing a number of enterprises planned, financed, and directed by the state. No one would claim that Ataturk was a Communist. Nor was he more than formally "correct" toward the U.S.S.R. Yet it is significant that he found it necessary to take some of the initial measures with which we have become familiar in Communist-ruled countries like Russia and Yugoslavia. Here, again, it should be noted that comparable circumstances tend to produce comparable policies—even though the basic ideologies may be completely different. And another thing we must note is that Turkey's modernization, political and economic, was launched by dictatorial, not by democratic, methods. It is important for us to bear this in mind when, as we look at other non-Western nations, we expect them, overnight, to develop democratic institutions like our own.

Since the death of Ataturk in 1938, his successors have moved in the direction of political democratization and away from a state-controlled economy. Instead of the one-party dictatorship established by Ataturk, Turkey now has a two-party system—the Republicans, who unlike their namesakes in the United States, favor more controls and planning, and the Democrats, who are comparable in their views to our Republicans. The government, under the leadership of the Democrats, has decentralized industrial development and has sold some of the former state-controlled enterprises to private owners. Today Turkey has a mixed economy, with some undertakings still under state control, notably the paper industry and a considerable number of shoe and metals factories. Cotton and copper, however, among other things, are in private hands. The government has also broken with an old European tradition by turning over the match industry, formerly a government monopoly, to private enterprise.

In the course of this transition from a state to a private economy, Turkey has run into a number of difficulties. It has found that it does not have enough trained managers. It has been faced by a shortage of investment capital. The Turkish people are still too poor, and not yet sufficiently advanced in industrial development, to accumulate capital out of their own resources. Turkey has had to turn to the United States, Britain, and West Germany for loans and credits. But the repayment of these loans and credits has proved burdensome, and Turkey, which at one and the same time has tried to build up its defense against the possibility of aggression by Russia, to develop industrialization, and to improve living standards, faces inflation at home and reluctance on the part of its foreign creditors to make further financial advances under existing conditions.

Turkey is fortunate in one important respect—it has a diversified economy. It produces tobacco and foodstuffs (notably figs and raisins), as well as strategic raw materials such as chrome, which it can use for export, the principal source of its foreign exchange. Turkey, however, is a latecomer on the world trade scene, and most of its exports must compete with the products of other countries—worst of all, often the countries to which Turkey owes money. For example, Turkish figs compete with the figs of California, and Turkish tobacco runs into the opposition of American tobacco growers. This is a problem which we find in other non-Western countries, and which calls for an "agonizing reappraisal" of the world trade policies of the Western powers.

In spite of its industrialization program, Turkey is still primarily an agrarian country, with 70 to 80 per cent of its people living on the land. Unlike Egypt, however, it has enough land for its present population needs, and it has gradually carried out the land reform adopted in 1946, which puts land into the hands of small cultivators.

Faced by grave economic problems, Turkey has found it increasingly difficult to maintain the practices of its as yet infant democracy. The government of Premier Adnan Menderes has been sensitive to criticism by the opposition Republican party, and has imposed restrictions on the press and on public expressions of discontent. Turkey's experience shows that in a newly independent country the delicately balanced processes of democratic institutions can be easily strained by economic setbacks and social maladjustments. It is an understandable temptation for a government which lacks the tradition of parliamentary rule familiar in Britain to jettison some of the procedures which may cause trouble or impede measures it wants to take in an authoritarian way.

Turkey's internal problems have been compounded by international anxieties. The dominant factor in Turkey's relations with the rest of the world is its historic fear of and hostility toward Russia, which in Tsarist as well as Communist hands had sought access to the Dardanelles and a position of influence in the eastern Mediterranean. Because of its traditional position about Russia, Turkey, which before had been an historic ally of Britain, has joined the United States since World War II in the creation of a policy designed to "contain" the U.S.S.R. A member of the North Atlantic Treaty Organization, to which its former enemy, Greece, belongs, Turkey is a participant in the Balkan pact which includes Greece and Communist Yugoslavia, and the Baghdad or "northern tier" pact concluded in 1955 with Britain, Iraq, Pakistan, and Iran.

Turkey's concern for its position in the eastern Mediterranean, at the gateway to the Middle East and Asia, also explains its attitude about the island of Cyprus, which lies only forty miles from its shores. This island, which Britain obtained from the Ottoman Empire in the nineteenth century, having its ownership confirmed by the Lausanne treaty of 1923, has a population of 100,000 Turks and 400,000 Greeks.

The Greeks have long been pressing Britain for self-determination, with eventual freedom to join Greece. Britain, for its part, having agreed to withdraw its troops from the Suez Canal Zone, is determined to hold on to Cyprus, its only remaining base in that area, which it regards as essential for the defense of Turkey and of its interests in the Middle East, with its reserves of oil essential for Britain's survival. The Cypriotes, led by Archbishop Makarios, have defied London through a resistance movement which, in scope and character, reminds one of the resistance of the Jews in Palestine before partition. Both Britain and Turkey fear that, if Cyprus joined Greece, this base would be lost to NATO and the defenses of the West, particularly since Greece, once a faithful supporter of the West, has been disaffected by Britain's Cyprus policy, and might conceivably turn to the Left in internal politics, and adopt the neutralist attitude of its neighbor Yugoslavia.

The anti-Greek riots which took place in Istanbul in the autumn of 1955 not only indicated the concern of Turks over Cyprus, but were also manifestations of deep-seated anti-Westernism, which re-emerged under the stress and strain of inflation. These riots, according to the Turkish government, were provoked and fanned by Communists—although the Communist party is outlawed in Turkey. According to Western observers on the scene, however, they reflected resentment over the maladjustments generated by a policy of simultaneously modernizing agriculture and raising the living standards of the masses of the people who live outside urban centers. It was also thought that the religious sentiment which Kemal Ataturk had successfully repressed during his secularization of the state may have reappeared in this altered political climate. Only the future will show whether Turkey, which more than any other Muslim country has tried to reconcile Islam with twentieth-century conditions and to create a national state outside the Islamic community, will succeed in its attempt at Westernization.

Meanwhile Egypt, thirty years after the revolution Kemal Ataturk effected in Turkey, is now in the process of carrying out a revolution of its own, under the leadership first of General Naguib and since 1953 of Colonel Nasser and his young group of officers, most of whom are under forty. The unrest long latent in Egypt became crystallized in 1950 into a many-faceted revolt against the corrupt regime of King Farouk, against the landowners and urban financiers, against politicians in general and most bitterly against the British, who had ruled the country since 1882. The event which finally brought about the revolt was Egypt's defeat in the Palestine war, when Israel, with a population of less than two million, easily defeated the Arab coalition, representing a total population of 40 million, of which Egypt was the acknowledged leader. The young officers who lived through this humiliating defeat attributed it to the incapacity of the country's parliamentary regime, to the corruption of King Farouk and his supporters among the moneyed group in Cairo and Alexandria, and to the alleged bias of Britain and the United States for the Jews as against the Arabs. They vowed to do away with the men and institutions which, in their opinion, had brought shame on Egypt, and to make sure that, in the future, Egypt would have the military and economic capacity to stand up against Israel and against its Western sponsors and supporters.

Subsequent events demonstrated that this revolt, triggered in the first instance by defeat on the battlefield, was not a flash in the pan, and that the young officers of Naguib and Nasser had made a careful study of Egypt's political, economic, and social conditions, with particular attention to projects for reform which had been urged from various sources under the monarchy, only to be pigeonholed by the authorities. These projects were promptly pulled out of their pigeonholes and put into effect. The military government of Egypt, like that of Turkey's Ataturk, is trying to modernize the state, to improve its economy, and to make Egypt conscious of its national identity and, most significant of all, of its Muslim mission in the twentieth-century world.

Egypt, however, faces several handicaps which Turkey did not have to overcome. To begin with, unlike Turkey, it does not have a homogeneous population such as the Turks acquired following the exchange of Greek-Turkish populations in 1923. Egypt's ancient civilization had been overlaid since the Middle Ages by the culture of its Turkish rulers under the Ottoman Empire. Then came the French in the wake of Napoleon's attempt at conquest—and although the French never actually ruled Egypt, it is their influence, rather than that of Britain, which affected those among Egypt's upper and middle class who dominated the country. Greeks, Italians, and other immigrants from Mediterranean lands have settled in Egypt, often without acquiring Egyptian citizenship. And since the breakup of the Ottoman Empire after World War I, Egypt has increasingly claimed the role of leader of the Muslim world from the eastern Mediterranean to the Pacific—a claim openly challenged only by Iraq, Britain's sole remaining ally in the Middle East. Since the revolution, Egypt has been trying to slough off outside influences, and to get back to the roots of its own "Egyptianism," which brings back memories of great cultural glories and military prowess. Premier Nasser expressed this attitude in a speech of March 29, 1955, when he said, invoking the Italian playwright, Pirandello, "Egypt is in search of a national personality." This search for its identity, which takes the form of vigorous assertiveness, explains much of Egypt's policy at home and abroad.

From 1882 to 1955 Egyptians concentrated all their energies on a single goal—to get rid of the British. During that period they did not have enough energy left over to undertake the internal reforms essential for the modernization of this Islamic nation, nor were they encouraged in that direction by the British, who in Egypt, as contrasted with their rule in India, were concerned almost entirely with strategic considerations, and showed no interest in developing Egypt's economy or improving its social conditions. It is interesting to speculate as to what Egypt would have done if, at the time when it came in contact with the Western world in the early nineteenth century, it had been in a position, like Japan, to control its own destiny, and to decide which aspects of Western development it would incorporate into its own society, and which it would reject.

As events turned out, the only aspect of the West which the Egyptians adopted promptly was its armed strength, in the belief that weapons represented the secret of the West's superiority over less advanced peoples. Mohammed Aly, whom the Ottoman Empire had sent to defend Egypt against Napoleon in 1799, so distinguished himself in combat that he was made Pasha of Egypt in 1806, and under his rule Egypt achieved a degree of autonomy within the Ottoman Empire until the British took over the newly-built Suez Canal in 1882. Mohammed Aly tried to Westernize Egypt, and in this respect he can be compared with Russia's Peter the Great. But most of his efforts were concentrated on modernization of the army—not on economic and social reforms. His preoccupation with military strength is interesting to recall today, when Egypt's officer rulers are determined to obtain modern weapons and learn how to use them as the first step in their endeavor to strengthen their country against the West, as symbolized by Israel.

Once the British had withdrawn from the Suez Canal in 1956, the Egyptians were confronted with two major problems: how to redirect the nation's energies, which for so many years had been concentrated on the negative policy of getting Britain out, to the positive policy of reforming Egypt's political system, economy, and social order; and, second, how to recreate a role in world affairs for modern Egypt within the context both of the Islamic community and of the international community of the twentieth century.

When it comes to economic and social reform, Egypt faces another serious handicap unknown in Turkey. This handicap is that it does not have enough arable land for its rapidly growing population. When Napoleon tried to conquer Egypt in 1799, it had 2.5 million people. By 1900 it had 11 million, and now it has passed the 23-million mark, with no relief yet in sight. It is estimated that before the end of this century Egypt will have to feed, clothe, and house 35 million people.

To meet the land hunger of the peasants, who form 90 per cent of the population and eke out a miserable and precarious living, the government has introduced a land reform, which provides for nationalization of land above 200 acres, in return for compensation, and its distribution among the land-poor peasants *(fellaheen)* at the rate of three to five acres per family. Land redistribution, however, is but a first step, as other countries at Egypt's stage of development have discovered to their sorrow. If the productivity of the land is to be improved, the peasant must have fertilizer, he must have insecticides, he must have at least a modest amount of machinery, he must have education, and, above all, he and his family must be helped to conquer the diseases which enfeeble the health of the Egyptians and reduce their capacity to work. Of these the two greatest scourges are schistosomiasis, produced by a fluke which lives in the water—where Egypt's cotton-growers must spend most of their working days—penetrating the system and gradually destroying it; and trachoma, an eye disease which causes blindness to thousands of children and adults.

Egypt's government must thus conduct a many-front campaign against poverty, illiteracy, filth, and disease if the country is to acquire a firm economic and social foundation on which it can build its security and maintain its national independence. To achieve this objective, Nasser and his young officers launched an ambitious program for the creation of community-development projects, ultimately to number eight hundred, which would bring to Egypt's "dark" villages education for children and adults, medical facilities, recreation, electricity, and training in various skills, from blacksmithing to beekeeping and dairying, thereby helping the *fellaheen* to achieve a diversified economy, as contrasted with their present dependence on the growing of cotton, which represents 90 per cent of the country's exports.

Egypt's community-development projects compare favorably with those established by India, but Egypt, like India, has discovered that it needs a large number of teachers, doctors, craftsmen, and other workers who not only are trained to man those projects, but also, once trained, are willing to leave the amenities of Cairo and Alexandria for a life of hardship in the villages. In this respect the dilemma of the young educated man or woman in Egypt is reminiscent of that faced by Russian intellectuals in the nineteenth century who, inspired by a spirt of dedication, wanted to "go to the villages"—as Turgenev well described in his novel, *Fathers and Sons*—yet faced difficult problems of personal adjustment.

Internal reforms are being planned and carried out in Egypt, as in Turkey under Kemal Ataturk, by a dictatorship. The announcement in January, 1956, of a new constitution, under which Egypt is to have a one-party government, with candidates to the legislature nominated on a single slate by the present rulers of the country, means that this dictatorship, until now military, may be shared with civilians, but it does not yet presage the adoption of democracy on the Western model.

Nor is it surprising that in Egypt, as in Turkey, the creation of democratic institutions faces great obstacles. The middle class of business and professions, which in Western nations developed over a period of centuries and played a powerful role in industrialization and democratization, is as yet small, and in the past has displayed little sense of civic responsibility. While dictatorship is distasteful to Western advocates of democracy for non-Western lands, it is possible to argue that a period of strong but reforming dictatorship may be an essential prerequisite for economic modernization and improvement of social welfare without which democratic institutions would be a sham. Egypt's dictatorship has, on the whole, refrained from bloodletting. The deposed pashas—Egypt's financial and landowning aristocracy, who supported Farouk, as well as fanatical leaders of the Muslim Brotherhood who would like to have Egypt return to its past—have been neutralized through "protective custody" whenever they have challenged the policies of the regime. The same fate has befallen Naguib, first leader of the revolution, whose course of action was not regarded as forceful enough by Nasser and his young officers. The new constitution envisages the creation of a legislative body where the population would be represented not by politicians but by spokesmen for various professions and occupations—a guild state, reminiscent of Fascist Italy and Franco Spain. This procedure might give an increased role to the as yet inchoate and weak middle class. If and when the economic position of the *fellaheen* is improved, and they are able to develop a money economy through diversified activities on the land, recruits to the middle class may begin to be drawn, as in advanced countries, from the ranks of the more prosperous peasants.

Meanwhile, Egypt, with limited financial resources, is determined to strengthen its role in world affairs. This it is doing by accepting military and financial aid from whatever source it may come from—East or West; and, in fact, Cairo has sought to play the Soviet bloc off against the Western powers in its ambitious plans for reform. Because of its one-crop economy, based on the production of long-staple cotton, Egypt is not in a position to obtain foreign exchange through trade with the United States, itself a cotton-producing and cotton-exporting country. It can therefore be expected to continue trading with those nations—Russia, the eastern European satellites, Communist China—which, for whatever purpose they may use their economic position, are genuinely in need of cotton imports. For the time being, arms produced by Czechoslovakia's famous Skoda armaments works will be regarded in Cairo as a satisfactory form of payment, particularly since Egypt does not have the dollars, and since Nasser's nationalization of Suez, the prospect, to purchase arms in the United States.

From the point of view of the West, as well as Israel, Egypt's arms purchases and the training of its military technicians by Russians, Czechs, and Poles in the use of these arms represent a great danger not only for the Middle East, but for the rest of the world. For through this contact with Egypt, the U.S.S.R. has leapfrogged over the Western-blessed pact arrangements in the Balkans and the Middle East which were designed to protect Turkey and the eastern Mediterranean, and this without moving a single soldier or firing a single gun. It is conceivable, however, that Egypt's ultimate purpose is not to direct these arms against Israel or against the West—unless, of course, the West again intervenes in the Middle East against Egypt by force of arms as it did during the Suez crisis—but rather to give Egypt the status of an important power whose leadership will be accepted by Muslims from North Africa to Indonesia.

Egypt, dreaming of its past glories—in this respect Nasser is an heir of the great nineteenth century Muslim leader, Jamal-ud-Din al-Afghani, who sought a far-ranging role for Islam—seeks a role greater than that of leader of the Arab countries. It is eager to play the role of leader of the Muslim world—and it is this ambition which explains Nasser's interest in the Bandung conference of Afro-Asian nations in April, 1955, and in the future of Indonesia, with its predominantly Muslim population. Egypt also sees a role for itself in Africa, of which it forms an integral part. Although it apparently no longer hopes to conquer the Sudan, which achieved independence in 1955, it may achieve influence over its neighbor to the south. It also has taken an active part in rousing the Arabs of French North Africa—in Tunisia, Morocco, and Algeria—against France by radio broadcasts and the activities of North African nationalists with headquarters in Cairo. Through its interest in North Africa, moreover, Egypt has developed contacts with Franco Spain, which, as ruler of Spanish Morocco, has, like Egypt, followed an anti-French policy in North Africa.

Thus, unlike Turkey, which seems to be satisfied territorially, after centuries of rule over other lands through the Ottoman Empire, Egypt, as it develops its "national personality," apparently hopes to combine reforms at home with a role of growing influence, even of cultural "imperialism," abroad. Whether it can achieve this combination on the narrow base of its present territory, inadequate for the bare needs of its growing population, or will once again dissipate its energies instead of concentrating them in endeavors which would improve the lot of its people, remains one of the major questions in the Middle East and North Africa. Meanwhile, Cairo's every move affects all Muslims in greater or lesser degree. As Marshal Lyautey, the great French Arabist, once said, the Arab world is like a drum; if you tap one end it reverberates all over.

For the time being, however, Israel feels itself the primary target of Egypt's drive for power. The dilemma of Israel is that it is a primarily non-Arab, non-Muslim country in the

Arab Muslim world of the Middle East. On the map it is a pinpoint, both geographically and in terms of its population of less than 2 million as compared with the 40 million of the Arab lands. Today in Israel's population of 1,800,000 there are only 170,000 Arabs, as contrasted with the 800,000 who lived in Palestine before partition. During the war which Israelis call the "War of Liberation" but which, from the Arab point of view, was a war of destruction and desolation for the Palestinian Arabs, 600,000 Arabs left Palestine, and now, increased to 900,000 they live in misery and apathy along the borders of Israel—in the Gaza strip between Israel and Egypt, in Jordan, in Syria. These refugees are kept barely alive by the United Nations Relief Agency, the bulk of whose funds is contributed by the United States. They represent a veritable tinderbox of future rebellion, which could as easily be directed against the Western powers, regarded by the Arabs as sponsors and supporters of Israel, as at Israel itself.

Meanwhile, the State of Israel, created in 1948, has absorbed 700,000 Jews from Arab lands where they were either oppressed or lived in fear of future oppression—primarily Yemen, Iraq, and French North Africa. The Israelis thus feel that, while 600,000 Arabs left Palestine, Israel has absorbed approximately the same number of Jews from Arab lands, which have thereby been relieved of responsibility of this number of people and, therefore, would or should be able to absorb the Arab refugees. This view, understandably, is not shared either by the Arab countries, which are reluctant to accept the responsibility for the refugees and see an advantage in keeping the issue alive as a form of pressure on Israel, or by the Arab refugees themselves, who have a natural desire to return to the homes, no matter how poor, where they were brought up, rather than to re-establish themselves in a new setting.

Palestine, before it was transformed into the state of Israel, had, like the Arab nations of the Middle East, been a part of the Ottoman Empire until 1919. The Jews had been well treated by their Turkish rulers—and it should be added one of the paradoxes of our times is that, in spite of the barbed-wire curtain between Israel and the Arab nations, Jews living in Egypt had been decently treated before the Suez crisis as were the Arabs remaining in Israel. After the breakup of the Ottoman Empire, Palestine was awarded as a mandate to Britain, which had promised, in the well-known Balfour Declaration of 1917, that the Jews would have a "homeland" in Palestine. This promise became a matter of life and death for thousands of Jews after Hitler's rise to power, when they sought a haven from Nazi persecution in the "promised land." If at that time of bitter need the Western world had opened its doors wide to the immigration of Jews from Germany and eastern Europe, it is conceivable that the problem of a Jewish home in Palestine would not have arisen in an acute form, and the Arab-Israeli conflict would not have occurred. The West, however, slow to rouse itself against Hitler, was also slow to respond to the disaster which faced Europe's Jews. From the Western point of view, Palestine seemed the most plausible answer to the Jewish problem—yet Britain, as the mandatory power, and as a nation which had leaned heavily on the Arabs' support during two world wars and depended on them for strategic bases as well as for the oil needed for its navy, was not eager to antagonize Arab leaders by opening the doors of Palestine to Jewish immigrants.

The outcome of this complex interplay of national interests and international clashes was that the Jews of Palestine decided to take fate into their own hands, not unlike the Cypriotes in 1955, and through a campaign of terrorism finally succeeded in driving Britain to relinquish the mandate and in convincing the world, both in and out of the United Nations, of the need to create the state of Israel through partition of Palestine. The UN's decision of 1948 to partition Palestine, which triggered the war between Israel and the Arab lands that ended with a resounding victory for the Israelis, has since then overshadowed all other developments in the Middle East, and has created a chasm between Israel and its neighbors which no efforts by outside powers or by the United Nations have as yet succeeded in bridging.

The resulting situation was a compound of two human tragedies: the tragedy of displaced Jews who, having discovered from their experience in Germany that no amount of adaptation could protect them against destruction, were determined to find a home of their own, from which they could never be ejected in the future; and the tragedy of displaced Arabs, who whether through their own free will, as claimed by the Israelis, or because of Jewish acts of terrorism during the "War of Liberation," as claimed by Arab spokesmen, left the territory of Palestine encouraged by the Cairo radio to believe that, once the Arabs had won the war, they would be able to return victorious and to push the Israelis into the sea.

Whatever the reasons which brought about the flight of the Arab refugees, the fact is that the miserable existence they eke out in camps as wards of the United Nations is comparable, in its tragic implications, to the terrible fate suffered by the Jews of Europe—and calls for comparable understanding and compassion, particularly on the part of those who, like many of the European Jews settled in Israel, have experienced the horrors of persecution and exile.

The Israelis, understandably, regard their settlement in ancient Palestine as the fulfillment of an age-old promise and prophecy. The Arabs, also understandably, regard it as an invasion, and an intrusion of elements foreign to the Middle East, into their ancient homeland. The problem is made all the more acute because, to the Israelis, the aid of Western nations, financial, military, and spiritual, appears essential for their survival, while to the Arabs this very aid represents an unwarranted intervention in their region—and, to make matters worse, an intervention by the western European powers which once ruled them, now joined by the United States, politically a newcomer to the Middle East. Israel is proud of its "Westernism," of its command of the techniques and ideas of the West. And the West, in turn, often speaks with pride and satisfaction about Israel as an "outpost of Western democracy" in the Middle East. To the Arabs, however, this emphasis on the Western character of Israel is like the proverbial red rag to a bull. It seems to re-emphasize their relative backwardness, their lack of Western know-how, which in the past has left them, as they see it, at the mercy of the West, and might do so again in the future, unless the Arab nations have an opportunity to become, technologically and militarily, the equals of the West.

Yet Israel itself is gradually becoming less Western than it was at the outset of its independent existence. Israel is an amazing laboratory where peoples of many lands, coming from the most diverse civilizations, are being rapidly molded into one nation. Here many centuries can be seen living side by side—technicians and scholars trained in Germany and eastern Europe, in South Africa and the United States, rub shoulders wtih primitive farmers and craftsmen from Yemen and Iraq or North Africa. The astonishing thing—and this is one of the most remarkable contributions of Israel in the short span of its existence—is that these primitive people who had never seen or used a tool of any kind before, have within a year or two been trained to work in modern factories, without noticeably raising the accident rate in industrial production.

The influx of immigrants from Yemen, Iraq, and other non-Western areas means that today 40 per cent of Israel's population is non-Western in origin. And since the fertility of Jews from Africa and the Middle East is higher than that of Jews from Europe, it is predicted that within a decade the population of the country will be 60 per cent non-Western. The more non-Western Israel becomes, the sooner and the more effectively it will fit into the Middle East—and we must remember that, whatever may be the intellectual and spiritual attachments of Israel's European-born population, the new state, for better or worse, must live in the Middle East, and not in Europe or the United States.

In another respect Israel faces a problem similar to that of its Arab neighbors, and that is the problem of state and church. The Israeli state is based on the common religion, Judaism, which unites Jews from many lands. But within Israel there is a far-reaching debate as to whether Orthodox Judaism should be as closely interwoven with the state in the future as it has been in the past—whether there should not, in effect, be a separation between church and state. Many people of the younger generation believe that overemphasis on Orthodox practices, which are rigid and authoritarian in character and, like Islam, constitute a way of life, not only a religious faith, may impede the economic and social advance of the new country, whose economy faces grave problems of survival.

Israel is the only nation in the Middle East which, while still dependent on agriculture, has developed a considerable industry, with 40 per cent of the national income derived from industrial sources. Despite the socialist government created by the ruling Mapai party of Premier and Defense Minister Ben-Gurion and former Premier Moshe Sharrett, and the tremendous influence wielded by the labor organization, Histradut, 80 per cent of industry is in private hands.

Even if there were no threat of war, Israel would face difficult problems in developing its economy. This small country, a good part of which is arid land that needs careful irrigation, has often been called by its well-wishers "the "Switzerland of the Middle East." This, however, is a comparison that might create dangerous illusions about Israel's future. Switzerland has many natural advantages which Israel cannot hope to achieve. Switzerland is an advanced industrial country with a skilled population which imports raw materials and processes them into manufactured goods of high quality for export, thereby acquiring the foreign exchange it needs for the purchase abroad of food and raw materials. Israel, on the other hand, is a non-Western area in which, though skilled technicians from the Western world have settled there, a large part of the population is still backward technologically and must be trained for the tasks of modern industry. Although this task is by no means impossible, as has been proved by Israel's success in training Yemenite Jews, Israel, unlike Switzerland, does not lie at the center of the world's industrial complex and must import its raw materials from long distances and, once it has processed them into manufactured goods, export them again over a long haul. This process raises the price at which Israel must sell its goods abroad and makes it difficult for the new nation to compete with more advanced industrial countries on world markets. Moreover, Switzerland has for centuries been a financial center for most of Europe, with its neutrality recognized and for financial and other reasons safeguarded by the great powers, which find it advantageous to preserve Switzerland as a haven impregnable to war. And Switzerland has derived a good deal of its economic strength from this very role of banking center for other nations. Israel, by contrast, has only limited financial resources of its own to draw on, and has so far had to rely on governmental and private grants and gifts, chiefly from the United States, and on reparations by West Germany. These outside contributions estimated at about 250 million dollars for 1957, made up Israel's foreign trade deficit of over 200 million dollars. If Israel is gradually to achieve economic viability, it will have to intensify the balanced development of its industry and agriculture, reduce imports of food which can be grown at home as well as imports of many consumer goods, and concentrate on the production of selected items which can be most readily sold in world markets.

Israel's dilemma in trying to achieve this objective is twofold. First, Israel is a backward country which is endeavoring to modernize its agriculture and to speed its industrialization while, at the same time, assuring to its population social welfare standards comparable to those achieved by the most advanced nations of the West. Whereas in the Western nations—Britain, the United States, the Scandinavian countries, Germany—such measures as social security, unemployment insurance, health protection, universal education, and so on, were the outgrowth of strong developed economies, in Israel these measures have been adopted and applied at a time when economic development is still under way. This welfare policy, which is not only desirable in human terms but is regarded as necessary by the socialist government of Israel and by the country's powerful labor organization, Histradut, imposes a strain on the economy which countries like Switzerland did not have to bear in the early days of their industrialization.

Second, Israel, unlike Switzerland, has lived in constant fear of war since the first day it was created. This threat of war not only diverted manpower and urgently needed financial resources from productive work in developing the country, but also resulted in the strangulation of Israel's export trade through the economic boycott imposed on it by the Arab countries since 1947 and the restrictions the Arabs placed on Israel's use of the main arteries of commerce in the area—the Suez Canal and the Gulf of Aqaba—over both of which Egypt claimed control.

This economic strangulation, if unrelieved, threatened to prove as disastrous for Israel as outright war. To overcome the difficulties of competing in the West, Israel sought to open up markets for its goods in Asia, notably Burma and India, and in East Africa; and for this purpose it built the new port of Elath on the Red Sea. Egypt and Jordan, however, threatened to block traffic through that port. This action raised questions about the legality, under international law, of interference by Arab states with passage through an international waterway, the Suez Canal, as well as about the use of territorial waters in the Red Sea. On these points of law the United States and Britain, which have traditonally taken a strong stand on questions of freedom of transit, and were quick to protest about Nasser's nationalization of Suez, remained strikingly reticent before Israel's invasion of Egypt in October 1956.

Their attitude strengthened the impression in Israel that the Western powers, although professing their belief in democracy, have been less than ardent in supporting the one nation in the Middle East which has developed democratic institutions, and have leaned over backwards not to antagonize the Arabs. In part, at least, it seems to Israelis that this policy is explained by the Western powers' concern—this is particularly true of Britain—to preserve the access they now have to the rich oil resources of the Middle East, notably in Saudi Arabia and Iraq. In part, this interpretation appears to indicate lack of understanding about the Arabs' views on the future of the Middle East. The Arab countries, particularly Egypt, have shown that they are profoundly opposed to political and military intervention by the Western powers, although ready to accept economic aid from whatever quarter it comes provided it is given without prior conditions. The one exception to this generalization—Iraq—has been a rival of Egypt for leadership of the Arab world; and the inclusion of Iraq in the Baghdad pact of 1955 which Britain—but not the United States—also joined, aroused Egypt's resentment to a degree surprising to the West.

One of the reasons for this reaction was that no sooner had the front door of the Suez Canal Zone been closed, the Baghdad pact opened the way for Britain's military return to the Middle East through the back door of Iraq. And this Egypt was determined to prevent at all costs. Another reason was the suspicion in Cairo that the pact was an effort to divert the attention of the Arab countries from opposition to Israel and to turn their eyes, instead, to the U.S.S.R. On both counts Egypt and its supporters in the Middle East considered the Baghdad pact a nefarious move.

Not only does Israel, with barbed wire running through the streets of New Jerusalem and dividing house from house in many border villages, feel constantly menaced by the Arab states, but it differs from them, and particularly from Egypt, as to the role of Russia in the Middle East. Egypt has welcomed the return of Russia to the strategic area where the Tsars once confronted Britain, because Moscow serves as a counterweight to the Western powers and enables Cairo to develop a balance-of-power policy which can serve its vast aspirations for influence in the Muslim world. Israel opposes Russia both because it believes in democracy and rejects totalitarianism, and because the Soviet government has taken an openly hostile stand against Zionism, until recently preventing the emigration of Jews from behind the Iron Curtain to Israel. Russia's attitude toward Zionism, which has hitherto been in harmony with its opposition to all international movements and organizations other than those of a Communist character, notably the Vatican, creates a common ground for Russians and Arabs. Moreover, while Russia does not need Middle East oil for its own use, it regards the withholding of oil from the West as a strategic advantage in the global great-power struggle. And, above all, it has no intention of being barred from the Middle East, where the Tsars, long before the Commissars, had been active for two centuries.

Under the circumstances, Israel feels squeezed between the upper and nether millstones of the West and the U.S.S.R., both of which, for diverse motives, have reason to cultivate the friendship of the Arab nations and, in Israel's view, have shown little courage in standing up to Arab demands, both in the United Nations and outside. In fact, the one great power which has won the admiration of the Israelis in this respect is West Germany—and this because Chancellor Konrad Adenauer stood firm in 1954 against Arab threats to boycott German goods if Bonn paid reparations to Jews now living in Israel. The Germans proceeded to pay reparations—and their trade in the Middle East, far from suffering as a result, has thrived and, indeed, has challenged the trade of other Western nations.

Living in daily fear of extinction, either through war or through economic strangulation, Israel has again and again been tempted to strike the first blow at the Arab countries before they had an opportunity to increase their military strength. The temptation became well-nigh irresistible in 1955, when Egypt began to purchase Czech arms and Soviet-made planes. At one danger-point in the autumn of that year Prime Minister Ben-Gurion, who is also Defense Minister, seemed on the verge of counseling "preventive war." Calmer counsels, given by their Foreign Minister Sharrett, however, prevailed, and Israel's international position, which had been seriously undermined by the appearance of aggressive designs, noticeably improved.

In October 1956, however, Israel decided it had to stop destructive guerrilla raids from Egyptian soil and to win free passage for ships and goods through the Gulf of Aqaba. It consequently invaded Egypt at approximately the same time that Britain and France attacked at Suez. This two-pronged drive into Egypt was checked by the action of the United States and the U.S.S.R. which found thmselves voting on the same side in the United Nations for a cease-fire, and by the creation of the UN Emergency Force which kept the belligerents apart. Early in 1957, however, it was not yet clear whether the UN would succeed in settling the Arab-Israeli controversy, or would merely attempt to restore the status quo.

Over the long run, the future of the Middle East depends, first and foremost, on the rapid economic development of an area which is still living in feudal times, politically and economically, but is reaching out for the better things of life promised by modern science and technology. In this process of development, the 900,000 Arab refugees crowded along Israel's borders must be resettled, in large part, in Arab lands—primarily Syria and Iraq—with funds which the United States should either lend or preferably give outright to Israel for transfer to the Arab governments which show willingness to undertake such resettlement, with perhaps a token number—50,000 to 100,000—returning to Israel. Such a program would also require regional, and not nation-by-nation, planned development; it would put the waters of the Jordan—as proposed by Eric Johnston, President Eisenhower's personal representative—at the disposal of both Israel and the Arab nations for irrigation, a situation essential to the "conquest of the desert" that remains one of the top problems on the agenda of both Israelis and Arabs. It calls, moreover, for a genuine pledge of security by the great powers—Russia as well as the West—given to both Israel and the Arab countries, with no prejudice to future frontier adjustments, but without insisting that such adjustments, which may take years to work out, be made a prerequisite for security.

The differences in religion, culture, and traditions of Jews and Arabs do not, of themselves, preclude eventual stabilization of the Middle East. In ancient times, and even in the turbulent period since 1948, Arabs and Jews have lived peacefully side by side, and they can do so again. What must be changed are the profound differences in the economic conditions of relatively advanced Israel and its backward Arab neighbors, and between Israel's democracy and the Arabs' predominantly dictatorial institutions. Such changes cannot be enforced by the Western powers. Nor can Israel set itself up as an example to its neighbors without exacerbating their hostility. But as the economies of the Arab nations are modernized, so ultimately will be their political systems and social conditions. And then, but only then, will the nations on both sides of the barbed-wire curtain achieve a common level of communication, like water flowing between two similar jars.

This goal, however, can be achieved only if both Israel and the Arab states come to think of themselves as modern states, not as nations based on exclusivist religions. And this, in turn, means that the Muslims, instead of rejecting coexistence on a basis of equality with peoples of other faiths, must come to accept fellowship with non-Muslim communities within nations as well as in the international community. The greatest test of their capacity and willingness to do this will come in India and Pakistan.

4

India and Pakistan: Anglo-Asian Synthesis

The most striking aspect of the Indian subcontinent, divided since 1947 into two states, India and Pakistan, each of which is still going through the painful process of unification—hampered, in the former, by linguistic differences, and in the latter by geographic division—is the extent to which here East and West have become fused into what one might call an Anglo-Asian synthesis.

When the British, after decades of pressure by the Indian Nationalists, finally relinquished their vast empire and sailed home in August, 1947, ending three centuries of British "presence," it looked as if India would turn its back on its former rulers—as Egypt did when Britain withdrew from the Suez Canal Zone in June 1956—and shut the door on its experience with Britain. Yet, as events proved, nothing could have been further from the truth. The moment the British left, the Indians were free to express their admiration for the practices and institutions Britain had brought to the subcontinent. Today there is little doubt that India's ideal of democracy is not the United States, but Britain—an ideal which the Indians strive to approach, meanwhile deploring their own shortcomings as judged by British standards.

The basic problem of the Indian subcontinent since the days when Muslim conquerors invaded it from the north in the fifteenth century, establishing the Mogul Empire on the ruins of divided and clashing Hindu principalities, has been the need to reconcile the two principal groups of its vast population, Hindus and Muslims. The differences between these two groups are profound—not only because of differences in their religions, but because their religious and philosophical concepts deeply affect their respective ways of life and their attitudes toward the rest of the world.

When a Westerner first looks at Hinduism and at Islam, the

differences seem far more striking and far-reaching than the similarities. The Hindus believe in a secular state, and oppose the concept of a state founded on religion. This was the basis for the objections of Nehru and Gandhi to the demand of Mohammed Ali Jinnah, the lawyer who played a key role in the creation of Pakistan, for the establishment of a Muslim state when India achieved independence from Britain in 1947. On the other hand, the Muslims of the Indian subcontinent, like their coreligionists elsewhere, think in terms of a religious state. Not only did they insist on the separation of a Muslim state from India, but, once free, they decided that the constitution of Pakistan, with its population of 70 million Muslims and 10 million Hindus, should be squarely based on the Koran, the sacred book of Islam. In this respect, Pakistan has followed the course of other Muslim states, with the notable exception of Turkey. However, even though, as pointed out in Chapter III, Islam has not had a reformation comparable to that of Christianity in the sixteenth century, the religious leaders of Pakistan have gone further than their colleagues of other Muslim states in trying to reaffirm the relations of church and state in the modern world, and in seeking to discover how the precepts of the Koran, through reinterpretation, might be adapted without undue controversy to the recognized needs of the twentieth century. More important, the 40 million Muslims who remained in India are struggling to find a way to preserve their faith and at the same time to achieve political and economic integration with a non-Muslim, predominately Hindu majority.

Hinduism is, in essence, an all-inclusive and all-absorptive religion. It has survived war and civil strife for thousands of years, through countless crises, invasions and conquests, largely because it has proved to be "all things to all men." Within its over-all framework there is room, at one and the same time, in the twentieth century as well as in the distant past, for the beliefs of primitive peoples who worship the forces of nature, believing, like the ancient Greeks, that the Godhead is present in all things, animate and inanimate; yet it also satisfies sophisticated Hindus who want to believe in a supreme being, since it holds that the Godhead is made manifest in human form, notably in the form of Krishna, chief spokesman in the *Bhagavad-Gita*. This brief book, a gem of Hindu literature, is the main part of the *Mahabharata*, one of India's two great epics, the other being the *Ramayana*. The Hindus can indulge at great length in abstract thinking, which to their Western friends often sounds thin-spun and elusive. Yet they can also portray their gods in the most realistic manner, as men who share human experience, in the colorful paintings of the Ajanta caves, as well as in the impressive and often sensual sculptures that decorate Hindu temples. The Hindus have always sought to find the common denominator in the many faiths which have flowed into their country from north, east, and west. And even those beliefs which at first appeared to challenge Hinduism on grounds of ideas and practices such as the caste system—notably Buddhism—have ultimately been absorbed into Hinduism and have all but disappeared in India.

By contrast, Islam is a monotheistic faith. When the prophet Mohammed, in the sixth century A.D., interpreted the will of Allah, he thought first of all in terms of purifying Arabic thought of the polytheistic excrescences with which it had become overlaid. It is true that the Koran lists a long roster of prophets drawn from the traditions of other faiths—Christianity and Judaism—including Abraham, Jesus Christ, and the Angel Gabriel, but all these prophets are on a lower level than Allah, the one and only God. And unlike the Hindus, the Muslims do not permit the portrayal of Allah or of his prophet Mohammed.

The devout Hindu is inward-looking. His principal endeavor is to improve himself through pursuit of the path of duty *(dharma)* and the performance of good deeds *(karma)* until such time, with intervening transmigrations of soul, as he can become free of all strife and change, and experience the bliss of *nirvana,* non-being. The Hindu finds nothing peculiar in spending long periods of time in meditation. He is convinced that every deed starts a chain reaction, producing successive resulting situations, and is therefore at great pains to weigh every decision he takes.

At first glance the Muslim seems more akin to the Westerner than the Hindu because of the outward-looking character of his religion. Yet the difference is not as profound as it sometimes appears. In the *Bhagavad-Gita* the god Krishna tells the warrior Arjuna who seeks his counsel on the battlefield that he must act and, if he acts right, he will be reborn. The Muslim, too, is enjoined by the Koran to do good deeds, from giving contributions to religious foundations and alms to the poor to the final and most important act—the journey to Mecca—comparable for the Muslim to the Hindu's pilgrimage to the holy places of his faith, of which the most important is the city of Benares on the Ganges. The Hindus seem to think in abstract terms about good and evil, the retribution of being reborn in an unpleasant form or the rewards of *nirvana*—yet both punishment and reward are vividly anticipated, and practical actions must be taken to achieve the latter rather than the former. Among these is self-training, the use of various disciplines, of which Yoga is one of the best known. The Muslims depict heaven and hell in graphic terms, not unlike those of medieval Christian chronicles. Yet while they represent Allah as a stern taskmaster, the Koran also emphasizes that Allah can be merciful, and that the sinner can obtain mercy by good works. Thus the concepts of life and ethical prescriptions of the two faiths are not, in actuality, as far apart as is sometimes thought in the West.

Hindus seem to differ from Muslims by their emphasis on non-violence (*ahimsa*) to men and beasts, which is a deeply ingrained principle of Hindu philosophy, as embodied in the Rock Edicts of Hindu Emperor Asoka, and ancient Hindu writings. Because of the injunction not to kill animals, meat eating is prohibited, and respect is enjoined for all animals, but particularly those regarded as sacred—the cow, the snake, and the monkey. The Jains, a reformist Hindu sect, go so far as to forbid deep breathing, for fear that the intake of breath might kill insects invisible to the naked eye. It was this traditional principle of non-violence which Gandhi invoked when, on his return from South Africa in 1915, he spurred the Congress, organized by the Indian Nationalists, to adopt a policy of non-violent non-cooperation toward the British—a policy which eventually caused the British to withdraw from India.

The Muslims, by contrast, are believed, especially by Hindus, to approve the use of violence. Traditionally, it is true, the followers of Mohammed have supported the idea of waging a holy war—*jihad*—against the infidel. Such a war the Muslims waged against the Christian Crusaders in olden times, and today in Pakistan one can hear talk of *jihad* against India over Kashmir, while Israel fears a holy war against its territory by the Arab states. Yet violence cannot be regarded as an exclusive prerogative of the Muslims. The Hindus, too, have found it difficult to remain non-violent when their emotions have been deeply stirred. This was seen during the turbulent days of partition in 1947, when the Muslim-Hindu riots shocked and devastated the Indian subcontinent, leaving at the end five or six million homeless, propertyless refugees on both sides of the new border. Again in January, 1956, violence characterized the disturbances in Bombay and other leading cities of India, following Nehru's announcement of plans for the reorganization of the country on linguistic lines.

The most striking outward feature which distinguishes Hinduism from Islam in the subcontinent is the existence in India of a caste system, which has never been accepted by the Muslims, either when they lived in India under the British or in the new state of Pakistan. The Muslims believe in the intrinsic equality of man. For them all Muslims, irrespective of rank or wealth or education, are brothers. Only the infidel is an outsider.

In India the caste system, that to Westerners seems peculiar and repugnant, has a significance which is not merely religious, but is also political, economic, and social. It is an institution deeply rooted in the history of the Hindus. Originally the caste system appears to have developed at a time when waves of new immigrants or invaders poured into India. The indigenous people known from the earliest available records must have been small, squat, Negroid in appearance, flat-faced and bushy-haired—like some of the aborigines who still survive in Australia and the Philippines. Then came the Dravidians (around 3250 B.C.), also dark of skin, but taller and better-formed, who made use of the primitive peoples they found in India in a servile capacity. The Aryans (around 1720 B.C.) who entered from central Asia and were light-skinned and blue-eyed became, in effect, the ruling race, recruiting the natives they found in India to do their less palatable chores and assuming positions of distinctive authority in government, the armed forces, and trade. The result was that Hindu society became divided from top to bottom, according to the lightness or darkness of one's skin, or one's breed: the word *casta,* a Portuguese word, means "breed," while the Hindu word *varna,* used to describe caste, means "color."

The four castes which have persisted into our own times are:

1. *Brahmans* (or Brahmins), who constituted 6 per cent of the population of India before partition, and included in their ranks priests and educators. The Brahmins knew the *Vedas,* the ancient books of India's lore and wisdom, and transmitted their knowledge to selected young people, who perpetuated the existence of their caste. In our own times many Brahmans are members of other professions—doctors, lawyers, merchants—but distinguished scholars are still prominent in their ranks. Their members have a sense of *noblesse oblige* about

duty to the state which in Western nations has been the hallmark of an aristocracy.

2. *Kshatryias,* who are the rulers, nobles, and warriors, form the caste which engaged in civilian and military administration. It was into this caste that Buddha, who opposed the caste system and urged its reform, was born in the fifth century B.C.

3. *Vaishyas,* the caste which includes merchants and landowners, constitutes what we would call in Western societies the middle class.

4. *Sudras,* the workers and servants, were included in the caste system, but had to perform the lowly, hard tasks of Hindu society. This group, by our standards, would be the lower class, or in Marxist terms the proletariat.

This four-category caste structure should not seem alien to past Western experience. Similarities may be found between this structure and the gradations with which we are familiar in the Middle Ages—the king or prince flanked by the clergy, the lords of the manor who were also the warriors, the merchants who created the guilds, built up the towns, and eventually led the revolutions which brought about democracy in the West, and the serfs attached to the land and the landless peasants who drifted to the new towns and eventually became factory hands in the early days of the Industrial Revolution. The Western medieval system, however, had relatively more mobility than the caste system of India, and the Catholic Church, which held the view that all men are equal in the sight of God, made it possible for a serf to leap over intervening categories and rise to the ranks of the priesthood.

The unique feature of the Indian social system is the fifth group, which was not included in the caste system—the exterior castes also known by the British term "scheduled castes" and the derogatory Hindu phrase "untouchables." Gandhi, shocked by the existence of this sub-proletariat, who were regarded as unclean because they were condemned to perform "unclean" tasks—such as street-sweeping, scavenging, slaughter of animals, tanning, laundry, and so on—called for the abolition of untouchability, and spoke of them as "harijans," children of God.

What made the existence of the untouchables particularly painful was that the Hindu religion, which did not itself prescribe the caste system, nevertheless specified a wide range of prohibitions on contacts between the four castes and the "untouchables," who were confined to jobs regarded as unclean, such as scavenging, on the ground that contacts would bring about pollution of caste members. These prohibitions, in effect, condemned the untouchables to a ghetto existence—to a situation which, in the parlance of modern South African Nationalists, could be described as rigid *apartheid*. The untouchables were forbidden to enter Hindu temples, to use wells, to travel on public conveyances, to live in the same areas of villages and towns as members of other castes, to eat with them, or to intermarry with them, or even to offer them a drink of water. They were excluded from schools, and were even ordered to make a detour on the road if they saw members of castes drawing nigh. True, untouchables, like other Hindus, could achieve a better position through rebirth—but only if they behaved like good untouchables while alive and did not rebel against their lot. Under these circumstances, it is not surprising that some untouchables abandoned Hinduism and turned to other religious faiths.

In their struggle against the concept and practice of the caste system, Gandhi and Nehru won a resounding victory after independence, when the 1950 constitution of the Republic of India prohibited discrimination on grounds of race, religion, or caste. Although this provision has by no means been universally carried out, and many years will elapse before the caste system disappears in India, the system had begun to change even before independence and the adoption of the new constitution.

Many factors caused this process of change, among them the influence of British precept and practice, British insistence on the equality of all individuals before the law, and, above all, the introduction of industrialization, which has gradually whittled down caste restrictions on the use of buses, eating in common, working and living side by side, and other rules which worked a great hardship on untouchables. Moreover, the drift of the untouchables to faiths other then Hinduism—notably Christianity, which did not exclude them from places of worship, as well as to Islam and, more recently in 1956 to Buddhism—caused Hindu religious leaders to reconsider their opposition to the use of temples, and to urge modification of ancient rules. And the Indian government's insistence on equal educational opportunities for all is gradually breaking down the barriers, in schools and colleges, that once made it well-nigh impossible for untouchables to obtain the education without which they could not hope to gain the skills that, in turn, would make it possible for them to rise in the economic and social scale.

Thus, India is passing through a profound social revolution, which may ultimately bring about the breakdown of the caste system. This revolution should not be too rapid and violent according to responsible Indians, who point out that with all its reprehensible features, the caste system has served to hold together widely diverse populations, has provided a cement for a society which might otherwise disintegrate, and has acted as a voluntary social security system, with each member of a caste feeling responsibility for the poor or handicapped among his fellow caste members. Only when India has succeeded in providing substitutes for the advantages offered by the caste—such as its social security aspect—would it be wise, they feel, to discard the system. Moreover, some observers believe that, as India becomes industrialized, its population may divide along class, instead of caste, lines, and that then the newly emerging classes may clash with each other, as has happened in more advanced countries at comparable stages of economic and social development.

The two philosophies of Hinduism and Islam are reflected in the nature of the two new states—India and Pakistan—which emerged after the withdrawal of Britain in 1947. The Republic of India was established by a constitution proclaimed three years after partition. This constitution is squarely based on the principles of political democracy as developed in India under British rule, and enlarged by the Indians to include the concepts of economic and social democracy which in various forms have been incorporated into the constitution of the U.S.S.R. and the post-World War II constitution of the Fourth French Republic. The Indian constitution combines Gandhi's ideas about non-violence and the protection of minority groups, notably the untouchables; Nehru's belief in a moderate form of socialism, deeply influenced by the ideas and practices of the British Laborites; and some of the basic principles of British administration, particularly the rule of law. It thus represents a synthesis of the most advanced thinking of Britain and Asia.

The Republic of India is a secular state, within which, as already pointed out, there is to be no discrimination on grounds of religion. This is a life-or-death necessity for a country like India, which, even after partition and resettlement of populations, has 40 million Muslims out of a total of 380 million people, as well as adherents of various numerically smaller sects, notably the independent-minded Sikhs of the Punjab. The republic is a federal organization of states, each of which, under the constitution, exercises considerably more latitude in a number of fields than the states composing the United States. At the outset, Nehru and his associates were notably successful in integrating into a single nation the widely differing units of the British Empire in India—a part of which was directly ruled by the British, with another part subdivided into 582 princely states which had bilateral agreements with the British. This success is credited in large measure to the late S. V. Patel, first president of India, a skillful politician who succeeded in persuading the princes to integrate their states into the new nation in return for the assurance that they would retain their titles and receive a pension from New Delhi—the only two exceptions being Hyderabad and Junagadh, where India finally used military action to bring their rulers into line.

The maintenance of India's unity, however, has been threatened by the language differences which have developed over centuries in the sub-continent. India today has at least twelve major languages, several of which, notably Bengali, possess a distinguished literature. New Delhi's attempt, set forth in the constitution, to introduce Hindi as an official language for the entire nation aroused opposition in several areas, most vigorously of all in South India, whose inhabitants have something of the same feeling about North India, where Hindi originated, as the American Southerners have about the "Yankee" North. The Congress party, before independence, had promised linguistic autonomy once the British had left, and many of its supporters pressed for fulfillment of this pledge. The States Reorganization Commission in 1955 announced a plan for the reorganization of the 27 states listed in the constitution into 16, each organized on the basis of a different language.

This plan, however, provoked a violent explosion when it became known that the powerful and rich state of Bombay, where the Congress party first started, was to be divided into two states, one based on the Gujerati language and the other on the Marathi language, with the city of Bombay, India's principal port and intellectual center, to be placed under the direct rule of the central government in New Delhi. Protests came from other states as well, and for a time it looked as if India, having barely achieved independence from Britain and having developed a sense of national unity such as it had seldom enjoyed in its history, might be disrupted by linguistic clashes.

To avert what Nehru called a "catastrophe," New Delhi proposed the reorganization of the country into five states—north, south, east, west and center—in the hope of overcoming language barriers. Finally, however, the nation's reorganization into 17 states based on language was accepted. Although this controversy over languages may seem strange to Westerners, it is important for us to remember that it is this very kind of controversy which kept Europe aflame for several centuries, as the western Europeans sorted themselves out into the national states of France, Germany, Italy, the Netherlands, Belgium. In our own times eastern Europe has resounded to the clash of recrimination about the use of Polish, Czech, and other Slavic languages in the Austro-Hungarian Empire; and the Tsarist government was accused of trying to Russify the many national groups within its borders by forcing them all to learn Russian and forget their mother tongues. In size of territory and population, India exceeds Europe outside the U.S.S.R., and a number of its states, with populations of 30 to 40 million, are equal in population to independent national states of Europe, such as France, West Germany, and Italy. Time and patience will be necessary to alleviate the passions aroused by linguistic controversies.

The 1950 constitution provides in detail for the establishment in India of a welfare state, to be achieved by gradual, democratic methods, as contrasted with the rapid, totalitarian methods of Russia and Communist China. This goal is to be attained by means of planning, carried out through a series of Five-Year Plans, the first of which was completed in 1956. The resulting economy would have two main features. The first is a modernized agriculture, characterized by land redistribution, with plots over 30 or 50 acres (depending on the laws of the various states) taken from the big landowners in return for long-term compensation and redistributed to the peasants, and productivity increased through community development projects, which eventually are to cover the entire country, providing the peasants with medical, educational, and agronomic facilities of various kinds, developed not by fiat from above, but through voluntary cooperation between the peasants and the government. The second feature is an industrial "mixed economy," with some undertakings reserved to the public sector, controlled and directed by the government, and others left in the private sector, to be directed by private owners and developed through private investment.

In both these respects—voluntary agricultural development and the continuance of private enterprise in certain fields—the Indian type of development differs fundamentally from the Russian and Communist Chinese models. Two criticisms, however, have already been made of the Indian system as it has worked out thus far. One is that land reform has been proceeding too slowly to meet the needs of the peasants—partly because the government, both at the center and in the states, lacks the means to give financial compensation—and that more direct steps must be taken to put land at the peasants' disposal if resort to violence on the Communist pattern is to be avoided. This criticism has come most eloquently from Vinoba Bhave, a Sanskrit scholar and devoted follower of Gandhi, who has been going from village to village urging landowners to make gifts of land to the peasants, thereby avoiding both the danger of revolution and the necessity of compensation. —so far with only limited practical success. The other criticism comes from India's business community and from would-be foreign investors, who say that the line between public and private sectors has not been defined with sufficient clarity, and that this uncertainty, and the possibility that the government might suddenly nationalize undertakings once in the private sector—as was the case with life insurance in 1956—makes the development of private enterprise hazardous, and in the long run impossible. The government, for its part, contends that India's businessmen have not yet developed the sense of responsibility of their counterparts in Britain and the United States, and have been more interested in turning a quick rupee through speculation in commodities, such as sugar and cotton, than in taking the risk involved in building up established business concerns over a long period of time through investment of capital.

Whatever the criticisms that may be made of the Indian system, Nehru and his associates have acted on the belief that gradual economic development achieved without resort to violence represents the most effective method of defeating communism. This emphasis on gradualism is not only in line with India's own tradition of trying to absorb and reconcile various faiths and its predilection for non-violence, made world-famous by Gandhi, but also with the British policy, regarded with favor in India, of seeking to find a middle ground between clashing ideologies, and to discover a workable common denominator. In this respect, India has greatly benefited—as thoughtful Indians readily admit—by their experience with British administration, much as they resented it at the time. This administration gave India an opportunity gradually to develop democratic institutions, and to train the men who could direct such institutions—an experience lacking in the history of other great non-Western nations, such as Russia, China, and Japan, when they entered the era of industrialization.

The result has been that, when India achieved independence, its leaders were able to take over responsibility from the British, not without many problems, but with few of the sharp clashes which led to civil strife in Russia and China, or the political tug-of-war that occurred in French Indochina and Dutch Indonesia, where native leaders had not been prepared for the tasks of government.

India, however, has had to face the problems which understandably developed when the Indian National Congress, originally a catchall organization of all elements opposed to British rule except the Communists—who backed the British during World War II after Germany's invasion of Russia in 1941, and have since been in ill-repute for this reason—had to reorient its policy of opposition to Britain into a policy of reshaping the country to the heart's desire of the Indians. The influence of the Congress party remained unchallenged in the early years of independent India, principally because of the tremendous influence exercised by Gandhi and, after his death in 1948 at the hands of a Hindu religious fanatic, by Nehru. The Socialists, who for a time appeared to have the makings of something like Her Majesty's loyal opposition in Britain, proved unable to fill this role—partly because their thunder had been stolen by the socialism of Nehru, and partly because their most outstanding leader, American-educated Jayaprakash Narayan, decided in 1953 to abandon political life and to join Vinoba Bhave in his non-political campaign of *Bhoodan* (land-gift). The Congress party, although in a position to exercise authoritarian rule, has refrained from taking this course, and India's first national elections, held in 1951-52, with 70 per cent of the qualified voters going to the polls throughout the length and breadth of the land, were carried out in exemplary democratic fashion, resulting in a Congress party victory.

Since then, however, the party has been challenged by the small but active Communist party, particularly on linguistic issues, as in the state of Andhra (1953) and Bombay city

(1956) and in areas where extreme poverty combined with high literacy have created unrest, notably Travancore-Cochin in South India. The 1955 visit of Russia's Communist leaders, Premier Nikolai A. Bulganin and Communist Party Secretary Nikita M. Krushchev, was believed by some Indians—as well as by many foreign observers—to have reinforced the position of India's Communists. Others, however, contended that this visit had strengthened the hand of Prime Minister Nehru, who had shown no hesitation in repressing India's Communists, up to and including jail sentences, when it could be proved that Communists had created a direct threat to the state. Nehru, however, has observed the practice, followed also in Britain, of permitting the Communists freedom to speak and publish, and to be elected to India's parliament, the House of the People, where they hold 27 seats as a result of the 1951-52 elections.

The firmness with which Nehru has acted against Communists at home has seemed in sharp contrast to his policy of friendliness toward the Communist states, Russia and China, which he visited in 1955. When Peiping and Moscow leaders returned the visit, they spared no effort to enlist Nehru's public reaffirmation of the "five principles" enunciated by Nehru and Chou En-lai in Peiping, reiterated at the Afro-Asian Conference held in Bandung, Indonesia, in 1955, and reaffirmed in New Delhi during the Bulganin-Krushchev visit. Although Mr. Nehru's foreign policy often seems incomprehensible to Westerners, and has been denounced in the United States as pro-Communist and anti-Western—at least before the Eisenhower-Nehru talks of December 1956—it is understandable in terms of India's past traditions and present-day problems.

Mr. Nehru—and in this he has the support of most responsible Indians—is convinced that military blocs, whatever their origin or motivation, will sooner or later lead to the outbreak of war. War anywhere in Asia (Formosa has long been regarded by New Delhi as the principal danger spot) would, in his opinion, jeopardize, if not destroy, India's hopes, nurtured during three centuries of British presence, of building an independent, modern nation capable of fulfilling the aspirations of its people. It has therefore been Mr. Nehru's endeavor to keep a balance between the West, on the one hand, and Russia and China, on the other, and to avoid commitment to either side, which might force India to become aligned with one bloc against another. This policy has been described in the West as "neutralism," with the connotation that it is a negative and, according to John Foster Dulles, "immoral" policy because it does not espouse with positive enthusiasm the principles and objectives of the democratic West against totalitarian world communism. India's attitude, however, which Mr. Nehru calls "non-alignment," is by no means a negative approach to world problems—any more than Gandhi's policy of non-violent non-cooperation could be regarded as a negative attitude toward the British. Just as Gandhi's policy had the positive objective of building a new India once the British had relinquished their rule, so Mr. Nehru has thought in terms of helping to create a more stable world free from the threat of nuclear war, where underdeveloped new nations like India, and peoples still living under colonial rule who might eventually achieve nationhood, could develop their resources and perfect their institutions in an atmosphere of peace. Nor has India been "neutral" between democracy and communism. It has not only vigorously supported British democracy, but is a member of the Commonwealth.

Mr. Nehru's views of the world have unquestionably been affected by his opposition to colonialism, born out of his personal experience under the British. The West has castigated him for not taking an equally strong stand against the new colonialism of Russia, particularly with respect to the countries of eastern Europe. From the point of view of the Indians, however, Russia's relations with the countries of eastern Europe is an aspect of power politics in which all great powers have indulged in the past, whereas the rule of whites over non-whites arouses a deep revulsion on their part against what they regard as racialism. This revulsion has not, however, prevented independent India from developing a warm relationship with Britain since 1947—so warm, indeed, that Americans have often felt the Indians preferred the British, their former rulers, to the United States, which had supported India's struggle for independence. Nor have the Indians been slow to praise the British whenever Britain has moved, since 1947, to give greater independence to other non-white peoples—notably in the Gold Coast and in British Togoland. Moreover, Russia's ruthlessness in suppressing the Hungarian revolt of October 1956 brought official condemnation by Mr. Nehru.

By contrast to India, Pakistan adopted a constitution only in 1956. According to this constitution, the government of the Islamic Republic of Pakistan shall be based on the Koran, and all its activities must conform to Koranic principles. A commission has been appointed to study how this objective can be brought about.

The creation of a Pakistani constitutional system has been hampered by the geographical division of the country after partition into two segments—West Pakistan with the national capital at Karachi, a former small and insignificant seaport suddenly transformed into the center of a state, and East Pakistan, formerly part of the Indian province of Bengal, separated from each other by 1,000 miles of Indian territory. Within this divided state the Muslims have not completely achieved the dream of Pakistan's founder, Mohammed Ali Jinnah—a traditional Muslim dream—that the new state should be entirely Muslim in character. The Muslim League, which before 1947 corresponded, for Muslims, to what the Congress was for Hindus, was dedicated to the maintenance of Koranic principles. There is real opposition to this goal among thoughtful Pakistanis—and this opposition brought about in 1956 the breakup of the Muslim League.

Out of its total population of 80 million, Pakistan still has 10 million Hindus. The decision to base the constitution ultimately on the Koran gave rise to the fear that this Hindu minority would be put in the position of second-class citizens—a position which the Muslims, when they were still part of undivided India, feared might be theirs if they remained within a predominantly Hindu state after partition. However, the rigid views of the Muslim League have been challenged by the principal opposition group, the Awami League, leftist in character, which has urged that Hindus should be represented in the National Assembly proposed as Pakistan's legislature once the constitution has been adopted.

The authority of the Muslim League has been challenged also by spokesmen for East Pakistan, which is not only the principal source of the nation's wealth—jute and cotton—but is politically more advanced than West Pakistan. The East Pakistanis, in elections held in 1953, brought to the fore leaders who demanded a stronger voice in Karachi than had been previously accorded to their sector of the new nation. The Karachi government, claiming that these leaders threatened the security and stability of the country, put them in jail, but released them in 1955 when it agreed to include several of their number in the national cabinet.

Like India, Pakistan faces two serious political problems. The first is how to hold two sectors of the nation together—and in the case of Pakistan the physical separation of the two sectors creates an added complication. The other is how to reorient the Muslim League to the reconstruction of the state on lines which would permit peaceful coexistence between the Muslim majority and the Hindu minority, as well as the adjustment of Islam to modern times—the same problem which faces other Muslim countries from North Africa to Indonesia.

Although the Muslims, too, had had experience with British rule, and might eventually, like the Hindus, find it possible to bring about a synthesis of British and Asian ideas, their situation is more complex than that of the Hindus. There are two reasons for this. First, the Muslims took a longer time to adapt themselves to British principles and practices, in part because they were slower than the Hindus to learn English and therefore to enter administrative services where the use of English was required. And second the Pakistanis, like other Muslims, have a predisposition to authoritarianism, which is directly related to their reliance on the prescriptions of the Koran. This predisposition, contrary to assumptions in the United States, may make the Pakistanis more susceptible to Communist indoctrination at home than has been true of the Hindus, although hitherto Pakistan has been no less zealous than India in repressing native Communists.

In foreign policy Pakistan has adopted a position which is outwardly at the opposite pole from that of India. The Pakistani leaders have not accepted the concept of "non-alignment" on which Nehru has based his foreign policy. On the contrary, they have clearly taken their stand at the side of the West, and in token of this have concluded a military alliance with the United States, have sought and obtained American weapons, have joined the Southeast Asia Treaty Organization (SEATO), and have entered the Baghdad, or "northern tier," pact, which is designed to check aggression by Russia and/or China against Southeast Asia and the Middle East.

Pakistan's attitude in world affairs, however, has been determined less by irrevocable acceptance of the Western bloc than by its opposition to India, particularly concerning the issue of Kashmir, the only princely state of undivided India whose adherence to one or the other of the two new nations continues to be contested. This became increasingly clear after the Bandung conference of April, 1955, when Pakistan did not hesitate to send missions to Communist China, whose government it has recognized, and later grew restive when it discovered that the United States and Britain did not take up the cudgels on its behalf against India on the issue of Kashmir after Russia's visiting leaders had expressed their support of Nehru's Kashmir aspirations. It is not outside the bounds of possibility that when Pakistan sees other nations—notably Muslim Egypt—dealing advantageously with both Communist powers and the West, it will follow suit, hoping thereby to strengthen its position in Asia through closer ties with Communist China and Russia and, in any case, to avoid becoming the principal target in that area for the displeasure of Moscow and Peiping. Pakistan, moreover, hopes to find in the Soviet bloc countries an outlet for its principal exports, jute and cotton.

The controversy between India and Pakistan about Kashmir often gives the impression that the two nations of the Indian subcontinent are, and may remain, locked in mortal hostility toward each other. Yet India and Pakistan have many interests in common, and in this generation at least, their leading administrators have a strong link of mutual respect and similar training forged by participation side by side in the Indian Civil Service under British rule. No matter what storms may rage in New Delhi and Karachi about such issues as Kashmir, compensation for refugee property, the possibility that India might withhold water needed for the irrigation of Pakistan; no matter how vigorously the late Jinnah's sister, Fatima Jinnah, may call for *jihad* against India—the former civil servants of British India find a basis for understanding and cooperation across newly drawn frontiers and tariff lines.

Partition, moreover, has wrought great hardship on the economies of both nations. It left most of the jute and cotton of undivided India within the territory acquired by the Muslims, notably in East Pakistan, and most of the factories which once processed these raw materials into manufactured goods within the territory of the Republic of India. Had the two nations shown the political wisdom to forbear from imposing tariffs against each other, this situation would not have proved alarming. But it is apparently one of the great temptations of new nationhood—as well as old—to set up barriers against the trade of other states, and neither India nor Pakistan resisted this temptation. Customs duties, added to the differential between the Indian rupee, devalued at the time of Britain's devaluation of the pound sterling in 1950, and the Pakistani currency, which was allowed to maintain its previous value because of the world demand for jute during the Korean war, made trade between the two countries all but impossible. The result was that Pakistan initiated its own plans for the construction of factories to turn its jute and cotton into manufactured goods, while India, which desperately needed more food for its continuously growing population, turned to the cultivation of the jute and cotton it could no longer obtain from Pakistan without customs duties. Thus nationalist sentiment diverted both new states from the untrammeled economic development which could have greatly eased their problems. This situation, however, may be alleviated by the trade treaty the two nations signed in January 1957.

In contrast to Pakistan, which is relatively lacking in raw materials needed for modern industry, India, which lacks oil, does have iron ore, coal, and manganese, which have made possible the development of a modest steel industry that started with the Tata plant north of Calcutta, and is being expanded by the establishment of three new plants—to be built by Russia, Czechoslovakia, and West Germany. These, it is estimated, will raise India's steel production from 1 million tons to over 4 million. This is a small amount compared with the more than 100 million tons produced by the United States, or the 68 million tons projected by the Russians for the end of their sixth Five-Year Plan, but for India it represents an important step forward. Moreover, India, which looks eagerly to the development of atomic energy for peacetime purposes because of its lack of oil and limited quantities of coal, has thorium and mozanite sands, important ingredients of atomic energy output.

Both India and Pakistan, because of the relatively low level of production from which they started, must emphasize the development of agriculture as the first priority on their economic agenda, and only then dream of substantial industrialization. Some observers, impressed by Gandhi's hostility to British cotton products and his criticism of the ravages of slum life in urban centers, jumped to the conclusion that the Mahatma opposed industrialization in general. This was not the case. Gandhi, as well as his disciples, have favored the use of industry provided it could be located in proximity to villages, thereby making it possible for agricultural workers to supplement their farm labor, seasonal in character because of the incidence of droughts and monsoon rains, with earnings in nearby factories. The Indian government, with the cooperation of the Ford Foundation, has started to build small-scale industries within range of agricultural communities, and has thus made it possible for India's peasants, who constitute 80 per cent of the population, to think in terms of a diversified money economy, in which they can obtain cash for factory work, and gradually improve their fields and homes with the money thus earned, which in turn will spark the output of consumer goods. Pakistan will probably go through a similar experience. A new pattern may thus be evolved by the non-totalitarian Asian nations—a pattern which combines farming with industry, and avoids, to the extent that this is at all possible, the evils which village dwellers, untutored in the ways of big cities with neon lights, crime, immorality, and the other concomitants of modern industrial life, might otherwise face if they drifted to big cities like Bombay and Calcutta and fell prey to the temptations graphically described by the Indian writer Anand Mulk in his "proletarian" novels.

The historic issue which divides India and Pakistan and, in 1948, brought them to the verge of war, is the future of Kashmir, a princely state at least four-fifths of whose population are Muslims, but whose ruler at the time of partition, Maharajah Singh, was a Hindu. Singh found it difficult to decide in 1947 whether to link his state to India or Pakistan. The decision was made for him, on the one hand, by Hindu riots against Muslims which brought Pakistani warriors from the militant Punjab, armed with weapons from Pakistan to invade western Kashmir, where they set up a state known as Azad Kashmir, with its capital at Mufferabad; and on the other by the Indians, who in retaliation, sent in troops which still occupy the state of Kashmir, which includes the famed Vale of Kashmir, with its capital in Srinagar. Fighting between the two contending forces was averted by the establishment of a cease-fire line under United Nations auspices, which since then has served as the frontier between Pakistani-influenced and India-influenced Kashmir, with the state divided on a prolonged temporary basis somewhat like North and South Korea, or North and South Vietnam.

The Pakistanis believe that India hopes eventually to obtain all of Kashmir, while India is inclined to credit all rumors of Pakistani plots to annex Kashmir to Karachi. The issue is complicated by Pakistan's fears that India might use its position in Kashmir to divert the waters of the principal rivers and canal systems which serve to irrigate the arid plains of Pakistan, and thus in effect bring the Pakistanis to the verge of starvation. In actuality, the Chenab is the only one of Pakistan's three principal rivers—the Chenab, the Indus and the Jelum—which originates in Kashmir. Outside observers, notably experts sent by the World Bank, believe that an arrangement for division of waters between the two countries, similar to arrangements reached in comparable cases in other parts of the world, could be worked out between India and Pakistan, provided both sides are willing to accept a compromise.

Such a compromise has so far been precluded by Mr. Nehru's reluctance to authorize the plebiscite he had earlier promised on the basic issue of Kashmir's accession to India or Pakistan. Mr. Nehru, who comes of a Kashmiri Brahmin family, has a personal affection for Kashmir, which is reinforced by his firm belief that states should not be organized on religious lines—the belief that led him to oppose partition of India in 1947. He fears, moreover, that if a plebiscite should result in Kashmir's partition by religions, it would precipitate fresh clashes between Muslims and Hindus in both India and Pakistan, and thereby jeopardize the hard-won stability of India, where he hopes that the Muslim minority will settle down to a serene and fruitful participation in a multireligious state.

Although these sentiments and fears are understandable, even to his opponents, Mr. Nehru's reluctance to seek a solution of the Kashmir problem by peaceful means while urging other nations to compose their differences and avoid warfare in other trouble spots, such as Korea, the Formosa Strait, and Indochina, has caused his critics to accuse him of using a double standard in world affairs. Meanwhile, Pakistan fears India's ultimate intentions about Kashmir. It points out that New Delhi, in 1953, ousted the former ruler of Kashmir, Sheikh Abdullah, a Muslim, in spite of his former support of India, and replaced him with his deputy Prime Minister, Bakshi Ghulam Mohammed, suspected of being sympathetic to the Communists, who occupy a strong position in Kashmir's Constituent Assembly. An Indian government influenced by Communists, Pakistanis think, might some day oust Pakistan from Azad Kashmir. An alternative even more dreaded by Karachi is that native Communists will seize official control of Kashmir and then enter into close association with the U.S.S.R., which would then begin to put pressure on Pakistan, not only through Kashmir, but through neighboring Afghanistan, which has been pushing claims to Pushtunistan, now a part of Pakistan.

The importance of Kashmir in the relations between India and Pakistan, and even more on the world scene, has thus become vastly enhanced since 1948, out of proportion to its intrinsic position at the time of partition. A sharp explosion was precipitated on January 26, 1957, anniversary of India's establishment as a Republic, when Kashmir's 1947 accession to India was legalized through the new constitution of the state, without the plebiscite previously promised by Mr. Nehru and in defiance of the January 24 resolution of the UN Security Council, which declared that such accession was not internationally binding.

If a solution, now not in sight, could be found for the Kashmir controversy, it is conceivable that India and Pakistan could learn to live on amicable terms. Both have learned from harsh experience the value of independence, economic as well as political. Both are painfully aware of the need to assure their peoples a modicum of subsistence and a measure of social welfare if they are to escape the ravages of political extremism. Both have found it possible, in spite of profound aversion to communism at home, to deal with the Communist rulers of Moscow and Peiping. Both are able to draw on ancient faiths for a philosophy of life which has given them inner stamina to cope with the turmoil of the modern world. Both, in varying degree, see the need to accept and protect the existence of important minorities of the other's population.

Both have greatly benefited by the experience acquired under British rule, and are conscious of their debt to Britain. Both, of their own free will, decided to join the Commonwealth, and have remained loyal to it, and to Britain, in spite of the participation of the Union of South Africa, which has openly discriminated for years against people of color settled within its territory, notably Indians and Pakistanis. And both have benefited by the operation of the Colombo Plan for technical assistance in Southeast Asia initiated in 1950 by the members of the Commonwealth, but since then substantially aided by the United States. Each, naturally and deeply affected by its own respective traditions, philosophy of life, and religious beliefs, offers a striking example of how Western ideas of freedom and equality can be successfully blended with Asian practices, which in turn blend ancient customs with modern ideas of social welfare into a workable synthesis that represents the most telling challenge yet discovered to totalitarian communism. This situation sharply contrasts with that of Communist China.

5

China: Confucius and the Commissars

In the thirteenth century, the Venetian Marco Polo wrote a glowing report on the Chinese Empire—at that time actually ruled by an alien, Mongol, dynasty—for his astounded European readers. In it he described a civilization and a political organization far more refined, complex, and modern than anything medieval Europe had ever known.

Marco Polo's testimony to the grandeur of imperial China is of great importance to our understanding of a very central problem, often forgotten by Westerners today, but hardly ever by the Chinese themselves: that for many centuries China had been far more "modern" and far more advanced in almost all aspects of its cultural and political life than the West. The Chinese Empire had already existed for seventeen centuries at the time Marco Polo came face to face with it; it was to continue, pretty much unchanged, until its downfall in 1911, a bare half-century ago.

Nowhere else in the world has so large an area been politically held together for so long a time, and nowhere else has change, fundamental change in society and state, worked so slowly and imperceptibly. The Roman Empire had come and gone; Europe had passed through the Dark Ages and the Carolingian Empire; the centuries of medieval unity of Church and Empire had been followed by the storms of the Reformation; national states like Spain, France, and England had emerged and transformed the political map of the Western world.

Thousands of miles away, Chinese civilization, rarely touched at its outer fringes by contact with the West, had developed a world of its own—a world of basic unity, which reasserted itself after whatever inroads wars and civil strife might have made into it in the course of history. Even foreign conquests by invaders from the north had never been able to destroy that civilization. Instead of being really conquered from without, China had in the end always succeeded in assimilating its foreign overlords to its own way of life. The Chinese have, therefore, been justifiably proud of their unique and unparalleled achievement. Until well into the nineteenth century, they had, in fact, been convinced that they were the most highly civilized—if not the only civilized—people on this earth.

The basis of this intrinsic continuity of Chinese history lay in three important factors. In the first place, the social fabric of China had remained by and large stable over the centuries. Secondly, China had developed a viable political system which to a remarkable degree combined the advantages of a central bureaucracy with those of decentralized local government. Finally, it had found a meaningful set of ethical rules and values which dominated its social and political life for over two thousand years. Those three determining factors—social, political, and ideological—constituted the foundation of Chinese civilization from the third century before the Christian era until the early twentieth century.

Like many oriental societies and like Europe until the late Middle Ages, China is a land of peasants, who form the overwhelming majority of the population. Even the inhabitants of towns and cities in imperial times still had strong roots in the land, and many would return to their ancestral villages in their declining years. Similarly, the Chinese who have migrated overseas as a rule retain this sense of loyalty to the village of their origin, and many endeavor to return to it from distant lands after a lifetime spent abroad. These strong bonds with one's native soil are not to be explained solely by the agrarian character of Chinese society, but primarily perhaps by its familial character. The family, and beyond it the extended family, the clan, has traditionally been the basic social unit of China. The Chinese has always thought and acted in terms of the family, rather than those of the individual. The family molded the individual's life and determined his place in society; to it, the Chinese owed prime responsibility and loyalty. In exchange, he could rely on the family for help and advice at all times.

The family in China was not only psychologically of enormous significance; it performed, in addition, many important functions for its members, including their education and their social welfare. It was, indeed, for centuries a self-contained small community in its own right, a self-governing social group, which ordered its own affairs and even adjudicated disputes among its members. Chinese society was thus made up of a vast number of self-governing social cells, so to speak, each ruled by a patriarch.

In spite of the fact that there have always been wealthy landowners and poor peasants and tenant farmers in China, the cleavage between social classes was not rigid. Unlike India, China never developed a caste system which permanently confined individuals to one group in society. In fact, even the highest position in the land, that of the emperor, was open to the commoner, and not infrequently a new dynasty was founded by a resourceful man of peasant stock who had quickly risen in prominence in times of civil strife. Landownership, one of the criteria for social distinction in any agrarian society, was not exclusively confined to a small aristocracy. Although many wealthy families continued to hold prestige and influence for several generations and thus tended to form a class apart, their ranks were constantly invaded by newcomers from below. In short, Chinese society had developed a certain measure of mobility in the course of the centuries, which was no doubt one of the main reasons for its continued existence and internal cohesion.

The Chinese genius was perhaps best demonstrated in the field of government. It is true that the history of China, like that of other countries, is full of dynastic and civil wars as well as of invasions. But China is unique in having throughout these internal and external upheavals preserved one form of government for over two thousand years, from 211 B.C. until A.D. 1911. Perhaps one of the most important reasons for this unparalleled continuity of a single form of political order was that the central government—unlike present-day government in the West—had relatively few functions to perform. Since the Chinese family was, as we saw, really a self-governing local community, the emperor was left free to concentrate on such major tasks as tax collection, irrigation and flood control (one of the most crucial problems in China then and now), and defense.

In contrast to Japan, where the imperial title has throughout its history, right up to the present day, remained attached to one dynasty, China was constantly plagued by a lack of dynastic unity. Although the Chinese assumed that their emperors ruled by the so-called "Mandate of Heaven," this mandate changed, and at times rather rapidly, from one ruling house to another. In fact, for two long periods of its history, the imperial title was borne by non-Chinese dynasties; first, at the time of Marco Polo's visit to China, by Mongols, and later, from the seventeenth century until 1911, by the Manchus. We have already seen that at times a commoner might succeed in winning the "Mandate of Heaven" by staging a successful rebellion and thus founding a new imperial line. The Chinese, eminently practical people, quite readily accepted the successful usurper—even the foreign usurper—and his claims to having obtained the "mandate," as long as he could restore order and bring peace to the country.

But while the imperial title itself was subject to change, and often to violent and rapid change at that, permanence and continuity were assured by the Chinese bureaucracy. Although wholly dependent on the emperor for their status and offices, the bureaucrats were, at the same time, the real power behind the throne. No emperor could hope to retain his throne once the bureaucrats abandoned him.

The majority of these all-important officials came from families of the more well-to-do landowners, but commoners could often be found among them. In effect, the Chinese bureaucracy formed a coherent group not because they necessarily came from the same social class, but rather because they shared a common educational background, a schooling which entitled them to the administrative and political offices of the empire. China was, then, for centuries ruled by an academic elite, the so-called "scholar-gentry." Their education had, however, nothing to do with public administration or political science, but was humanistic, literary, and artistic rather than practical.

The third, ideological, factor among the bases of Chinese civilization is closely connected with the scholar-gentry class. Just as top-ranking British civil servants and colonial administrators receive their training in the Greek and Roman classics of the West, so the Chinese scholars in imperial times were steeped in the study of the Chinese classics, and in particular of the writings of Confucius, one of the world's greatest and—if judged by the influence he has wielded over the minds of a large body of men throughout the centuries—most important philosophers.

This great Chinese thinker was not primarily interested in problems of metaphysics or religion, but devoted most of his efforts to the solution of ethical, human, and social problems here on earth. Harmony in human relations might be called the key word in Confucian ethics. True harmony, so he argued, should be based on clear recognition of the principle of order and authority in family, society, and the state. Confucius enumerated five "relationships" as the lasting basis for the good society: subjects should obey their ruler; children should obey their parents; wives their husbands; younger brothers their elder brothers; and finally—an exception to the hierarchical order—Confucius placed great stress on friendship between man and man as a guarantee of social harmony. It will be noted that only one among these principles—the first—is directly concerned with government, while three are devoted to conduct among family members. Confucianism thus tended to underline the importance of the family in Chinese society. But since the family was, as we have already seen, the nucleus of social and political life in imperial China, the Confucian system was a guide to both social and political hamony—a harmony, however, based on the principle of authority rather than of individual liberty.

An intellectual doctrine, Confucianism elevated the scholar to the highest place in the social hierarchy, deprecating both manual labor and money making as occupations unworthy of the truly civilized gentleman.

The writings of Confucius and other important Chinese philosophers, together with the commentaries written on these works by later generations of sages, formed the core curriculum in the education of the scholar-gentry up to the end of the empire. The prospective candidates not only had to acquire a high standard of literacy—which, because of the highly complex Chinese system of writing in ideographs, in itself took many years of hard work—but a word-perfect memory of the classical literature. Since such thorough study requires leisure, it is obvious that sons of the well-to-do had an advantage over the commoners in preparing for the very exacting civil service examinations which gave entry to the service. Such, however, was the prestige attached to scholarship and public office that even poor families would pool all their meager resources, and even go into debt, in order to enable a promising youngster to devote himself to this arduous intellectual toil. For, if he succeeded, the whole family would be raised in status, and the successful student could, as behooved a Chinese, repay his family by providing them with minor positions and other advantages.

One more word should be said about Confucianism. It was, as we have seen, an ethical code rather than a religious creed.

By the same token, it was happily free from dogmatic intolerance. As long as people ordered their lives in accordance with it and professed it in public as a civic creed, they were free to embrace whatever private religion they might choose. China was thus, on the whole, saved from the disastrous religious wars which shook the Western world during and after the sixteenth century. It also had no need for forcing other peoples by means of the sword to accept Confucianism; if others adopted it, then they did so because they had become convinced of Chinese cultural superiority, rather than because they had been conquered in a religious crusade. In China itself, this attitude explains why Buddhism—the only important cultural importation from abroad, which spread to China from India and became especially prominent during the sixth century A.D.—could win adherents fairly rapidly, especially among the commoners, who found in its spiritual message of personal salvation a religious element absent in the more refined, intellectual teachings of Confucius. After some initial hostility, Confucianism "peacefully co-existed" with Buddhism in China, because of the intrinsic tolerance of the official ethic of the state.

The civilization of imperial China thus contained a great many strong features. The strongest point in its favor was that it had been able to exist for so long and provide a meaningful material and spiritual home for its millions of inhabitants. The Chinese family, in particular, had for centuries served as a solid social unit, providing security for the individual and serving as a buffer against disorganization and havoc in times of war and civil strife. Again, government by a perpetuating class of enlightened bureaucrats at local and central levels had led to a political stability unknown elsewhere in the world. Finally, although class distinctions did exist, they were not rigid and allowed some social mobility over the centuries. Poverty and famine, occasioned by droughts or floods, were by no means unknown; but the poor were never as downtrodden as, for example, the untouchables in India, or even as the medieval serfs in the West. Often enlightened rulers and officials applied themselves seriously and successfully to the task of controlling the great rivers and organizing food distribution in stricken areas. Even technologically, China was for centuries ahead of the West in such matters as irrigation and road construction. All these outstanding and positive achievements, combined with a brilliant cultural heritage in literature, painting and sculpture, and other fields, gave the Chinese good reason for taking pride in their civilization.

However, even before this ancient and glorious civilization found itself suddenly confronted with, and threatened by, a dynamic West in the nineteenth century, it was apparent that it also contained weaknesses, which made the task of successfully dealing with the West extremely difficult. To begin with, the Chinese family, for all its psychological and material advantages, prevented the growth of self-reliance and individualism. It tended to breed an exclusive respect for paternal authority and the ancestral tradition at the expense of individual motivation and the desire to experiment. This frame of mind was, if anything, strengthened by the all-powerful dictates of Confucianism, with its emphasis on tradition and authority in society and the state. In embracing these doctrines, the scholar-gentry in the course of the centuries came to place reliance on the virtues of the past. In the end, they were so imbued with those virtues that they failed to adapt themselves to the dictates of the present.

These factors in combination led to what was perhaps the most glaring of the weaknesses of Chinese civilization, namely the authoritarian tradition of Chinese government, which placed a premium on conformity rather than on individual initiative. Although imperial China had benefited from central government long before the West, it had stood still over the centuries. Its government continued to be in the hands of the few, while the mass of the people—or, for that matter, a part of the people, such as the trading class—were never allowed a say in political matters. While in the West the middle class in the course of time forced its way into government, in China both the small trading class and the peasantry continued to be ruled from above by an aloof court and a scholar-gentry.

Chinese government, then, never developed under the empire into government by the people. But what aggravated the situation in the course of the nineteenth century was that the imperial government ceased to be—as at one time it had been—a government for the people. Basking in the achievements of its glorious past, the court devoted less and less time to sound administration. After three hundred years, the Manchu dynasty had become corrupt and inefficient. At the same time, the Chinese population had rapidly increased during the last decades of Manchu rule—partly, no doubt, due to continued internal peace—and the pressure of people on the land was assuming serious proportions. In the 1850's, when the Western impact had already made itself felt, a huge peasant uprising shook, and almost destroyed, the empire.

These internal difficulties clearly indicated that, in order to survive, the rulers of imperial China would have had to introduce reforms by broadening the base of government and, in particular, by paying heed to the widespread peasant discontent. But the scholar-gentry took the side of the Manchus against the rebellious peasantry in an endeavor to restore the *status quo*—a goal which was temporarily achieved with great cruelty.

This grave situation was compounded by the sudden pressure exerted on the Chinese government by Western powers, led by Britain. What the British and other Westerners wanted from China was, in the first place, trade. In the mid-nineteenth century, Western traders were scanning the world for new markets, and the immense populations of the Far East seemed to hold vast promises for extensive exports of industrial goods from the West. If trade was the most important motive for dynamic overseas expansion, a vigorous Christian missionary zeal was next in importance. Businessmen and missionaries thus appeared almost simultaneously at the doors of the empire, eager and determined to win its inhabitants for the goods, material and spiritual, of the West.

For this encounter the Chinese were totally unprepared. Neither the scholar-gentry nor the imperial court could understand the importance attached to trade and the Christian missions in the West. As we have seen, traders and businessmen had never played an important role in China; if anything, they had been held in low esteem in a society based on agriculture and governed by scholars. Thus the ruling classes of China resented the demands of Western traders who regarded trading as a right to be claimed of any country. They resented no less the missionaries whose gospel appeared to them to carry a subversive message of equality, undermining the Confucian order.

But above all, the rulers of China did not realize in time that behind missionaries and traders stood the armed might of the West. Meeting haughty resistance, both invoked the aid and protection of their governments. Even then, Chinese reactions betrayed the unpreparedness of the court and the bureaucrats to deal with the West, which, in order to safeguard what it assumed to be its rightful interests, demanded the establishment of diplomatic relations with China. The Chinese, however, had never dealt with other peoples as their equals.

In Chinese eyes, all foreigners were less civilized "barbarians," owing allegiance to the world's only real suzerain, the Chinese emperor. Westerners, to them, fell into the same category.

The Chinese thus fatally underestimated the West, and the resulting misunderstandings were bound to lead to armed clashes, which started in the 1840's and continued, with many periods of uneasy truce or peace, into the present century. Because of the West's vast military superiority, China was forced step by step to open its doors to the foreigners, to make concessions to the traders, and to establish diplomatic relations. Westerners had to be granted "extraterritorial rights," which meant that Western residents in China would live under their own laws instead of those of China. In the end, even the Chinese customs service was placed under foreign control, to ensure the well-nigh free entry of Western goods into China. With these swift hammerblows the West undermined the prestige of the old order in China and imprinted lastingly on the Chinese mind the technological, military, and economic superiority of the West.

The empire, already rocked by internal troubles, rapidly started to disintegrate; its life was—ironically and humiliatingly—prolonged for a few decades by the very Western powers themselves, who aided the dynasty in suppressing the vast peasant uprising of the 1850's. But continued incompetence and corruption, coupled with further military defeats suffered as a consequence of the court's renewed reluctance to meet Western demands, sealed the fate of imperial China. In 1911, the Manchu dynasty was overthrown by Chinese revolutionaries, who immediately proclaimed China a republic.

The downfall of the empire brought with it the collapse of the world's oldest political order, and with it, that of the Confucian system and its propounders, the scholar-gentry. But the real tragedy of the revolution which toppled the Manchu dynasty was that of itself it could not provide a new order for China. With the empire China had, so to speak, temporarily lost its soul and its sense of direction. Many thoughtful Chinese felt the urgent need for spectacular and rapid change, which would place China on a footing of equality not only with the West, but also with Japan, which, by adopting Westernization, had forced the empire into humiliating territorial concessions in the 1890's. But in the chaos after 1911, few Chinese knew where to seek salvation, whether in copying Western constitutional models—such as a republic—or in adopting Western technology, science, or again, mass education. In its search for a new and meaningful order, China tried to find an answer in most of these solutions; but the predominant and most important ideological force proved to be nationalism.

The men who placed themselves at the helm of China after 1911 came from two different groups. On the one hand, there emerged powerful military leaders, especially those few who had acquainted themselves with the use of Western military equipment and methods in the declining decades of the empire. Because they were the only holders of real, physical power, they soon occupied the most important places in republican China. But instead of uniting in a common cause, these "war lords" started to carve up the former empire into quasi-independent satrapies and engaged in long and bitter feuds for predominance among themselves. In spite of their military power, however, the war lords failed to make a constructive contribution to the new China.

The other group of leaders was of an entirely different caliber. These were educated young men, often sons of gentry families, who had become convinced of the need for reform and Westernization and had rebelled against the old order—often at the risk of their lives. They were the leaders of modern Chinese nationalism, smarting under the humiliation inflicted on China by the West and by Japan. Just as some of the military leaders had desired to copy Western technology for their own purposes, so these young intellectuals, some of whom had actually studied overseas, set out to copy from the West the tools of political organization. To this group belonged modern China's first national leader, Sun Yat-sen, who became first president of the republic in 1911, and who founded the first modern political party in China, the Kuomintang, or Nationalist party.

Unfortunately, these nationalist leaders had more enthusiasm than political experience. Their main support came, understandably enough, from the coastal cities, where direct contact with the West had resulted in an atmosphere congenial to change, especially among the Chinese business community, students, clerks, and workers. But outside these urban centers, the war lords reigned supreme over the rest of the country, including the capital, Peking. For a short time only the intellectuals and the most prominent military leaders agreed to work together. Once this brief alliance was broken up by the military leaders, China entered a decade of civil war. It thus became apparent that it had been easier to overthrow the empire than to replace it with a well-functioning political system.

China, although roused by the spirit of nationalism, remained powerless in the face of foreign encroachments. Although the Western nations and Japan recognized the new republic, they were primarily concerned with safeguards for their trading interests. In the face of its internal weaknesses, they proceeded to carve China up with great vigor into "spheres of influence"; yet although the "territorial integrity" of China was respected in the sense that no outright annexations took place after 1911, China was never treated as an equal by the great powers. But whereas the Western powers—jealous of each other's concessions—were content with exerting indirect control over China, Japan during World War I, endeavored to force the young republic into far-reaching and humiliating concessions, which only pressure from the other powers finally averted.

In retrospect it is tragic and fateful that the Western world, preoccupied with its own problems after 1919, and unaware of the far-reaching importance of the changes within China, did not come to the aid of Sun Yat-sen and his party in those years. Indeed, whenever the great powers had to choose between him and the war lords, they threw their financial support behind the most powerful military leaders in the belief that these would be better able to maintain some kind of law and order, and therewith protect Western commercial interests in China. The selfish war lords, however, were incapable of building a modern, new China, the task to which Sun Yat-sen was devoting all his energies. His program—spelled out in the so-called Three People's Principles—called for national unification, popular government, and social reforms leading to a higher standard of living.

These goals could not be attained as long as chaos prevailed in China. The Nationalists needed help from abroad in order to organize and strengthen their party as a prerequisite for the establishment of a new, truly national government. Having failed to obtain such help in the West, Sun had to look for help and advice elsewhere, and he got both, for a time, from Soviet Russia, which had itself only recently emerged from prolonged civil war. The Russian leaders eagerly responded to Sun's appeals for political and military aid. With the aid of Soviet political advisers, the Kuomintang was molded into an efficient and well-organized party, closely modeled on the Bolshevik party in Russia. With Russian aid, the Kuomintang also established a military academy in South China, which placed a well-disciplined and politically indoctrinated army at the disposal of the Nationalists.

Sun welcomed this Soviet cooperation without himself in the least becoming a Communist. A small Communist party had, it is true, existed in China since the early 1920's, and its leaders—in line with Soviet aid to the Nationalists—pledged their collaboration with the Kuomintang. For a few years, Nationalists and Communists were allies in the struggle for the unification and modernization of China.

Sun Yat-sen died in 1925. Two years after his death, the Nationalists with their new political and military organizations felt strong enough to attempt the unification of China from their southern strongholds. The party's new leader, Chiang Kai-shek, trained at the Kuomintang military academy, conducted a brilliant campaign against the war lords in the North, many of whom surrendered to the Nationalists. The campaign turned into a victory march to Peking (Peiping), and even though many outlying provinces remained to be brought under the control of the new central government, Nationalist China had become a reality.

It was then that the Communists proved to have been only temporary allies of the Kuomintang. Making use of the revolutionary upsurge, they incited workers in many cities to armed rebellion against foreign and Chinese "capitalists." This well-planned action threatened to alienate valuable support for the Nationalists from important sectors of the Chinese community; more fatally, it also threatened to bring in its train punitive expeditions from the Western powers, a danger which the new regime could ill afford at that moment. Lastly, it represented a direct challenge to the new government itself. Chiang reacted swiftly and with deadly vengeance exterminated a great number of Communist leaders, expelling at the same time his Soviet advisers. The short-lived marriage between Nationalists and Communists thus came to an abrupt end.

The Kuomintang victory of 1927 constituted the fulfillment, by and large, of Sun's First Principle—that of national unification. In the succeeding years, the new government started to lay the groundwork for attainment of the other two principles—that of popular government and, ultimately, of a better economic life. A new centralized administration was taking shape under strict party control. Gradually, China appeared to be approaching the brink of progress toward modern nationhood, led by a vigorous group of new men, inspired by a nationalist ideology, and at long last enjoying relative—though by no means absolute—internal peace.

But this vision, so greatly sought ever since 1911, turned out to be a mirage. Two important factors stood in the way of its realization. In the first place communism, although it had suffered a setback after 1927, was by no means entirely defeated. Having been ousted from their urban strongholds in such cities as Shanghai and Canton, the Chinese Communists had regrouped in the interior, where they proclaimed the first Chinese "Soviet Republic." After several military campaigns, Chiang Kai-shek succeeded in forcing them out of that state-within-the-state. In the end, the Communists retreated from incessant Nationalist pursuits to the far north of China. This "Long March," as it was called, toughened the Communist leadership, among them many of today's top leaders such as Mao Tse-tung and Chu Teh, for later encounters. Equally important in the light of later developments, the forced withdrawal of Communist cadres from the cities after 1927 impelled them to live among the peasantry and to make themselves acceptable to the Chinese rural population. Unwittingly, the Nationalists had thus given their foes a chance to learn an inestimable lesson—a lesson, moreover, which Chiang and his lieutenants were very tardy in learning themselves.

The continued internal division was soon overshadowed in importance by renewed Japanese aggression. Foiled in their expansionist endeavors after World War I, the Japanese now realized that a united China under Nationalist leadership might within a few years become strong enough to resist Japanese demands. Therefore, their military leaders decided to strike before it was too late. In 1931 they occupied Manchuria, in natural resources one of the richest parts of China. Manchuria was declared an independent state, which was given the name of Manchukuo, but it was, in effect, a Japanese colony ruled by a puppet emperor. Having swallowed Manchuria, which was turned into a huge industrial supply base for Japan's needs, the Japanese in 1937 invaded China proper, in an endeavor to subjugate the entire country to their rule.

Unequal to the military superiority of the aggressor, and failing to obtain both large-scale military aid from the West and intervention from the League of Nations, Chiang's government was forced to abandon to the Japanese the richest and most advanced parts of the country—including the coastal cities in Southern China and important centers such as Nanking and Peiping. Although the greater part of China, including the wartime capital Chungking, remained outside the area of Japanese supremacy, the conquered part of the country became, like Manchuria, a puppet state under a former colleague of Chiang's, Wang Ching-wei.

This Japanese encroachment was a crippling blow to the young Chinese republic. Instead of consolidating its newly established nationalist revolution and devoting its strength to the fulfillment of the Kuomintang program of political and economic reorganization, China had to divert its energies entirely to defense. In the face of this deadly challenge, Chiang, after many hesitations, decided to call off his anti-Communist drive, and for the second time Communists and Nationalists entered on an uneasy alliance, or United Front, against Japan. It will, perhaps, never be decided which of the two bore the major brunt of the struggle against the Japanese, but there can be little doubt that the Communists gained widespread support among millions of Chinese for leading with great skill, whatever their ulterior motives, the anti-Japanese resistance in those areas which their armies and guerrilla bands liberated from Japanese rule.

In December, 1941, after the attack on Pearl Harbor, the United States and its allies entered the war against Japan. The war which China had waged single-handed for ten years thus became part of the second world war, and ultimate deliverance from the Japanese yoke was at long last in sight. For the first time since 1911, the Chinese Republic was recognized as an ally and equal partner of the Western powers, a position which China's leaders had in vain craved for a long period. Two years later, in 1943, the Western allies at long last gave official recognition to this equality by relinquishing their "extraterritorial rights" in China.

Before we continue with our examination of external events, a few words should be said about some internal problems created by the Japanese invasion of China. The loss of the wealthiest and most modernized parts of the country deprived the Nationalist government not only of finanical support, but, far more important, it also cut it off from the most dynamic elements in China, on whom the rise of the nationalist movement had to so large a degree depended. It was in the coastal cities, primarily, that Chinese businessmen, white-collar workers, students, and intellectuals in general had formed the bulk of an educated following for the Nationalist cause, as well as a reservoir of staunch party workers. Only a very small number of these people followed Chiang to Chungking. Cut off from these vital nerve centers, the party soon started to stagnate intellectually. Before the invasion its dictatorship had rested squarely on the support of the country's most vocal and progressive urban elements; now it was gradually transformed into a military dictatorship pure and simple. More and more Chiang turned to his military aides for advice, and more and more he was led to rely on war lords and landowners in the unconquered interior of China as his allies. Under the circumstances, this reorientation was perhaps inevitable; but it led to a moral stagnation which tended to replace the true revolutionary fervor of the Kuomintang's halcyon days.

For the future development of events, this profound change in the character of the Nationalist government proved to be fatal. Ideological and political stagnation at the top stood in marked contrast to the renewed fervor of Communist propaganda, which, because of the military advances made by Communist troops, found an ever-wider audience among millions of Chinese during the war against Japan. Communist propagandists had, as we have already mentioned, learned one invaluable lesson from their enforced exile in the Chinese countryside—namely, that no revolution could hope to succeed in China unless its leaders knew how to speak to the Chinese peasant and to win his support. This the Nationalist leaders were far slower to grasp.

Yet there can be little doubt that ever since the mid-nineteenth century the Chinese peasant had been demanding change and betterment of his lot, which had markedly deteriorated since the establishment of the republic. We saw that already before 1911, the empire had experienced widespread peasant rebellions, because the rapid increase in the rural population, combined with corrupt and inefficient government, had created serious agrarian problems. But while the Nationalist revolution had triumphed in the cities, its aftermath had continued to take a heavy toll from the Chinese peasant. For long years, military bands of innumerable war lords were ransacking the countryside, exacting tribute in food and labor from the peasantry. Many a peasant youth was forced to join these roving bands because his ancestral village could no longer provide a living for him. This situation grew much worse still during the war. In the areas overrun by the Japanese, a harsh military regime pressed relentlessly on the peasant population with demands for forced labor and rice deliveries. Inflation, willfully caused by Japanese printing presses, added to economic disintegration. In the areas under Nationalist rule, similar, if not equally ruthless, conditions prevailed, particularly with regard to inflation. Thus the tides of revolution, civil strife, and war turned the peasants, the overwhelming majority of the population, into hapless victims of an era of rapid change.

This was the situation in China when the Allies, in August, 1945, forced Japan to surrender, thus ending quite suddenly the Japanese puppet regimes in China. After fourteen years, China seemed to be given a second chance to realize Sun Yat-sen's dreams for a strong and united China. But even at the outset, this second chance looked far less propitious than the first of 1927. Not only was the country in a far worse plight economically than ever before, but the political and social upheaval had been vastly accelerated during the intervening years. At the same time, the means for accomplishing more things more quickly in 1945 than in 1927 were desperately lacking. In 1927, the Kuomintang had been the major unifying factor in China, carrying with it large sectors of at least the urban population. By 1945, this party had become alienated from these vital groups by sheer distance and, more important, by that moral and ideological stagnation already referred to. Returning from Chungking, Chiang Kai-shek and his government failed to recapture the essential bases of support for one-party rule.

The problems facing the Nationalists were rendered far more complex still by the wartime successes of their Communist competitors. Where in 1927 the Communists had merely constituted a small band of determined leaders and a few thousand followers, in 1945 they virtually emerged as an alternative government, with vast areas of China—including Manchuria—under their firm control, and with a weathered and experienced army at their disposal. Their successes against the Japanese, coupled with their administrative experience had also attracted many non-Communists to their side, particularly young men burning with enthusiasm. The Communists had also profited from the Soviet Union's entry into the war against Japan just a few days before the Japanese surrender, when Russian troops had swiftly occupied Manchuria; a good deal of the arms and military equipment captured by the U.S.S.R. had passed into the hands of the Chinese Communists.

A repetition of the successful anti-Communist military campaigns of the late 1920's was, therefore, out of the question. For two years after the end of World War II, Chiang and the Communist leadership tried to arrive at a compromise solution, a continuation of the United Front which had prevailed during the war against Japan. But these endeavors ended in deadlock. Even during the war, the United Front had shown many cracks; it was now impossible to reconstruct it. Thus China, still bleeding profusely from the wounds of the war against Japan, rapidly drifted into bloody civil strife. Until the very end, a small segment of Chinese intellectuals had hoped to achieve a compromise between Nationalists and Communists; but neither of the two contending camps heeded this Third Force, as it called itself. Such a compromise solution was strongly recommended by General George C. Marshall, whom the American government had dispatched to China as a mediator between the two parties. But Marshall's mission, for all his strenuous endeavors to avert civil war, failed. To understand this failure we must remember that a compromise between two parties, each dominated by a militant creed and each equipped with well-organized armies, is at all times problematical, if not impossible. There was, consequently, a dreadful logic in the refusal of Nationalists and Communists alike to surrender what they felt was already theirs, and to forgo what they were certain to attain by renewed armed struggle for ultimate predominance.

In fact, the last phase of this struggle was much shorter than many outside observers had expected. By mid-1949, the Nationalist regime on the mainland of China was defeated and was forced to seek refuge on the island of Taiwan (Formosa). The final victory of communism on the mainland was not due to military successes so much as to a rapid disintegration of the Nationalist armies, part of which surrendered to the Communists in spite of the superior armaments with which, largely through American military aid, they had been equipped. This military debacle was paralleled by large-scale defections of important groups of civilians, primarily again of intellectuals, to the side of the Communists after 1948.

It has sometimes been argued in the West that large-scale military intervention from the outside might have been able to halt the Communist conquest of China. But any such intervention would have had to be on such a massive scale that few Western powers, and in particular the United States, would have willingly undertaken it at that time. Even had it taken place, however, it is doubtful whether the fate of the Nationalist regime would in the end have been substantially different. The Communists had to all intents and purposes won over to their side the minds and hearts of too many Chinese for outside military intervention to redress the balance. They had, moreover, in the course of the last decade developed a military strategy and mobile tactics far superior to those adopted by their adversaries. In spite of the undoubted fact that the Chinese Communists owed their military predominance in part to the substantial help received from Russian forces in Manchuria after 1945, the fate of 500 million Chinese was in the end not decided by Moscow or Washington, but by the Chinese themselves. In a cruel ballot, fought over for many years, they had at long last abandoned the Nationalists.

There are several factors which may account for the victory of communism in China. The most important among them is almost certainly the Communists' recognition of the widespread discontent among the peasantry and their astute manipulation of agrarian unrest for their own purposes. By redistributing the land in areas occupied by them, by maintaining iron discipline among their troops with regard to peasant property, and by giving the villagers a voice in local government organs, the Communists brought about significant changes which, coupled with an end of corruption and inflation, were doubtless welcomed by the peasantry. Ever since the Japanese invasions of the 1930's, the Chinese Communists had been able to attract an ever-increasing number of the Chinese intelligentsia by an appeal to their patriotism no less than by the ideological certainty implicit in the Marxist-Leninist gospel. Finally, in the years after World War II, many Chinese in the urban centers—workers, white-collar workers, and even businessmen—came to support the Communists as the only alternative to the chaos which the Japanese occupation had left behind and which the returning Nationalists appeared unable or unwilling to cure.

But beyond these tangible factors, the Chinese Communists profited from other, no less important, circumstances. Paramount among these is the fierce national pride of the Chinese, which the Communists have adroitly channeled into a militant nationalism and aggressive anti-Westernism. This has made it possible for the Communists to pose successfully as the true disciples, not only of Karl Marx, but also of Sun Yat-sen. Their promise of rapid industrialization, modernization, and social change, projected against the achievements—real or alleged—of communism in the Soviet Union, was almost certainly another major attraction to millions of Chinese who for decades had been yearning for equality with—if not superiority over—the West.

In several respects, too, Chinese traditions may have facilitated the victory of communism. Thus the severities of Communist dictatorial rule may at the outset have appeared as a change in degree rather than in substance in the perspective of the history of Chinese authoritarianism—an authoritarianism deeply ingrained, as we saw, in imperial China no less than in Nationalist China. It is, in fact, not unlikely that the long decades of chaos during which the Chinese people had struggled in vain for a new pattern of life made the very rigidities of Communist totalitarianism appear as the harbingers of order, guaranteeing a meaningful life to all strata of society. Even the fact that most of the new leaders were intellectuals—and at that, doctrinaire intellectuals imbued with a highly complex social ethic—placed them well within the traditional Chinese pattern. Similarly, the Communists' ideological disdain for the bourgeoisie and for capitalism echoes the low esteem in which the traders had been held by the Confucian scholars. Moreover, unlike their Russian and European comrades, the Chinese Communists were not confronted by powerful religious opposition. No organized church stood in their way, pitting the allegiance of its believers against Marxist-Leninist materialism. On the contrary, the waning of the Confucian ethic had left an ideological vacuum which the combination of nationalism and communism could apparently easily fill. Finally, the long tradition established by the doctrine of the "mandate of heaven" may have been instrumental in eroding loyalty to the established government faster than in other parts of the world. Once the Nationalist government was losing ground, it may have been interpreted as a clear sign that the "mandate" had, in fact, been transferred to the Communists.

But if the combination of all these favorable factors may go some way toward explaining why communism proved to be successful against its competitor, and even why it has undoubtedly generated enthusiasm and released springs of energy among many Chinese, it is as yet too early to know whether China is willing to pay the price for communism and whether, even if that price be extorted through sheer force and compulsion, the people of China will ultimately find in communism what they have so desperately sought since 1911—a combination of personal and national dignity accompanied by rapid social and material advancement.

Communism in China, as in the Soviet Union, is wedded to the Western belief in progress—to be realized, if need be, by violent and ruthless means. Education, technology, and industrialization—all of them part of the Nationalists' program—have been vastly accelerated since 1949. More important still, the creation of a centralized Communist state calls for a citizenry whose loyalty to that state and its political leadership must at all costs be assured. The Chinese Communists have demonstrated their awareness of the vast problems confronting them in the rapid attainment of these goals. These problems amount to nothing less than the almost complete transformation of the very roots of one of the oldest civilizations on earth. In other words, although the Communists could win acceptance from many Chinese in the absence of a viable alternative in the postwar years, to remold Chinese society in accordance with their own blueprint they must overcome—by whatever means—those Chinese traits which may significantly obstruct the realization of that blueprint.

Foremost among these obstacles stands the vast majority of the Chinese people, the peasantry, on whose very backs, so to speak, the Communists rode to power. It was one thing to lead and exploit agrarian unrest, and to satisfy the land hunger of downtrodden and bewildered peasants; it is quite another thing to deprive them of their barely won piece of land by the ruthless process of collectivization which will reduce the proud landowners of yesterday to the status of an agrarian proletariat of tomorrow. In any case, the rapidity of collectivization leaves no doubt that to China's new masters the modernization of the country means the destruction of the peasantry as an independent social force. It is difficult to believe that the kaleidoscopic rate of change brutally imposed on the Chinese peasant has not generated antagonism and fear. We do not know whether these have offset the benefits which Communism at the outset brought to the peasantry, and whether they will prove strong enough to force on the Communists a revision of the vast social experiment on which they have embarked.

Beyond this in itself staggering and awesome problem lurks the even more profound resistance to rapid modernization embedded both in the Confucian tradition and in the familial pattern of Chinese society. Both are, therefore, prime targets of the new government, which cannot allow competing allegiances to persist in Communist China. Again, it is impossible from outside to judge the effect of the concerted attacks on the fabric of Chinese society, in particular on the family as a primary social unit of mutual loyalties. No doubt any effective Chinese government would have been confronted by the task of transforming these basic attitudes in order to educate the Chinese into citizens of a modern state; but only the Communists have felt the need for a frontal and cruel attack on tradition and family, extinguishing the past and forcing children to denounce their parents, in both cases as a service to the Communist state.

The answers to these crucial questions can only be provided by the Chinese people in the years to come. They are vitally important not only to the Chinese at home, but also to the millions of Chinese outside China's borders, who still possess the freedom of choice—a freedom even more significant because of the fact that the majority of them live among other non-Western peoples in Asia. For many of these non-Western nations are watching Communist China as one possible example to copy in their search for rapid modernization and change. Another example is westernized Japan.

6

Japan: Asian Westernism

More than any other country in Asia, Japan has adopted the ways of the West. With modern Western science, technology, business methods, military arts, even Western sports, music, and now pinball machines at its disposal, Japan has been recognized for half a century as one of the powers in world affairs—for a while, in fact, one of the great powers. Contemporary Japan presents a sharp contrast to the Japan of 1854, when Commodore Matthew Perry of the United States Navy, in command of eight American warships, induced a reluctant Japanese government to sign the Treaty of Kanagawa, bringing to an end over two centuries of Japanese isolation and relative stagnation. Yet in recent years Japan has demonstrated that important elements of feudal spirit and culture persist, despite modern machines and ways of living.

The high-water mark of Japanese power was reached early in 1942. After a decade of aggression in China, the attack on Pearl Harbor signaled Japan's final wave of expansion. Japanese forces quickly seized the Philippines, Indochina, Malaya, the Netherlands East Indies and other areas, overthrowing in a short space of two months Western colonial control that had existed for periods ranging up to more than four centuries. Yet the Japanese troops who made these conquests still lived by a feudal code so strict as to permit incidents such as that reported by an officer of the United States Marines as they moved in on a Pacific island being captured from the Japanese late in World War II. A file of Japanese soldiers was observed moving slowly toward the end of a point of land, where their lieutenant was ceremoniously chopping off their heads with his traditional two-handed sword.

Paradoxes such as this have long caused Westerners much difficulty in their attempts to know Japan. American opinion, both public and official, understated Japan's strength consistently up to the time of Pearl Harbor. That attack came as a surprise to Americans, even many who had seriously studied Japanese history. From Pearl Harbor until Japan's surrender in 1945, American opinion, both public and official, consistently overestimated Japanese strength, especially economic strength, and toward the end of the war American planes bombed Japanese factories which were already idle for lack of raw materials, whose import had become impossible because most of Japan's seagoing cargo ships had been sunk.

Conversely, failure to understand the West had proved extremely costly to Japan, despite its startling record of successfully copying Western technology. The attack on Pearl Harbor was itself based on the false assumption that the United States, delayed by naval losses in undertaking to dislodge Japanese forces from occupied territory, would not have the perseverance to carry the war to a victorious conclusion, against determined Japanese defensive action.

In the commercial sphere, Japanese exports have reached large volume, reflecting mass production, yet Japanese merchandising techniques have been such as to arouse opposition in most of the countries of the world. And Japanese officials have at times shown a notable propensity to antagonize Americans and other non-Japanese, including Asians.

Geography exercises an important influence on Japanese affairs, both directly in the limitations and opportunities felt today, and indirectly through its influence on Japanese history and culture. Japan's main geographic feature is its island position off the coast of Asia. The water barrier separating Japan's four main islands from the mainland has prevented armed conquest from the continent, although not without a close call when Kublai Khan attempted invasion (1274 and 1281), and the Japanese themselves have more than once launched aggressive ventures across these waters. This insular position has given Japan an extraordinary degree of control over its own affairs, including the choice of whether and how Japan should deal with China, Korea, and other neighboring countries.

Nature is often violent in Japan. Earthquakes, typhoons, and floods, to say nothing of man-made fires that rage out of control, frequently bring sudden and widespread destruction. The earthquake and fire of September, 1923, wrought great devastation in the densely settled Tokyo-Yokohama area, and over 100,000 persons are thought to have been killed. Smaller catastrophes take place every year, and the ever-present hazard of their occurrence has a profound influence on Japanese life and character.

Other geographic features of special significance are the mountainous terrain, volcanic soil, temperate climate, ample rainfall, and sparsity of industrial resources. No more than a sixth of the land area of the islands can be cultivated, and today Japan, despite high yields achieved with Asia's most advanced agricultural techniques, produces only about 80 per cent of its own food, and virtually none of its fiber requirements except for a portion of wood pulp. Forest and fishery resources are very important under the circumstances. In industry Japan is one of the world's more developed countries, but domestic sources today provide only about a fifth of its total raw-materials consumption.

The Japanese people now number 90 million, three times the estimated total for Commodore Perry's day. The present population is over half that of the United States, but the area of Japan is about equal to that of California. More than half of Japan's population lives in cities, crowded together in such a way that a Westerner finds it hard to believe so many can live in such a limited space. Rural villages also are crowded to an extreme degree. This pressure of many people in very small space is not new, even though modernization has permitted rapid increase. Japanese manners and customs, even the Japanese language, are permeated with elements, especially sense of duty, formality, and politeness, that go with crowding.

The racial origins of the Japanese are not completely known, although an important Malaysian element appears to be present, as evidenced not only in the physical appearance of the Japanese people, but also in their mythology and in the construction of their houses, which are more appropriate for warm climates than for Japanese winters. Both racially and culturally, the Japanese people are extraordinarily homogeneous. Among the traits so widely found as to be characteristic are great industry and skill in a wide range of artistic and utilitarian fields. The Japanese are also a highly emotional people, despite customs that put a very high premium on impassivity.

Borrowing from abroad is the source of many of the principal features of Japanese life. In times past, China has provided the most extensive and profound influences, either by direct transfer or by way of Korea. In modern times, Western influences have added a heavy top layer to Japan's complex culture. The process of learning from abroad has taken place in waves, each of which has deposited an enduring layer of culture. Because of Japan's physical separation from land contact with other civilizations, foreign impact has been both intermittent and obvious, in contrast to the situation of most countries, which are influenced more or less continuously and imperceptibly. Three major eras of intensive borrowing can be identified in Japan's history, and the century since Perry is only the latest of these. In these periods, the Japanese have very quickly accepted new ways. Borrowing has been selective, however, and old ways have tended to persist, side by side with the new. Between periods of active culture import, Japan has turned its attention inward, glorifying Japanese traditions and resisting foreign influence, most notably during the two hundred years preceding Commodore Perry's arrival.

Japan's religion is a mixture of many elements. Buddhism came from China, at different times and in various forms, some of which gave rise to sects more Japanese than Chinese or Indian. Today, five Buddhist sects have major importance. Confucianism was also taken from China and enjoyed special prominence and favor during the Tokugawa Era (1603-1867), but with important changes that conformed to Japan's feudal structure. Christianity gained an important following in the sixteenth century, was suppressed by the Tokugawas, and returned with other Western ways after Perry. Today Christianity has significant influence in Japan, although the number of Christians is very small. Shinto, a Japanese religion with very ancient origins, enjoyed great favor in the modern era. Sectarian Shinto has developed through the ages from a simple, primitive animism. State Shinto was fostered and sponsored by the Japanese government after the Meiji Restoration of 1868, as a means of stimulating fanatical devotion to the state. Impressive Shinto pageantry and ceremonies reminded the Japanese of their national traditions and stressed the need for complete devotion to the emperor and his officials. Today Shinto—demilitarized since World War II—and Buddhism dominate religious life; in fact, most Japanese follow both Buddhism and Shinto simultaneously.

The family is the center of Japanese society. Family loyalties are very strong, and great efforts are made to continue the family line. The father is traditionally the head of the house, with many obligations and privileges. He has ultimate financial responsibility for all. He represents the family in its dealings with others. The position of head of the house has customarily gone to the eldest son, with younger sons displaced and expected to make their own way, although with continuing responsibility to support the parental family financially and submit to the family council, and with right to assistance in time of distress. Since World War II, along with a weakening of the position of head of the house, the legal foundations of primogeniture have been removed, and heads of families may now leave their estates as they choose. Women have at times been virtual servants in their own homes, subject to the will not only of the head of the house but of all males and older females. Since World War II, however, women have acquired more rights, including the right to vote, and their degree of independence is growing. Marriages, for instance, are no longer exclusively the result of parental arrangement, but frequently reflect the wishes of the young couples themselves.

Loyalty to family is not the only or even the highest loyalty in Japan. The individual has numerous obligations, and these at times conflict. In feudal Japan loyalty to the lord was for all practical purposes a man's highest obligation; in modern times it has been loyalty to the emperor. Other loyalties are owed to teachers, supervisors, and employers. Obligations are of many different sorts, from the unlimited debts owed to parents and emperor to quite specific obligations incurred in daily interpersonal contacts. Many of these latter require payment in gifts, for which there are numerous occasions. Conflicting loyalties are a favorite theme in Japanese literature, and one of the most popular of Japanese tales is the *Forty-Seven Ronin,* a story of military retainers who sacrificed their families in order to avenge the death of their lord. Japan did not follow China in the idea of the mandate of Heaven, which justified the rule of Chinese emperors when they ruled properly, but also justified the overthrow of dynasties which were deemed to rule improperly. No such withdrawal of the mandate of Heaven was possible in Japan, where the emperor *was* Heaven. Only since World War II has the Japanese emperor declared himself not to be divine.

The life of a Japanese is so full of duties that he must be on guard every minute. Many duties are ceremonial, such as bowing on meeting others, and many are matters of language—as shown by the delicate nuances of Japan's uncomplicated poetry—for the correct phrase and degree of respect must be used on each occasion. All duties tend to be defined specifically, so that Japanese ethics are called situational, applying only to particular situations. Learning all the rules is therefore very difficult, but even after an individual has mastered the rules he may be unable to cope with a situation that is not covered by them. In such a situation a Japanese has little tradition of individual self-reliance or general moral principles to guide him. Thus, when something goes wrong, a Japanese in a position of responsibility tends to feel shame because of the "loss of face," or dishonor. This appears to have been the general reaction to defeat in World War II. The Japanese do not show much sense of guilt for wrongdoing in that war.

Because of the importance of face, Japanese tend to avoid clear-cut issues. Even formal government committees and corporate boards of directors work more by general consensus than by formal votes, in which someone would lose face by being voted down. Yet this apparently vague procedure of consensus instead of dramatic leadership succeeds remarkably well. Japanese work well in groups, even in situations that may cause consternation to individuals.

When Perry arrived in 1853, a feudal dictatorship prevailed in Japan. This regime, headed by a shogun or military dictator, of the Tokugawa clan, had ruled for two and a half centuries by methods approaching those of modern totalitarianism. Major policies sought to assure stability and continuance of effective control by the shogun. Contact with the outside world was prohibited, except for very restricted trade with the Chinese and Dutch at Nagasaki in western Japan. The country was ruled through daimyo, feudal barons, each of whom had his own soldiers (samurai) who performed not only military but also administrative duties. Daimyo were controlled by severe measures, including the requirement that they spend half of each year at the shogun's court in Edo (now Tokyo) and leave their families at the court during the other half-year. Peasants tilled the soil and paid feudal dues in the form of rice, enough to support all the ruling classes.

Distress and dissatisfaction affected most groups in Japan at the time of Perry's visit. The shogun was in financial difficulties, and his control over some of the daimyo, especially in southwestern Japan, was weak. The daimyo were in many cases unable to meet both the growing exactions of the shogun and their normal or growing payments to their retainers. The samurai were in many cases not receiving their full dues, and in a large number of cases were hopelessly in debt to the merchants. The mass of peasants were in such distress that they sought to relieve their burden by recurrent uprisings. Even the merchants, who found many of their loans uncollectible, were dissatisfied. During the generation before 1854 an intellectual ferment had developed, challenging the authority of the shogun and seeking real power for the emperor, who had been relegated to powerless though august poverty in Kyoto while the shogun ruled in his name.

Thus Japan was ripe for change when Perry arrived. The shogun resisted Perry's demands briefly, but had no choice when faced with the guns of his "Black Ships." The 1854 Treaty of Kanagawa opened certain ports to American ships and trade and permitted appointment of an American consul. Later treaties with the United States and other Western powers increased these concessions and extended them to other nations.

The shogun's weakness before foreigners and his consequent reversal of the seclusion policy that had been in force for over two hundred years cleared the way for dissident daimyo to work for the overthrow of the shogun. Western daimyo led this revolt, seeking the restoration of the emperor to his full authority. Many new activities required additional expenditures, and the financial weakness of the shogun became extreme. The emperor, supported by the growing power of the western clans, increasingly made his influence felt to limit the shogun. Finally in November, 1867, the shogun resigned. Thus the old order was swept out of national, political, and military power in short order and with very limited fighting. Japanese economic and social organization remained much the same as before, with a great deal of strength, cohesiveness, and restless energy, but through contact with the West it was freed from the dead weight of feudal exactions, confinements, and repressions.

Continuity with the past and a profoundly important focus for loyalties were provided by the Emperor. The overthrow of the shogun involved not a destructive political revolution, but a remarkable restoration of the emperor as a national leader and symbol. A youth of fifteen—Mutsuhito—had just succeeded to the imperial throne. On January 3, 1868, his reign was proclaimed by the name Meiji (Enlightened Peace), and the shogunate was declared abolished. This Meiji Restoration marks the starting point of modern Japan. In the forty-four years of the Meiji era Japan became one of the world's great powers.

The Meiji leaders who wrought this modernization were an extraordinarily able and devoted group, mostly samurai from four southwestern clans, along with other supporters of the emperor. Some of them had been abroad, bringing back a remarkably keen perception of how Western countries might contribute to Japan's development. This group governed under the emperor with only limited challenges to divert their attention from the central objective of modernization in the shortest possible time. The motives that inspired these men seem to have been patriotic rather than personal. Their attitude was that Japan must become strong in order to prevent further encroachments from Europe and America, especially such humiliations as the treaty ports and other concessions Western countries had imposed on China. Some of the Meiji leaders may from the start have harbored notions of Japanese imperialist aggrandizement. In any case, the means of Japan's growth was to be adoption of Western technology.

The most pressing problems encountered during the first years were economic. The new government needed first to obtain means of adequate support, the lack of which had been an important factor in the decay of the Tokugawa shogunate. A modern tax system was impossible as long as the traditional feudal dues persisted. The commutation of these dues was undertaken by the issuance of government bonds to the recipients of the feudal income. The feudal obligations of the peasants were converted into taxes payable to the government in money. The interest on the bonds delivered was far below the income derived from the new heavy taxes, and a basis for orderly government finance was established. But this income was still not adequate. Government expenses for development were greater than the new taxes could cover. Inflationary currency issue was resorted to for a number of years, despite knowledge that such practices under the shogunate had brought serious consequences. But economic activity in the early years of Meiji expanded so rapidly that the expansion of the currency had only a limited inflationary effect.

The establishment of a banking system was necessary if savings were to be stimulated and mobilized and credit was to be made available for business as well as government needs. Various financial institutions were created, including commercial and agricultural banks and, in 1882, a central bank. A postal savings system early succeeded in mobilizing small savings from all over Japan. The Bank of Japan became the center of a modern banking, credit, and currency system, providing specialized services of many kinds in addition to ordinary banking operations. Funds necessary for economic development thus came from taxes, small savings, and inflationary finance. In addition, the early success of trade and other enterprises soon produced profits, the reinvestment of which provided a growing source of capital for development purposes. Some confiscation and forced loans were imposed. Small amounts of foreign capital made a limited but significant addition.

Industry was a field of very high priority in Meiji Japan. Building on the pre-Meiji beginnings of various daimyo and even the shogunate itself, the government established a number of modern factories, especially for the manufacture of munitions and other products considered vital to the power objectives of the regime. Cotton textile mills, mines, railroads, and a telegraph system were developed largely by the same method. Ocean shipping, too, was started by direct government purchase of ships from abroad. These were at first privately operated on behalf of the government on an expedition to Taiwan (Formosa) in 1874, and then sold cheaply to the private operators to form the nucleus of the Mitsubishi interests. Most of the factories and other government enterprises were also sold before long at low prices to private owners. Thus business enterprises were established quickly, and yet continued bureaucratic operation was avoided. Private initiative and capital also went into new industries and unsponsored enterprises, especially small firms.

Agriculture was sufficiently modernized to raise yields sharply. With very little increase in acreage, total food production during the Meiji Era expanded enough to feed a rapidly growing population at somewhat improved levels. Foreign trade, a major object of Commodore Perry's visit, grew in the Meiji Era on foundations laid before 1868. Silk, especially raw silk, soon took the lead among Japanese exports, a position that was retained until the depression of the 1930's. A silkworm disease in Europe boosted the market for raw silk, and also provided a temporary market for silkworm eggs. Other exports included tea, copper, and a few minor products. Imports were varied, including cloth, yarn, machinery, and other metal manufactures.

Education and specialized training were undertaken to provide industrial workers, technicians, and managers. A system of universal education reduced illiteracy in one generation to a small proportion of the population. Commercial colleges, technical colleges, and universities were established and soon produced a flow of remarkably well-qualified manpower.

Managerial personnel in the early years of the Meiji Era were mostly samurai, the merchants providing less modern entrepreneurial talent than might have been expected. But business enterprise was not confined to a few large firms assisted by the government. Small enterprises were very numerous from the start, and remain so today. Many thousands of independent business careers contributed vastly to the economic development of Japan. In other fields also, personnel was available in quantity and showed an eager ability to learn. Foreign technicians and teachers contributed a great deal, and Japanese in substantial numbers went abroad for study.

Military affairs were of great importance in the eyes of the Meiji leaders. Universal conscription was introduced in 1873, imposing on the lowliest peasant a period of compulsory military service, whereas only a few years earlier the bearing of arms had been the carefully restricted right of a superior class, the samurai. With foreign advisers, army and navy forces and facilities were soon brought into being. Their effectiveness was made known to the world when Japan defeated China in 1895, and then Russia in 1905.

Political evolution was rapid during the Meiji Era, but the oligarchy that overthrew the shogun continued to rule. Their power was challenged, notably in the Satsuma Rebellion of 1877, but for the most part the energies and resources of Japan were available for national development. The authoritarian character of the Meiji government was formalized in the constitution of 1889. Handed down without prior public discussion, this constitution was in form the expression of an absolute ruler, the emperor, in whom rested all sovereign power, military and civilian, legislative, executive, and judicial. The constitution provided certain ways for exercising this power in practice, including a bicameral diet, the lower house of which was to be elected by the people. A cabinet minister was required to countersign all political documents signed by the emperor. But numerous checks on the diet meant that in fact it had very limited power. The cabinet was subjected to military veto by an imperial ordinance issued in 1900, requiring that the army and navy ministers be officers of the two highest ranks on active duty. Thus any army or navy decision to withdraw its minister would bring down a cabinet.

Manners and customs showed many outward changes. Topknots, kimonos, and swords gave way to Western haircuts, business suits, military and school uniforms, and, in recent times, briefcases. Baseball, ballroom dancing, and other

Western sports and recreations soon appeared, along with Western music and painting. New ways made an uneven impact, in some cases spreading throughout Japan quickly, in other cases affecting only a narrow circle in Tokyo and other large cities. Most of the new ways were simply added to the old.

Old ways tended not to die out but often continued side by side with the new. Businessmen and military officers would wear Western clothes at work, and use chairs, desks, and tables. But at home they would change to loose-fitting Japanese garments, sit on the matted floor, and live according to traditional customs. In the cities there was a gradual but very limited development of Western attitudes toward life, including ideas of freedom and democracy and interest in political parties and labor unions. In the rural villages very little fundamental change in attitudes was to be found, even long after Meiji times.

With improved health and increasing agricultural production, Japan's population rose, but the rural villages did not expand much. Younger sons found employment in the growing cities and new industrial centers. Even daughters were in many cases sent to these centers for employment. Such country people in the cities tended to retain their village ties, returning for visits, for marriage (usually arranged by the parents), and in time of trouble. Whether in village or city, Japan's common people clung to their habits of thrift, hard work, and intense loyalty. And urban employers, for their part, acted paternally, somewhat in the tradition of the feudal lords, caring for workers in ways virtually unknown in Western countries during the early stages of industrialization.

Thus in the space of a single generation, Japan accomplished what most of the non-Western world seems to be seeking today —rapid modernization in the physical aspects of life, and the military strength and national prestige of one of the world's great powers, but without undermining unduly the essential character of the nation. From a feudal kingdom hardly able to control internal forces, let alone resist the armed overtures of Western powers, Japan grew strong enough not only for self-defense, but also for aggression against neighboring countries. Western technology and teachers, and Japanese leadership, learning, and hard work had brought about a hitherto unprecedented change. After the death of Emperor Meiji in 1912, Janpan's record was no longer that of a weak struggling new country, but of a power making its own decisions about its national course, except for the temporary foreign occupation of 1945-52.

The years immediately after 1912 were relatively easy for Japan. Already in possession of Taiwan and Korea, South Sakhalin and the Kuriles, and with an important foothold in Manchuria, Japan expanded farther during World War I, occupying the German Pacific islands and extending its encroachments on China. Exports boomed, and Japan experienced great economic prosperity for the first time. Following World War I, however, Japan's position became difficult. Financial troubles arising in 1920 had not been wholly liquidated when the earthquake of 1923 struck, destroying more property and killing more people than any similar catastrophe had ever done before. The financial repercussions of the earthquake were, in turn, still being felt in 1927, when a banking crisis occurred. And in 1930 and 1931 Japan's economy suffered acutely from the world depression.

During the decade 1921-31, Western political, social, and economic policies were more popular in Japan than at any other time before 1945. Party government enjoyed its greatest development, and civilian influence in politics gained in relation to military influence. Universal manhood suffrage and other reforms were adopted. Labor and liberal movements gained their first foothold. Finally, despite all the financial difficulties of these years, Japan's adherence to "sound" financial policies was manifested in its return to the gold standard in January, 1930. But many of these achievements, so impressive to Western observers at the time, were very unpopular in Japan. Party politics produced not responsible maturity, but rather a large degree of bickering, which to many Japanese seemed unpatriotic, and some scandals served to undermine the already insecure prestige of the political parties. And the financial policies that led to resumption of the gold standard after the world depression had already started, exacerbated the very sharp effects of that depression in Japan.

The Japanese military intervened by launching operations in Manchuria in September, 1931. This attack opened a period of military influence and imperialist ventures that spread Japanese forces over much of China, all the major Southeast Asian areas, and many Pacific islands, and ended only with the Japanese surrender aboard the U.S.S. *Missouri* in September, 1945. During this period party government was superseded progressively by military control. Liberal tendencies were checked. Skillful management of inflationary factors in the economy between 1932 and 1936 brought Japan out of the world depression faster than any other major trading nation, and the late thirties were a period of great economic prosperity, giving way after the start of war in Europe in 1939 to progressive wartime privations. The *zaibatsu,* huge family cartels, countered military influence to a substantial extent before 1937. But after war was extended to China proper in that year, increasingly fewer brakes were applied on military control of the Japanese government.

The Pacific war, opened by the attack on Pearl Harbor in December, 1941, brought Japan an initial series of dramatic successes. But from mid-1942 on Japan experienced reverses, as American military potential was rapidly mobilized. Japan's plan was to seize Southeast Asia and important Pacific Ocean areas, to defend these areas vigorously, and to exploit them for Japan's military and economic advantage. This plan failed when determined Japanese defense proved inadequate, and efforts to exploit Southeast Asia yielded much less than had been anticipated. It was not until a year had passed after the attack on Pearl Harbor that the Japanese leaders realized their country's plight and undertook maximum mobilization. This great effort proved inadequate, primarily because of the vulnerability of Japan's island economy to blockade. By the spring of 1945, the few Japanese ships that could still put to sea sought cargoes of food for a hungry population, as efforts to import industrial raw materials were virtually abandoned. Japan's home islands came under catastrophic attack. The nuclear bombings of Hiroshima and Nagasaki were a last stroke that put an end to extended debate in the Japanese government. The emperor himself decided on surrender.

The emperor's surrender order stunned troops and civilians alike, but they obeyed loyally. General Douglas MacArthur was appointed Supreme Commander for the Allied Powers (SCAP), under directives that called for demobilization of Japanese military forces, disarmament, and various types of reform. War leaders were removed from public life and subjected to trial as war criminals, and large numbers of subordinate personnel were prohibted from engaging in stipulated kinds of public employment and business. Occupation controls were exercised through the Japanese government, which continued to function, although with new leaders, under the emperor. Destruction, disorganization, and demoralization were so great that reconstruction came slowly. Economic recovery was handicapped by shortages of practically everything, by lack of leadership, and by cessation of foreign trade other than United States aid shipments. Political recovery was hampered by a tendency of the Japanese to defer to SCAP, by the shortage of qualified personnel untainted by the war, and by the psychological unpreparedness of all Japanese for their nation's new role. Social organization suffered from the dismay of defeat, the disgrace of the military, and general uncertainty as to the future, compounded by acute economic distress and disorganization.

Occupation reforms were aimed at removing from Japan's life the militarism that had dominated so much of its history and at building the social, economic, and political basis for a peaceful and progressive nation. Women were given the vote, labor was encouraged to form unions, freedom of speech was permitted, education was reorganized without militarist and ultra-nationalist elements, and political parties were encouraged. An agrarian reform restricted the amount of land one person could own, limited rents, and weakened the control of the landlords. Police organization was decentralized, steps were taken to break up the huge family combines, the zaibatsu, and a few industrial facilities were removed as reparations.

On the Occupation's insistence, a new constitution was drafted, and after several months of discussion, was adopted, effective May 3, 1947. In sharp contrast with the constitution of 1889, the new document declares that sovereign power resides with the people; makes the emperor a symbol of the state; renounces war and prohibits maintenance of military forces; grants many rights to the people; reconstitutes the diet as the highest organ of state power, with two popularly elected houses; and contains other provisions of a similar character.

Economic problems loomed large from the time of surrender, but Occupation economic activities were at first confined to limited aid for the prevention of disease and unrest and to measures aimed at demilitarizing economic life. Early in 1947 attention turned increasingly to rehabilitation and recovery, aimed at strengthening Japan to support the side of the Western democracies in the developing worldwide struggle against communism. Recovery took place very slowly, until 1950, when the Korean war placed sudden heavy demands on the Japanese economy, especially in the form of procurement orders for United States, South Korean, and other Allied military forces. With this fortuitous stimulus, Japan enjoyed a moderate degree of prosperity during the last two years of the Occupation.

A peace treaty to end Japan's role in World War II proved impossible to negotiate in the early years after the surrender, as growing disagreements and tensions emerged among Japan's victors. With the outbreak of the Korean war, however, the United States set out to get an early treaty even if some countries did not sign it. A draft treaty worked out in a series of bilateral negotiations was signed at a peace conference in San Francisco in September, 1951, and came into force, after ratification, on April 28, 1952. The treaty ended Japan's state of war with the United States and most of the other Allies, and brought the occupation to an end.

Because of disagreement over the Communist regime in China, Russia and China did not sign the treaty. Because of reparation disagreements, several countries in Southeast Asia, too, withheld their signatures. But by October 1956, when Russia signed an agreement ending its technical state of eleven years of war with Japan, Tokyo had re-established some sort of formal relations with most of its World War II enemies. Following reparations and peace agreements with the Philippines in mid-1956, Japan looked forward to settling in due course with Indonesia. But Japan's relations with Communist China remained uncertain, even though tentative overtures had been made by each side.

The San Francisco treaty restricts Japanese sovereignty to the four main islands, related smaller islands, and a few outlying island areas; confirms Japan's obligation to pay war reparations; specifically recognizes Japan's right of self-defense; and requires withdrawal of occupation forces but permits stationing of foreign troops in Japan in accordance with bilateral agreements. Such a bilateral agreement was signed by Japan and the United States on the same day as the peace treaty, and American troops still serve in Japan as security forces under this agreement.

Since the end of the occupation, Japan has again faced some of the questions raised a century ago about the character of the Japanese state, its means of support, and its relations with other countries. It is too early, and too many conflicting forces are now at work, to say what the answers to these questions will be. Japanese society is slowly evolving from what it has been in past centuries into something more consistent with the world of today. Occupation reforms have left a deep impression, but many of these reforms are already being modified or even undone. It seems clear that women will retain an improved status, and that labor will continue to exercise much greater influence that before 1945. The agrarian reforms are standing so far, with less legal change than most other reforms, and Japanese farmers look forward to a continuation of their improved position. Political parties have developed somewhat, but so far show neither the vitality nor the leadership that many observers consider necessary for effective democracy. Conservatives continue to dominate the government and have held power ever since 1945, except for a year of Socialist government early in the occupation. The purge has been abolished, a centralized police force has been re-established, and the zaibatsu have gone far in rebuilding their former business empires.

Economic factors are very important and may prove to be decisive in determining Japan's future. Ninety million people cannot live on Japan's rocky islands without a large flow of imported food and raw materials. To pay for these, Japan must export manufactured goods, the production of which requires additional quantities of imported materials. Japan's attempt to assure itself markets by military and political control of much of Asia was frustrated by defeat in World War II.

Trade recovery has been hampered by economic and political disorder in much of Asia and by Communist control of large areas potentially important in Japanese trade. Japanese exports have suffered also from high costs of production, low quality, poor marketing, and other difficulties which make these products non-competitive or marginal in important markets. Solution of production and cost problems has involved technical improvements, heavy capital investments, a national program of financial austerity adopted in 1953, and world-wide prosperity. Since 1953 Japan's production and exports have been booming, and per capita income has exceeded its highest prewar level. It is now evident that Japan has the capacity to produce enough exports to pay for necessary imports. Another development, a sharp decline in Japan's birthrate since 1947, gives a basis for the hope that its future population growth will remain within the supporting capacity of the nation's economy.

What is not yet evident is how readily foreign markets will accept Japanese goods in the years to come. Two major threats exist: world depression and trade barriers. Depression is considered by many economists to be less of a threat today than in times past, because there is an awareness of the problem and governmental readiness in the United States and elsewhere to take prompt and vigorous counter measures when the threat of an economic decline appears. But trade barriers remain a very serious problem for Japan. Japan's most important trading partner, the United States, administered a rebuff to Tokyo after rapid increases in Japanese textile sales in the American market aroused vigorous protests from American producers. These protests were discussed by the American and Japanese governments. As a result, and in order to avoid the imposition of even more severe trade limitations by the United States, Japanese authorities announced during 1956 a series of quotas on exports of specified cotton textile products to the American market in the years ahead. The role of the United States government in bringing these quotas into being makes it clear that Washington is not prepared to permit foreign cotton manufactures to provide a large share of the American market.

Japan's foreign relations reflect the uncertainties and difficulties of a strategically important but vulnerable country in a highly unstable world. Co-operation with the United States is providing defense forces while the Japanese slowly and reluctantly rebuild defenses of their own. Strong neutralist elements have from the start viewed the struggle between the Western democracies and the Communist world as essentially outside Japan's interest, which is deemed to call for avoidance of involvement on either side. The Japanese people, on the whole, did not regard the Korean War as of direct concern to them.

Signs of new vigor and spirit are becoming apparent. Nationalist sentiment, even in racist forms reminiscent of the period of military aggrandizement, is reappearing, displacing the numbness that followed defeat and the compliant acceptance that was given to foreign rule during the Occupation. Where this nationalism will lead cannot now be foreseen, but it seems consistent with the assertive character of the Japanese nation.

The re-emergence of Japan as an active participant in world affairs is being vigorously pushed. Diplomatic and economic relations have been re-established with most countries, including most of the new governments of Asia. Japan participates in a large number of international organizations. Tokyo's keen disappointment at exclusion from the list of countries admitted to the United Nations in 1955 gave way to satisfaction when Japan was admitted in the autumn of 1956, with the support promised by Russia in the agreement ending the state of war with Japan, signed in October 1956. Relations with Communist China have been restricted to limited trade since 1950 when China intervened in the Korean War, but there is strong business pressure in Japan for expanding trade and some sentiment for opening diplomatic relations.

Sentiment in favor of communism and of Communist regimes is fostered by the small Communist party in Japan, and by the larger and more influential left-wing element in the Socialist party. Marxism is enjoying a vogue among Japanese intellectuals. The diplomatic course recommended by these different groups, and by neutralists and others as well, is not so much an active or close relationship with Communist countries as dissolution of present close relations with the United States. Thus, despite the great economic advantage Japan gains from the presence of United States security forces, their departure is being sought with increasing vigor.

Japan, the most Western of Asian countries, remains today a country in between—between the tremendous power of neighboring Communist regimes and the presumably even greater power of the United States across the Pacific Ocean, between traditional Asian and modern Western ways, between memories of privation and hopes for prosperity, between authoritarian traditions and possible new social and political forms, and between past militarism and some new orientation not yet determined.

7

Southeast Asia: Non-Western Pluralism in Transition

The emergence of Southeast Asian countries into independent nationhood has been one of the most dramatic developments of the postwar era, which was highlighted by the fact that the first conference of Asian and African nations in 1955 was convened at Bandung in Indonesia, the largest of the new nations in Southeast Asia. In the span of a few years, between 150 and 180 million people, the vast majority of whom had lived under Western colonial rule for decades or centuries, changed their political status. Independence came, often after struggle against the former colonial masters, as the culmination of a long process set in motion by the contact of this huge non-Western area with the West.

Geographically, Southeast Asia reaches from the three northern states of Thailand, Burma, and Vietnam, which border on China, to the island republics of the Philippines and Indonesia, with Malaya forming, as it were, a bridge between mainland and islands. By virtue of its geographic position, Southeast Asia has from time immemorial been a crucially important gateway between the Indian and Pacific Oceans—a gateway coveted by merchants, adventurers, and conquerors bent on securing trading posts in its vital transit harbors, and —equally important—bent on obtaining economic and political control over an area rich in natural resources. In former centuries, the islands of the Indonesian archipelago, in particular, throve on the lucrative spice trade. In modern times, Southeast Asia has in addition become a prominent producer of such export commodities as rubber, tin, oil, rice, sugar, tea, quinine, teakwood, tobacco, and hemp. These strategic and economic factors account for the fact that Southeast Asia has been not only a gateway but also a crossroads; they explain why control over the area has been of such vital importance to the Western powers and why Japan sought to subjugate it during World War II. These factors play an important role today.

The vast geographical expanse of the region is paralleled by enormous differences between the individual countries of Southeast Asia. The highlands of Burma, for example, are very sparsely populated, while, by contrast, Java—the political center of Indonesia—is among the most densely inhabited and cultivated regions in the entire world. Even within the same country, population density sometimes varies, so that overcrowded areas can be found side by side with empty lands. Sumatra, for example, many times the size of neighboring Java, is still underpopulated, just as Mindanao can absorb the population surplus of Luzon, the main island in the Philippines. In fact, population pressure is so far not so much a general problem in Southeast Asia as a regional one. Thailand, Burma, and Vietnam—with populations ranging from 16 to 20-odd million—still have ample lands beyond the most fertile river delta regions; Indonesia, with 80-odd million, has enough space outside of Java, which alone accounts for almost 50 million of its inhabitants.

Of even greater importance than the diversity in geography and population are the ethnic, linguistic and religious differences among Southeast Asians. There is no racial homogeneity between Burmese and Indonesians, for example, or even between Vietnamese and Cambodians, who are close neighbors. Siamese (Thais) and Malays cannot find common traces in their respective languages, but even where such traces do exist—as is the case with Filipinos and Indonesians—they do not suffice to make communication easy. From the point of view of religion, again, Southeast Asia contains such predominantly Buddhist countries as Burma, Thailand, and Cambodia, and an almost entirely Catholic country—the Philippines—while Indonesia, the most populous state in the region, is predominantly Muslim. The tiny island of Bali (a part of Indonesia) alone has retained the Hindu religion which at one time counted hundreds of thousands of adherents in Southeast Asia. In Vietnam, beside Buddhism and Catholicism, a whole range of religious sects are thriving to this day. Malaya, almost evenly divided between Malays and Chinese, presents yet another mixture of religions and cultures in a relatively small area.

These diversities are indicative of the many cultural, economic, and political influences which have impinged on Southeast Asia in the course of its history. Before the advent of the West, the region was vitally affected by India and China, but from the sixteenth century onward and until quite recent times, Western peoples—Portuguese, Spaniards, Dutch, British, French, and Americans—have played a predominant role in the region. For many centuries, then, Southeast Asia was a recipient rather than a generator, and alien, particularly Western, influence—whether indirect or direct—fostered diversity rather than unity. Even today, although the Southeast Asian countries have at long last attained independence, they have so far shown relatively little regional cohesion or solidarity.

Yet in spite of these differences, the states of the region share several significant characteristics which not only justify a regional treatment of Southeast Asia as such, but which also —because of their combined effect—make the area unique and distinct from other parts of Asia and the rest of the non-Western world. These characteristics are a common economic base and a similar social pattern, both the result of near-identical historical developments, and a political experience in modern times—in particular, Western colonialism and Japanese military occupation—shared by most, if not all, of Southeast Asia. It is because of these factors that the problems facing the countries of the area today are strikingly similar.

Economically, Southeast Asia shows a dual development. In the first place, the vast majority of the population are peasants engaged in rice cultivation for their own subsistence. But ever since Southeast Asia has been drawn into the world market—roughly speaking, from the late nineteenth century onwards—a "dual economy" has existed in many parts of the area; for alongside the age-old native economy, new agrarian enterprises have been established, applying Western capitalism and scientific techniques to Southeast Asia's rich soils and resources. These new enterprises have given rise to the cultivation of export crops, including rubber, tea, sugar, tobacco, coffee, and other tropical produce. The opening of Southeast Asia to the world market also stimulated the commerical cultivation of rice and rubber by individual native agriculturists and entrepreneurs, who abandoned their traditional, consumer-directed village economy in favor of growing cash crops for export. Thailand, Vietnam, and Burma thus became the "rice bowl" of Asia, and Malaya and Indonesia the world's largest exporters of tin and rubber, much of the latter being grown by small cultivators.

Estate agriculture by Western-organized enterprises has introduced Indonesian and Philippine sugar, tobacco, tea, coffee, quinine, and hemp to the world market.

The traditional social structure of Southeast Asia was characterized by a rather rigid division between, on the one hand, rulers and court aristocracies, and, on the other, the vast mass of the population, the peasants. In some areas, such as parts of Indonesia, this stratified and authoritarian relationship was even expressed by the use of different languages between superior and inferior. In part, this social pattern was an inheritance of centuries of Indian influence in the area, even though the Hindu caste system was hardly ever fully copied and maintained in Southeast Asia. A priestly class, often allied to the ruling houses and of great importance to the legitimation of kingship, existed in many parts of the area. In early times religion was a court affair, while the peasantry remained on the fringes of the official creed of the nobility, adhering to age-old animistic beliefs which to this day—although often overlaid with later religious practices—have remained characteristic of Southeast Asian peoples. In later centuries, however, religion did gain important footholds among the peasant population and came to play a role in political development. Quite apart from their subsequent political significance, however, Southeast Asian religions often became—in part because of their close alliance with native aristocracies—important propagators of an other-wordly, spiritual, and anti-materialistic ethos which militated against the growth of a vigorous economic individualism.

Side by side with this native structure we find another unique social phenomenon. Over the centuries many foreign traders, particularly Indian and Chinese, stayed on as permanent settlers, and by virtue of their economic activities soon began to occupy prominent positions in most of the countries. Neither of these ethnic groups has tended to assimilate with the local population to a noticeable extent. In the course of time, both Chinese and Indians thus developed into a trading or business class in societies which had by and large no such native elements. They performed important services, but at the same time they often obtained a stranglehold over the native population as moneylenders and landowners, and this was—and still is—bitterly resented.

With the gradual opening of Southeast Asia to Western trade from the sixteenth century onward, this social structure underwent further change, since to the already existing racial elements a new, Western, layer was being added. By the nineteenth century, large-scale Western enterprise had not only introduced the "dual economy" already mentioned. It had also brought European and American business managers, planters, and traders who promptly arrogated to themselves a superior rung in the social ladder with respect to both the native populations and the Indians and Chinese. Indeed, in some countries Western colonial rule brought with it an expansion of these two Asian groups, since the colonial powers at times encouraged the immigration of Indians (as the British did in Burma) and Chinese (as was done by the Dutch in Indonesia). These immigrants were welcomed as laborers in mines and on estates, but some of them were also employed in more important and better-paid positions. Quite a few readily "caught on" to the new economy introduced by Western capitalist enterprise and found their way into trading occupations. Seemingly favored by the colonial rulers, their presence and activities only aggravated the centuries-old racial antagonisms.

Thus the establishment of Western colonial rule in Southeast Asia has given rise to what has been called a "plural society"—a society, that is, in which the division of labor as well as the division of wealth does not so much coincide with class lines but rather with racial, ethnic lines. Westerners, alien Asians, and native Southeast Asians live side by side in these countries, but there is little to hold them together and give them a common loyalty. Large-scale enterprise is in the hands of Westerners, while the immigrant Asians—Chinese and Indians, and before 1939 also a few Japanese, together with a sprinkling of Arabs and other nationalities—occupy as a rule middle-class positions, such as artisans, moneylenders, storekeepers and clerks. Within this strange and multiracial social pyramid the native aristocracies in some countries continued to occupy prominent positions for many decades; but in the measure that Western political control became solidly established in the latter part of the last century, their prestige rapidly started to wane.

Almost everywhere in Southeast Asia the coming of Western powers was met by armed resistance; but because of superiority in arms and technology, in part also because of internal divisions among Southeast Asian ruling houses, the West invariably triumphed. First among European colonial powers came the Portuguese in the early sixteenth century, soon followed by the Spaniards and the Dutch. While the Portuguese were forced out of their strongholds in Malacca by the Dutch, the Spaniards continued to occupy the Philippines until the end of the nineteenth century when, as one result of the Spanish-American War, the United States took over the islands. The Dutch made Java their main base of operations and ultimately expanded their Pacific empire over almost the entire Indonesian archipelago. The British occupied Malaya and, during the nineteenth century, Burma. The French, finally, subjugated Annam, Laos, and Cambodia, which, together with Tonkin, became known as French Indochina. Of all Southeast Asian countries, only Thailand escaped annexation by a Western power.

The nature of these colonial conquests, as well as that of subsequent colonial rule itself, varied from country to country. In some areas, as for example in Indonesia, a commercial enterprise, the Dutch East India Company, arrived on the scene long before the government of the metropolitan country itself became interested in assuming direct political control. Elsewhere, as for example in the Philippines, colonization was from the outset a governmental venture. Christian missionaries sometimes played a significant role, both in the Philippines—which is the only predominantly Christian, Catholic country in the area—and in Indochina, while in Burma commercial interests far overshadowed missionary endeavors in importance.

There were similar differences between the ways in which these newly acquired colonies were ruled by Western powers. The Dutch in many parts of Indonesia imposed "indirect rule," a system by which native rulers were outwardly left in control, while in fact they were shorn of all real power, which the colonial masters exercised for and through them. The British in Burma, by contrast, abolished the native monarchy, replacing it by "direct rule" of British administrators. Of greater importance still were the different philosophies underlying the colonial policies pursued by Dutchmen, Britishers, Frenchmen, and Americans. Primarily by means of education, both the British and Americans prepared their "wards" for increasing autonomy and ultimate independence far more rapidly than did the Dutch and French, both of whom adhered to a more gradual, and even paternalistic, approach to the ultimate emancipation of their colonies. As a result of these divergent policies Indonesia and Vietnam are today facing greater obstacles in staffing governmental and other public services with adequately trained personnel than are either the Philippines or Burma.

But even though these distinctions were important and far-reaching, the total effect of Western colonial rule was strikingly similar throughout Southeast Asia. Whether that rule was "direct" or "indirect," it ended to all intents and purposes the sovereignty formerly exercised by Southeast Asian kings, sultans, rajahs and other potentates, thus reducing the court nobilities at best to decorative survivors of a bygone political system. This does not mean that the replacement of the traditional regimes by Western administrations necessarily constituted everywhere a change for the worse. In fact, by abolishing some of the worst features of many Southeast Asian autocratic governments—their frequently harsh arbitrariness, the endemic fratricidal warfare among contenders for political power, and the ruthless and naked exploitation of the peasantry, and more particularly of slaves—the colonial powers laid the groundwork for a more modern, national development. Not infrequently it was Western colonial rule which for the first time created new territorial entities—as for example in Indonesia and the Philippines—out of petty and often warring native principalities. Such changes as the introduction of efficient and at times quite enlightened administrations, the extirpation of the worst forms of corruption and nepotism, the creation of modern systems of communication, as well as the spread of health measures and of Western education—whether sponsored by colonial governments or by missionaries—may be counted among the more positive results of colonialism in many parts of Southeast Asia.

These achievements, however, were outweighed by the negative aspects of colonialism. First and foremost, colonial rule was rule by aliens, however benevolent some may have been. The political degradation inflicted by Western supremacy left a deep and lasting scar on the minds of Southeast Asians of all strata. Second, colonialism, which ultimately relied on military predominance, continued and perhaps even strengthened the very authoritarian form of government which Southeast Asia inherited from its own tradition. Only during the present century, and even then only in parts of the area, were some liberal and democratic features introduced by the colonial powers in Southeast Asia, but never in a sufficient measure to affect the basically authoritarian relationship between mother country and colony. Third, in spite of the fact that under the aegis of colonialism Western enterprise extracted vast profit from Southeast Asian countries, the living standards of the population as a whole did not appreciably rise. Most of the wealth, instead of being reinvested on the spot, was allowed to flow to stockholders in the West. Thus the contrast between rich and poor remained stark, and in the peculiar context of the plural society this economic contrast was rendered starker still by the fact that Westerners —and, to a lesser extent, alien Asians—became increasingly identified with wealth, the native peoples with poverty.

Yet Western rule in Southeast Asia set in motion certain processes which in the end undermined the continued existence of colonialism itself, thus preparing the road to national independence. In the first place the requirements of both colonial and business administration had led to the gradual spread of Western education among Southeast Asians. Although most colonial powers only very cautiously introduced this education, it brought into existence an entirely new social group in Southeast Asia, the native intelligentsia. At no time numerically important, some of these young intellectuals soon became the principal anti-colonial spokesmen and leaders in their countries. This result of Western education was, indeed, unavoidable, since contact with the intellectual tradition of the West—particularly in the universities of the metropolitan countries, which some few Southeast Asians were starting to attend after the turn of this century—brought with it acquaintance with the theories of nationalism, democracy, and socialism, including, of course, Marxism.

This contact between West and non-West had the most far-reaching consequences for Southeast Asia, as it had for other parts of the non-Western world. The young students not only absorbed the teachings of the West; they also learned to appreciate the political systems of European states, and the role which political organizations, such as parties, played in the West. On their return many proceeded to translate both the symbols and practices of Europe and America into meaningful Southeast Asian terms, creating nationalist ideologies as well as nationalist, Western-organized parties and movements. In the twentieth century, resistance to Western dominance, which had been endemic in the region ever since the beginnings of colonial times, was for the first time organized along modern lines into a conscious struggle.

It is not surprising that the great majority of Southeast Asian intellectuals were as profoundly influenced by Western socialist ideas as they were by those of nationalism, and that some few among them, impressed by the victory of the Bolsheviks in the Soviet Union, embraced communism from the early 1920's onward. From their point of view, capitalism was intimately linked with the economic exploitation of their own countries by the West. In the absence of a powerful native middle class in the plural societies of the colonies, there were in fact few, if any, Southeast Asians with a vested interest in capitalism. In addition, the socioreligious tradition in Southeast Asia provided, as we saw, an unfavorable climate for economic individualism. Socialistic doctrines could fairly easily be assimilated to the traditional distrust of the capitalist, a distrust by no means alien to the new leaders, many of whom came from aristocratic—and thus inherently anti-capitalistic—families. In attacking colonialism, the new leaders were almost invariably led to attack capitalism as well, and to advocate a socialist economy and national independence at the same time. Largely however, because of the fact that the intellectual inspiration of these new leaders was predominantly derived from the West rather than from Russia, only a small minority of them turned to communism. Even then, however, nationalism and communism often seemed to go hand in hand in their attacks on the common enemy—Western dominance over Southeast Asia. This relationship is of the utmost importance for present-day developments in many parts of the area.

Neither nationalists nor Communists, however, were immediately successful in addressing themselves to the vast majority of the peasantry. Indeed, in some parts of the area, notably in Burma and in Indonesia, they remained for some time second in importance to religious—Buddhist and Muslim—leaders. The decay of native political authority had actually left Southeast Asians for many decades with no other leadership than that provided by religious spokesmen. Almost everywhere native religious sentiment had gained strength in reaction to Christian missionary endeavors encouraged by colonial governments. Rather ironically, the expansion of communications which Western rule had brought with it had also helped to carry religion to even the remotest hamlets and villages of Southeast Asia.

Resistance to foreign rule and to economic exploitation by aliens had often in the past been sparked by local religious leaders, and traditional religious appeals continued to be more effective rallying points for the illiterate peasantry than were such intrinsically Western ideas as nationalism and socialism. But even though nationalism and communism were at the outset almost exclusively urban-centered, already in the first two decades of the twentieth century links between them and religious movements showed that they were united in a deep-seated hostility to Western rule, and that each had a distinct contribution to make to the common struggle: nationalists and Communists—new and powerful ideologies and modern organizational methods; religious leaders—mass support among the rural population. As a result, colonial governments took repressive action whenever any of these radical movements openly and violently challenged the status quo, as happened repeatedly in the 1920's and 1930's in many parts of Southeast Asia.

While only a very small minority of Southeast Asians was affected by high-school, college, or university education, many more received a lower education, which sufficed to fit them for clerical positions in the colonial administration or in Western enterprises. This kind of education, although not as spectacular as academic training, was yet of far-reaching importance. For it brought a degree of Westernization and urbanization to thousands of Southeast Asians, who gradually grew into a small native white-collar class, ranking below professional people like doctors, lawyers, and engineers. It was among this new lower middle class that the appeal of nationalism and communism proved particularly strong. Only some very few went into business, where they would have to compete against Chinese and Indians; but very slowly a Southeast Asian trading class came into being, able and willing to provide financial backing for nationalist and religious, and at times even Communist, movements.

Among the vast majority of the population, the peasantry, the impact of Western economic and political forces proceeded at a far slower pace; but over the decades the cumulative effect of this impact led to serious inroads on the village-centered way of life. The prime factor of change was the introduction of the Western capitalist economy. In areas close to urban centers, employment possibilities were opened up in factories and other business enterprises. These attracted considerable numbers of villagers by the promise of money wages. Beyond the urban centers, work in mines, oilfields, and Western estate agriculture acted as a similar magnet. Thus both a city and rural proletariat came into being, who depended on a cash, rather than a subsistence, economy.

The traditional village pattern was further disrupted when many peasants changed from subsistence farming to the commerical cultivation of food crops and other tropical produce which in times of boom yielded handsome returns. Such small-scale native farming became especially significant in the delta regions of Lower Burma, Thailand, and Indochina, which developed into important rice exporters, and in Malaya and Indonesia, where, in response to growing world demand, natural rubber was being tapped by native producers on an ever-increasing scale. But though the promise of prosperity lured many Southeast Asians into these new fields, sudden price fluctuations often played havoc with the new-baked agrarian entrepreneurs in Southeast Asia, who at no time grasped the intricacies of world trade for which they had so willingly become suppliers. Forfeiture of land titles and indebtedness to moneylenders were thus often the harsh price exacted by the inexorable movements of an incomprehensible trade cycle. These sudden ups and downs continue to cause serious hardship in some areas of Southeast Asia to this very day.

The imposition of Western capitalism on Southeast Asia, instead of taking place gradually within a normal social evolution—as had happened in the West—thus led to a disintegration of village life and to much bewilderment and misery among the victims of the new economic processes. Coupled with the rapid population growth in the course of the nineteenth century—among other factors, a result of improved hygiene and preventive medicine—this disintegrative process undermined the traditional pattern of life of the peasantry. Agrarian unrest was the result of this ever more widespread social upheaval; on several occasions it reached serious proportions in the last two decades of colonial rule. As we have already pointed out, religious leaders often placed themselves at the helm of such uprisings. And although the link between this agrarian ground swell and the urban nationalist leaders was still weak, on at least two occasions in the 1920's outbursts of agrarian unrest were spearheaded by local Communist parties.

In the span of a few short months the era of Western colonialism was suddenly ended by the Japanese conquest of all of Southeast Asia in the early stages of the Pacific war. In spite of the brevity of Japanese military occupation—it only lasted some forty months, from late in 1941 to mid-1945—Southeast Asia emerged from it changed in so many vital respects that a return of Western colonialism after Japan's defeat was rendered very hazardous, if not impossible. Japanese rule decisively affected almost all aspects of life, primarily the political, and vastly accelerated the processes which had started to take shape in colonial times. It is not unlikely that parts of Southeast Asia would have evolved toward independent nationhood under colonial rule; but the attainment would have been delayed by decades had it not been for the Japanese interregnum in the area.

The most immediate result of the Japanese conquest was the rapid elimination of the Western top-layer from governmental and business positions, which followed in the wake of the defeat inflicted by the Japanese on the colonial defense forces. This visible destruction of Western prestige by a non-Western, Asian, nation, eradicated the age-old myth of Western supremacy. Most Europeans and Americans—men, women and children—in Southeast Asia were in subsequent years removed from public life, imprisoned or interned by the Japanese, and often forced to perform hard physical labor. Such sudden and public degradation of Westerners presented a stark contrast to the prominence they had occupied in the plural society of colonial days. It was bound to produce lasting impressions among wide layers of the native population, especially since it was followed by systematic anti-Western propaganda through newspapers and the radio, carried by public loudspeakers to even faraway villages.

Although the Japanese claimed to have liberated Southeast Asia from the yoke of Western colonialism, they proceeded to impose on the conquered territories a colonialism of their own. In many respects, this new Japanese military colonialism was harsher and more ruthless than European and American rule had been since the turn of the century. For where Westerners had primarily been interested in commercial exploitation and the preservation of law and order, the Japanese were out to mobilize the entire population for their war effort. The recruitment of forced labor and auxiliary troops caused grave hardships for millions of people. Exactions of food supplies for Japanese armies and administrators bore heavily on the livelihood of the peasantry, whose economic condition rapidly deteriorated. In addition, the paper currencies put in circulation by the occupation forces led to a spiraling inflation. Agrarian discontent, already widespread before the Japanese invasion, was given added impetus by these adverse economic developments. In spite of brutal repression, the Japanese could not prevent the flare-up of agrarian revolts, particularly in Burma, Indonesia, and the Philippines, during the later stages of the occupation.

But these negative and even tragic consequences of the occupation were by no means the only important result of Japanese rule in Southeast Asia. In the first place, the removal of Westerners from high places gave rise to an upward move among Southeast Asian government officials. Although the very top positions remained for a long time in Japanese hands, there were not enough Japanese in the area to occupy all the posts forcibly vacated by Europeans and Americans. In this way the occupation brought promotions and added administrative experience as well as prestige to a good many who had been denied such advancement under Western colonial rule. When, after initial successes, the fortunes of war started to turn, the Japanese created paramilitary youth organizations and even native armies, officered in part by Southeast Asians, which were to aid in the defense against eventual Allied attacks in the area. This was a most important change, since—with the exception of the Philippines—Western powers had denied large-scale military training to Southeast Asians. This Japanese move created a trained military leadership which, after the war, proved invaluable in the struggle against the attempted restoration of Western colonialism in such countries as Burma and Indonesia. The military profession, moreover, provided not a few energetic and resourceful young people with a career outside the traditional avenues of social prestige. A new class of potential leaders thus arose in the short years of Japanese rule, and these leaders have come to play a crucial, although not invariably constructive, role in the new nation-states of the area.

Finally, Japanese occupation policies decisively affected the political future of Southeast Asia. Eager to win to their side as many Southeast Asian leaders as possible, and skillfully exploiting the deep-seated anti-Western sentiment of many of these leaders, the Japanese almost from the outset courted religious and political spokesmen in the countries they occupied. Some of these leaders, who had openly resisted the colonial governments, were actually freed by Japanese troops from exile or jail; they as well as the majority of other leaders had little choice in the matter of collaborating with their new masters. Although the measure of freedom granted to nationalist and religious movements varied from country to country, on the whole nationalism benefited from this calculated Japanese policy, even though Southeast Asians were only very slowly given positions of real power. Late in 1943, Burma and the Philippines were actually granted their "independence" by the Japanese in the face of anticipated Allied counterattacks in both these countries. Elsewhere, as in Indonesia and Indochina, this political evolution was far slower, and in Malaya it had barely begun when the occupation ended. But irrespective of actual political concessions, nationalism in all of Southeast Asia enjoyed relatively greater official sanction during the occupation than it had ever had before.

Communism, in contrast, was even less tolerated by the Japanese than it had been by the Western colonial governments. Known Communists were hunted down and often executed by the military authorities, but many went underground and played a leading role in anti-Japanese guerrilla warfare; others managed to infiltrate the officially tolerated nationalist organizations and, in particular, the youth organizations and national armies created by the Japanese. Both provided excellent opportunities for broadening the appeal of communism, particularly among the young generation and among the peasantry. Not unexpectedly, the Communists exploited these wartime gains in later years.

Only the Philippines and parts of Burma had been liberated from Japanese rule when the Allies forced the surrender of Japan in August, 1945. The Japanese thus suddenly forfeited their new empire in Southeast Asia while still in actual possession of the greater part of the area, and at a time when Britain, the Netherlands, and France had neither sufficient manpower nor sufficient shipping at their disposal for the immediate reoccupation of their former colonies. A fateful power vacuum had thus arisen, which provided a unique opportunity for the nationalist movements all over Southeast Asia. Aided by the Japanese-trained armies and youth corps and supported by widespread nationalist enthusiasm, nationalist leaders firmly seized the reins of government from local Japanese military commanders, who either voluntarily abdicated, or were forced to abdicate their control, often amidst bloodshed and acts of vengeance against the Japanese.

When at long last the colonial powers were ready to claim their former possessions by force of arms, they were met all over Southeast Asia by nationalist governments which had proclaimed their independence and demanded recognition of the new national states. Armed conflict ensued between nationalists and their former colonial rulers in Indonesia and Vietnam. In the Philippines no such conflict ever arose, since the United States had before the war promised Philippine independence for 1946; in Burma war was averted by British recognition of Burmese independence in 1947. Two years later the Dutch transferred sovereignty over Indonesia to the nationalist regime, and the French reluctantly followed suit in Vietnam, but only after protracted and bitter fighting. Today, Malaya remains the only colonial area in Southeast Asia, but even there negotiations have now been completed, providing for independence during 1957. After long centuries of alien domination, the nations of Southeast Asia have at long last become masters of their own destinies and equal members of the community of nations; with the exception of Vietnam (still divided between two opposing regimes) and Malaya, all these states are members of the United Nations.

The decade since the end of World War II has witnessed remarkable developments in Southeast Asia under the impetus of newly won national independence. The triumph of nationalism has released enormous resources of energy and enthusiasm. It has generated a widespread desire to speed modernization and to rid the area of all vestiges of colonialism. These years, however, have also revealed the innumerable and vexing tasks confronting the new leaders, now that their prime goal of national independence has been achieved.

So far, political change has by far outpaced social and economic change, and this disequilibrium is hampering the fulfillment of nationalist aspirations. The plural societies continue to present serious obstacles to national integration, and in many respects the cleavages within these societies have deepened in postwar years. While Westerners have, of course, been excluded from their erstwhile functions in government since the attainment of independence, they have returned to their economic positions in banking, commerce, and estate agriculture. Although politically disfranchised, as it were, they thus again wield decisive economic power and occupy a prominent place in the social hierarchy. To a lesser extent this is also true of the Eurasians in Southeast Asia. Although born and bred in the area, they have as a rule been loath to forego the claims to a privileged status which they had occupied under colonial rule on account of their racial and cultural identification with the West, and because of the educational and vocational advantages open to them in colonial times.

The alien Asian groups, mainly Chinese and Indians, have generally maintained their privileged place in the economy, even though during the war and later, the foreign traders, landowners, and moneylenders have often been the targets of peasant rebellions. In some areas, above all in Malaya, the Japanese occupation brought with it a sharpening of racial conflicts. Since independence, nationalist leaders have often urged that these Asian and Eurasian residents merge their interests with those of the new nation-states and become true citizens of their countries of domicile. But while the Eurasians, without continuing moral or material aid from the former metropolitan countries, may ultimately be forced to transfer their allegiance to the national states of Southeast Asia, the case is entirely different with Indians and Chinese. Indeed, the reluctance of both these groups to abandon their ties with their ancestral homelands in favor of assimilation in the Southeast Asian host countries has been reinforced by the rising political stature of both India and China since the last war. Southeast Asian statesmen thus have to grapple with a very complex problem involving dual cultural—and in some cases even political—allegiances of some of their economically most powerful inhabitants. The gravity of this problem was illustrated by a series of discussions concerning the status of Chinese residents in some Southeast Asian countries during the Bandung Conference of April, 1955. Even if agreement can ultimately be reached at the governmental level, it will still take many years before the alien Asian elements will be integrated with, and accepted by, the new nation-states.

Behind these age-old racial antagonisms stand the realities of economic life, with which the phenomenon of the plural society is so intimately intertwined. The political changes wrought by the nationalist revolutions have not, so far, supplanted the dual economy which has been so characteristic of Southeast Asia for the last few decades. Subsistence agriculture continues to form the economic base of the entire region, but the ravages of the Japanese occupation and of the postwar years have in many parts of the area led to a serious worsening of the peasant's economic situation. Agrarian reforms to alleviate the lot of tenants, laborers, and small-holders have been attempted by the new governments but with varying degrees of vigor and success. The prospect of obtaining substantial savings for purposes of industrialization from the vast majority of the population is therefore at best no brighter now than it was in the past. Whatever funds can be accumulated must come through earnings from exports. Not only, however, is Southeast Asian export trade still predominantly in the hands of foreigners, but—and this is one of the harshest economic facts—export commodities continue to be subject to the ups and downs of international trade, rather than to the laws and statutes promulgated by the new governments in the area.

No amount of internal economic planning can be expected to obviate the dire effects which these unpredictable and often disastrous movements on the world market have on millions of Southeast Asian cultivators. For example, a worldwide food shortage led to a steep rise in rice prices in the immediate postwar years, soon to be followed by a glut which sharply reduced peasant incomes. For some years now the governments of Burma and Thailand have consequently been confronted with the difficult task of disposing of huge rice surpluses while at the same time cushioning the adverse effects of decreased prices on their rice cultivators. Similarly, when the Korean war sent rubber prices skyrocketing for a few years after 1950, thousands of Malayans and Indonesians sought to profit from the sudden boom. With the end of hostilities, rubber prices fell as steeply as they had risen, and widespread misery followed in the wake of this decline.

If the transition from an inherently colonial to a national—and in part at least socialist—economy has thus understandably become one of the main goals of the new political leadership, this transition, because of Southeast Asia's continuing dependence on international trade, is far more easily planned than translated into economic fact. As a first step, some leaders have pleaded for the establishment of international pools for their vital primary exports which could give a measure of sorely needed stabilization of prices. Since these pleas have so far fallen on deaf ears in the West, several Southeast Asian countries have gladly accepted offers for bulk purchases of rice and other staples from the Communist bloc. In the case of rubber, however, these offers have greatly perturbed the West, which unsuccessfully tried to embargo exports of this strategically vital raw material to Communist-dominated areas. Economic difficulties have thus been compounded by problems of international politics.

Most Southeast Asian countries lack adequate mineral resources—mainly coal and iron ore—which would make industrialization feasible on a scale sufficiently large to alter the nature of the economy and signally increase the standard of living. What mineral wealth the area produces—such as tin, oil, and bauxite, for example—is, moreover, again in the hands of foreigners. The new governments, many of them pledged to programs of nationalization of Western-owned enterprises, have found themselves confronted by difficult alternatives. On the one hand, where nationalization has been carried out, it has proved politically rather than economically profitable, in that it has satisfied nationalist aspirations at the expense of economic efficiency. In other words, it has often misfired because of inadequately trained Southeast Asian managerial personnel. No less important, nationalization has tended to frighten away new private capital investment from overseas; where the prospects for accumulating substantial domestic savings are, as we have said, extremely limited, this development is economically detrimental to the new countries of Southeast Asia, even though it may, again, be politically quite welcome.

Another problem, facing foreign and nationalized enterprises alike, has arisen with the growing demands of organized labor for higher wages and shorter hours. These demands are in themselves a natural and wholesome sign of the rapid social development of Southeast Asian labor; but they often cripple production at a time when the national economy can ill afford the luxury of labor disputes. Often, too, strikes are used for political rather than economic ends in countries where Communists have gained control over important unions.

Other approaches to economic reform have been tried in recent years, among them the encouragement of native business enterprise by a system of preferential quotas and licenses weighted in favor of nationals at the expense of foreigners, and combined with the granting of generous governmental credit facilities. Although it is too early to assess the long-range effect of these measures, so far they do not appear to have brought into existence a substantial and competitive Southeast Asian enterpreneurial class, a result which governmental planners had expected to follow from their policies. The absence of such an indigenous class of capitalists, together with the prevailing hostility of foreign capitalism, makes it very probable that the modernization and industrialization of Southeast Asia will be undertaken by direct governmental sponsorship and management of new enterprises, financed partly by national savings derived from taxation, and partly by loans and grants from other countries and international organizations. In addition, agreement has at long last been reached on the payment of Japanese reparations for damages inflicted on Burma, Indonesia, and the Philippines during the occupation. These payments—in cash, machinery, credits, and services—will substantially contribute to economic recovery and industrialization.

The fundamental problem of the immediate future is whether the economic aspirations of the peoples of Southeast Asia will be realized by the peaceful but less spectacular methods of democratic planning, or by the swifter and far more drastic methods of totalitarianism, which involve a callous disregard of human liberty and dignity.

Up to now, most of the new nation-states of Southeast Asia have exhibited a marked preference for political democracy. Since gaining their independence, the Philippines, Burma, and Indonesia have held free parliamentary elections which augur well for the growth of responsible and democratic government. Unlike the Philippines, Burma and Indonesia have shown a marked preference for socialist planning and regulation of economic life, without, however, shutting the door to foreign or domestic private enterprise. A similar pattern is likely to emerge in Malaya, once it gains independence in 1957. Thailand, at no time a colony and less affected by the Japanese occupation and subsequent revolutionary unheavals than its neighbors, continues as a constitutional monarchy ruled by a benevolent and somewhat paternalistic military dictatorship. The ancient monarchies of Laos and Cambodia have recently broken their last remaining ties with France and are rapidly progressing toward a new constitutional order.

Vietnam is the only country in Southeast Asia in which one of the most ruthless alternatives to democracy, communism, has so far been able to claim a significant, although as yet only incomplete, victory. In part this is due to repressive French colonial policies before the war, which impeded the growth of a democratic nationalist movement. Driven underground, Vietnamese nationalism became far more closely allied with the equally suppressed Communist movement than was the case elsewhere in Southeast Asia. The partial merger of nationalism and communism was, it is true, actively resisted by many staunch nationalists. Yet it enabled a resourceful and capable Communist, Ho Chi Minh, to become the most powerful leader of the anti-colonial resistance, who after the

Japanese occupation emerged as the head of a provisional government and spokesman for Vietnamese independence.

The bitter fighting which followed the attempted re-establishment of French colonial rule after the war was at once a nationalist struggle against France and a Communist bid for control of the country, rendered far more menacing by the material and military aid which the Vietnamese Communists received from their Chinese comrades after 1949. A complex and explosive situation had arisen which threatened to turn Vietnam into a second Korea, involving the Western powers as well as Communist China. In the end, a large-scale conflagration was averted by an interim solution negotiated at an international conference in Geneva in 1954. Ever since, Vietnam has been divided between a northern, Communist-dominated part and a southern part in which a non-Communist nationalist regime, aided by the United States, is slowly laying the groundwork for democratic government.

One of the most serous internal problems—although by no means the only one—is the Communist challenge to the young democratic regimes. In terms of electoral support in those countries where they are officially allowed to operate, the strength of the Communist parties is on the whole not yet perturbing. Even in Indonesia, one of their oldest strongholds in Southeast Asia, the Communists obtained less than 20 per cent of all votes cast in the elections of 1955, placing them fourth among leading political parties. But in the generally unstable political atmosphere generated by revolution, racial antagonism, and economic imbalance, communism in Southeast Asia poses a greater challenge than voting figures may indicate. In particular, many young people below voting age, uprooted by the bewildering experiences of the last decade, may be attracted by Communist propaganda.

As we have seen, in parts of the area the Communists have from pre-war days had experience in mobilizing or exploiting peasant unrest, and the Japanese occupation gave them almost everywhere added opportunities for broadening their appeal among the peasantry, urban workers, the military, and the young generation in general. Relying on these advantages, and acting on instructions from overseas, Communist leaders all over Southeast Asia made an open but uniformly unsuccessful bid for power by fomenting armed insurrections against the new nationalist governments in the immediate postwar years. The failure of these abortive attempts forced most Communist parties temporarily at least to abandon revolution in favor of parliamentary methods and collaboration with other parties. In Indonesia, for example, the new parliamentary tactics have already started to pay dividends. On the other hand, although open rebellion has not yet ceased in Malaya, Burma, and the Philippines, the governments of these countries have been successful in steadily reducing the armed threat to their authority. The Communist leaders in Burma, faced by their waning military fortunes, may decide to follow in the footsteps of the Indonesian party.

Nationalist leaders in the area differ in their attitudes toward communism. Although all of them have, when necessary, taken drastic measures in suppressing Communist-led rebellions, some feel that the Communist parties should be allowed to participate freely in the political arena as long as they abide by the rules of parliamentary democracy. This point of view involves a belief that, as conditions improve, nationalist as well as religious parties will continue to attract an increasing majority of voters, and that "peaceful coexistence" with communism, both local and foreign, is preferable to suppression at home and to participation in anti-Communist alliances with other nations. Following the example of India, both Indonesia and Burma have adopted this policy toward communism. By contrast, the leaders of Thailand and the Philippines regard communism, in spite of its new tactics, as a subversive movement dedicated to the violent overthrow of their regimes and as an international conspiracy to be fought by military and other means all over the world. They have consequently not lifted the bans on Communist movements in their countries. Moreover, in contrast to the neutralism professed by Indonesia, the Philippines and Thailand have—together with Pakistan, Australia, New Zealand, France, Britain, and the United States—joined SEATO (the Southeast Asia Treaty Organization).

Because of the aid which communism in the area is undeniably receiving from abroad and, more threateningly still, because of the military support which the Chinese government can—as became apparent in Vietnam—extend to Communist leaders in countries adjacent to its borders, the Communist challenge to Southeast Asian democracies is a matter of serious concern. Yet the continued, if not growing, appeal of communism is primarily an internal phenomenon. It is, in fact, symptomatic of a profound yearning among millions of Southeast Asians for the fulfillment of the many hopes and expectations which the nationalist revolutions have aroused in them. To these bewildered and impatient seekers for a new and meaningful order, the Communists are presenting the regimented modernization of Soviet Russia and Communist China as an alluring alternative to democracy, without, of course, revealing the human cost at which these achievements were brought about.

But democarcy in Southeast Asia is under attack not only from the Communists. Other vocal and often equally ruthless critics—even though some of them are, or at least pretend to be, staunch anti-Communists—are no less anxious to profit from the impatience and restiveness engendered by the dangerously slow rate of progress. In Indonesia and partly also in Vietnam and Burma, religious fanatics have incited their followers to armed and bloody resistance; in some parts of these countries, whole areas have come under the control of such zealots as well as of other dissident minority groups. Quite apart from these festering wounds, however, personal and ideological cleavages between political leaders have at times assumed such profound proportions that national unity, welded in the struggle against colonialism, has more than once seemed to be in jeopardy. Thus, Indonesians, like Pakistanis, have often bitterly quarreled over the issue of the Muslim state which some Islamic spokesmen in Indonesia sincerely believe to be the only suitable political framework for a country predominantly inhabited by Muslims.

More serious still than these continuing disputes among political groups, however, is the threat to civilian authority of any kind from ambitious individuals in the armed services. Having borne the brunt of the fighting against the colonial armies, some of these men have earned the gratitude and admiration of their peoples. But with the end of armed conflict, not a few of them have been reluctant to adjust to peacetime conditions and to submit to political superiors. Supported by hundreds of thousands of former guerrilla fighters, and conceivably influenced by developments in Egypt, they have here and there unsuccessfully endeavored to capitalize on their widespread popularity by taking matters into their own hands, promising to achieve by military rule what the slow process of politics has so far failed to produce.

All these internal difficulties have, in turn, diverted much time and energy from the arduous constructive work which must be the prime consideration of Southeast Asian statesmen today and in the years to come, if the goals of achieving the integration of their plural societies into prospering nation-states with a more balanced and equitable economy are to be realized in time. Unless the pace of change is visibly and substantially accelerated in the near future, the reliance which both governors and governed originally placed on democracy may yet be undermined by growing impatience, cynicism, and frustration.

Viewed against the background of these disheartening, if not ominous, factors, the record of democracy in Southeast Asia to date is nothing short of miraculous. In spite of dire forebodings, the new nation-states have not only survived rebellions, economic crises, and political cleavages; they have even succeeded in cushioning the effects of these internal threats by a slow yet steady growth of democratic institutions combined with social reforms and economic planning. They have been able to achieve these remarkable results largely through the good fortune of having a sufficient reservoir of devoted national leaders whose dedication to the ideals of democratic government is matched by the esteem in which they are held by the overwhelming majority of their peoples. Without men like U Nu, Sukarno, and Magsaysay—to mention the three most prominent figures in contemporary Burma, Indonesia, and the Philippines—the political future of Southeast Asia might be far less promising than it is today.

8

Africa: The Impact of the West

In the vast continent of Africa with its startling variety of more than fifty territories and eight hundred languages, life is changing rapidly under the impact of the West. From place to place and time to time the pace of change varies, but even in remote areas where people still live in the old way, those revolutionary instruments, the Western school, the Christian church, and the machine have penetrated. In Dakar on June 14, 1956, High Commissioner Cornut-Gentille told the Grand Council that French West Africa had changed more in the last ten years than in the previous two thousand and that French rule by direct administration was a thing of the past. Europeans in the area, he said, would have to become more African in thought while the Africans become more European in method. Such a mental transformation, however, is not so easy as it sounds, for both black and white have tremendous difficulty in understanding each other's behavior.

Although Africa south of the Sahara had undergone many changes before the coming of Europe, it emerged late into the mainstream of modern civilization because of its climate and topography and a long isolation which retarded the contacts between civilizations that stimulate growth. Today, however, the response of its peoples to the Western challenge is demonstrating their capacities as bishops, judges, doctors, journalists, craftsmen, technicians, and now even prime ministers. None of Toynbee's twenty-one civilizations was the creation of "black" peoples, but it is probably an "accident of history," as Raymond Leslie Buell once wrote, that the black man did not awake to the "need for progress" as soon as the white man. The natural environment and historical circumstance, rather than innate genetic differences, are primarily responsible for such cultural differences between races as do exist.

The size and complexity of Africa make generalizations risky and comparisons difficult. In an area nearly four times the size of the United States lie snow-capped mountains in the north, in the south, and even at the equator; steaming jungles in the equatorial rain forest; the broad sweep of savanna grasslands both north and south of the equatorial zone; the pleasant climate of the high plateaus in the east, stretching southward from Ethiopia to South Africa; and the arid desert and semi-desert areas of the Sahara, the east African horn, and the Kalahari. These geographical differences have influenced Africa's history, including the pattern of European settlement, which, in turn, affects the colonial policies of the European powers.

From this limited point of view there are at least four Africas: (1) the temperate Mediterranean belt, which has cultural and historical ties with the Arab world as well as Europe, and is largely outside the scope of this chapter; (2) the great bulge of black Africa on the West Coast down through the Congo; (3) the highlands of eastern and central Africa, where there are enough Europeans and Asians to arouse hopes and fears for a permanent multiracial society; and (4) the Union of South Africa, where the white man is already well established. In parts of western Africa there are three thousand blacks to one white, while in South Africa the ratio is less than four to one, in Southern Rhodesia fourteen to one, and in Kenya perhaps a hundred and fifty to one. These statistics symbolize a vital difference in racial problems and must be taken into account in any generalizations about or comparisons of British, French, Belgian, Portuguese, and South African policies. From a broader point of view there are, of course, many differences between the indigenous peoples of Africa which may prove more significant in the long run than the contrasts between the black areas and the areas of white settlement.

Along with these differences, however, there are many similarities. Most Africans throughout the continent still live in rural areas in tribal societies held together by complex systems of moral, ritual, and legal sanctions. A higher percentage of the people are engaged in agriculture than in any other continent, and the per capita income, while varying widely from area to area, averages probably less than fifty dollars a year. Productive efficiency is low, and Africa accounts for only about 7 per cent of world trade. At the same time a prodigious economic development all over the continent is bringing a high percentage of Africans out of the subsistence economy of tribal life into the life of industrial wage-workers, with repercussions in many ways. The astonishing growth of towns, new and old, and the remarkable educational expansion in recent years are producing a volatile, aggressive town population avid for further and faster change. The desire for a better life is also rising in the countryside, where it has led the people in certain areas to organize "improvement associations" such as those of the Ibo rural villages of eastern Nigeria.

To appreciate fully the nature of changing Africa it is helpful if one first understands how Africans lived before the advent of Europeans, a way of life that still continues in much of the continent. This information comes largely from anthropologists, for the historians of Africa, unlike those of Europe and Asia, are handicapped by the absence of written records. Scholars have not even solved the riddle of who built the massive granite structures of the Great Zimbabwe Ruins which still stand in Southern Rhodesia as an imposing vestige of a past culture that apparently thrived six to eight hundred years ago. From the sparse records of early Arab travelers and the later work of archeologists and other students, it is also clear that some remarkable societies flourished in the early kingdoms of Ghana and Mali and the Songhai Empire in the western Sudan beginning at least a thousand years ago. The attraction of gold evidently played a significant role in the establishment of these early civilizations in both the western Sudan and Southern Rhodesia.

Whether man originated in Africa, as new evidence suggests, or whether Africa's earliest peoples came from Asia, the continent was the scene of many migrations which ultimately carried some people westward through the flat lands of the Sudan—the "Broadway of Africa"—while others went southward through the beautiful highlands and great lakes into central and southern Africa. Aside from the aboriginal Bushmen, Hottentots, and Pygmies, who still survive in small numbers, most of Africa's remaining 200 million people may be divided into the Semites and Hamites of the north and northeast, the Negroes of West Africa, and the Bantu-speaking peoples of central and southern Africa, although this is only a rule of thumb classification which has many exceptions because of the continual mingling of peoples over many centuries. The non-literate peoples of Africa south of the Sahara speak about eight hundred vernacular languages, which have been divided into sixteen linguistic families. Languages like Hausa and Mandingo in western Africa each have several million speakers, but there are areas like the Nuba hills of Kordofan, where there is one language for each hill and even an instance where one language is spoken by the people at the top of the hill and another by those at the bottom.

In general, the political structure of African society has developed out of the family as the basic social unit. Within the extended family, which usually consists of a group of families of immediate blood relatives inhabiting the same locale, the elders discuss local problems and together with the head of the family reach decisions that must be obeyed by all. When the head of the family discusses village affairs with the village head or chief and the other family heads, decisions are made for the whole village. And in the more highly organized political systems, a paramount chief may make decisions for a large political unit in consultation with the lesser chiefs. While this political pattern was often upset by wars of conquest, real autocrats like the Kings of Dahomey were rare in the traditional society of Africa. The force or threat of force necessary to enforce decisions might come from the moral sanction of public opinion, or the ritual sanction or curse of a ritual leader with magical powers, or, in the more highly organized societies, the legal sanction of a state organization with an administrative hierarchy.

The "primitive states" of the Zulu in South Africa, the Bemba in Northern Rhodesia, and the Ankole in Uganda, for example, all had a central government with administrative machinery and judicial institutions, and a society with differences determined by wealth, privilege and status. In West Africa, Benin, Ashanti, Dahomey, and the Yoruba kingdoms had highly developed dynasties. On the other hand, the "stateless societies," like the Tallensi in the northern Gold Coast, had no central government and no sharp divisions in rank, status, or wealth. They were societies, or "lineages," of people who considered themselves descended from a common ancestor of several generations earlier, and whose relations, customs, and behavior were usually governed by moral and ritual rather than legal sanctions.

There were still other very small societies with neither states nor lineage systems, but only political units composed of all the people who were united by ties of kinship. And among the Nilo-Hamitic peoples like the Nandi-Suk in Kenya, the framework of the political system is provided by what the anthropologists call the "age system," in which there are no chiefs, and where influence, prestige, and authority depend primarily on the seniority of the age class to which the individual belongs, the age class being composed of all those initiated into a particular age group over a period of fifteen to twenty years. In such societies, age is equated with wisdom.

Within this diversity, what aspects do African cultures have in common? One of the best generalizations applicable to the remote tribes of the interior as well as to the skilled craftsmen of Western Africa, is that of an anthropologist who writes that African society is so organized that it provides a system of kinship and other relationships which can give people help and security when they need it. In these non-industrial societies, "status" within social groups provides more security than "control of investments"; it provides for security of life and property, the nurture and maintenance of children, assistance in sickness and old age, help for economic activities beyond the scope of the individual, and for unforeseen accidents, payment of legal claims, and medical and funeral expenses. When European governments took over many of the political functions of the old kinship and lineage systems, they did not provide adequate substitutes for the social and economic balance, harmony, and security of the old regime. Consequently the African still relies on the building up of personal obligations to himself through the old system of social relationships. As Elizabeth Colson has said in *Africa Today* (Baltimore: Johns Hopkins, 1955), "What to Western eyes may seem the foolish dissipation of wealth through casual gifts or the unthinking waste of time, may to the African be a calculated investment against the future and a method of obtaining immediate social status which in turn will lead to an increase either in followers or in potential assistance."

If status is important, so is land, which leads us to another common aspect of African cultures. As the producer and sustainer of life, and the receiver of the dead, land is an object of veneration. It is a symbol of the community and in many places the link between the generations, dead, living, and yet unborn. It is also the main form of capital, and, in many areas, the only means of livelihood. For these reasons, land in Africa belongs to the community, and the Western idea of private ownership is regarded as a threat to the existence of the community. Every member of the community is entitled to use the land, however, and is given security of tenure over what he needs to sustain himself and his family. Nevertheless, in certain areas like the rich cocoa lands of the Gold Coast, individual ownership of private property has been developing for some time, and Africans spend many thousands of pounds sterling in land litigation.

In addition to agricultural rights and pastoral rights for cattle grazing, an African in some areas may own trees if he plants them or, for example, if he undertakes the laborious task of preparing a wild palm tree for tapping palm wine. If he plants a tree, he may summon village elders as witnesses, particularly if the land does not belong to him. If he leaves his village, he loses his land rights but not his tree rights. According to C. K. Meek, *Land Law and Custom in the Colonies* (London: Oxford University Press, 1946), among the Yoruba of Nigeria, "a tenant should not raise his eyes upward." People in need of money may also pawn valuable trees for loans, a practice that may give rise to confusion and litigation, especially when the land and the trees on it have different owners.

In the main cattle areas, Africans usually do not raise cattle for meat and hides but consider them a form of wealth which gives their owners not only prestige but rights over persons. Sometimes cattle are used for marriage payments that bind the families of husband and wife in a system of mutual obligations. In Ruanda-Urundi, cattle are an object of veneration and are the basis of an interesting social relationship that in some respects has similarities to the feudal system of medieval Europe. The lord or master who owns cattle turns them over to his dependent or serf in a contract which establishes a relationship of allegiance and protection that goes on from generation to generation. One who gets cattle in this way may hand some of them down to other dependents. The *Mwami* or king, at the top of this pyramid, according to tradition, owned all the cattle. The more cattle a man has, the more important he is. He does not normally own them, but has a long-term right of use.

This custom in Ruanda-Urundi, a trust territory administered by Belgium under the supervision of the United Nations Trusteeship Council, has been frequently criticized in the Council because it causes serious overstocking of cattle and consequent exhaustion of the soil by erosion and intensive deforestation. It is especially bad because Ruanda-Urundi is the most densely populated territory in Africa and occasionally suffers from famine. Nevertheless, this system is such an integral part of the social structure that Belgian efforts to change it meet tenacious resistance from the people.

In this brief account of economic life in the old Africa, special mention should be made of the peoples of western Africa, who are mainly farmers but have a passion for trading and have achieved the highest development of the arts and crafts south of the Sahara. The colorful native markets of western Africa are a wonderful sight that the visitor to southern Africa misses. The Yoruba people of southern Nigeria have one of the most diversified economies in western Africa and have long had relatively highly developed organizations of skilled craftsmen. Yoruba country is noted for its many large towns, the greatest of which is Ibadan, site of Nigeria's new university and a city now approaching half a million. In northern Nigeria, the Muslim emirates also have some remarkable towns, the most noted of which is Kano, whose "Morocco" leatherwork and other crafts are well developed.

To ties of kinship, desire for status, and attachment to the land, religion must be added as another vital aspect of African life. Since the temples and idols of Asia are missing, the early missionaries had difficulty in accustoming themselves to the importance of the traditional religion. As one of them, however, Edwin W. Smith, has said in *Knowing the African* (London, United Society for Christian Literature, 1946), they came to recognize that religion was everywhere, "not as an organized cult separable from the rest of life, but as part and parcel of it, all-pervasive, motivating, controlling, guiding, strengthening." No doubt Africa has always had its skeptics and agnostics, but all tribes had their religion, whether in a simple form of ancestor worship or a more complex hierarchy of gods such as those of the more highly developed societies of the Yoruba in Nigeria and of the Baganda in Uganda. Although Christianity and Islam have made many converts, a majority of Africans are still animists who believe that all objects in nature have souls or spirits, and that these spirits cause practically everything that happens. It is believed that a man's success and happiness in life depend on the benevolence of the good spirits, and on his ability to placate or neutralize the bad spirits. Ancestor worship is an important element of this religion. Africans believe that the community consists of both the living and the dead, and many of them also believe in reincarnation. Their attachment to the land is strengthened by the belief that the spirits of the ancestors buried in the soil still hover about it. The traditional religion also includes faith in a Supreme Being, although belief varies as to whether this Supreme Being is a person or an impersonal force pervading the universe. In fact, the elaborate theologies that have been developed in some areas are far removed from the rather simple concept implied in the term "spirit."

Related at least in some respects to this animistic religion is the good and evil magic of Africa—the taboos, curses, omens, talismans, amulets, medicines, divination, witchcraft, and ritual murder. The belief in the mystic or supernatural power of fetishes and charms is still held by many Africans who leave their tribal environment and move into the towns. College students are known to have purchased charms in order to help them pass their examinations—a belief that is not far, perhaps, from the rabbit's foot that brings luck to the American student.

After the end of World War II, several outbreaks of ritual murders occurred in areas widely removed from each other, including the leopard murders of Nigeria, the lion murders of Tanganyika, and the medicine murders of Basutoland. In the Basuto murders, which have received the most recent publicity, people were murdered in order to obtain human flesh and blood for mixing into a substance thought to have magical powers. In Nigeria, where by the end of 1947, seventy leopard killers had been duly tried, convicted and executed, the victims were badly mutilated by killers who made footprints resembling a leopard's on the ground around the body. Often the head and one arm of the victim were severed and skinned and the heart, lungs, and other internal organs removed. When evidence was discovered that the flesh of the victims was sold to the leaders of the secret *Idiong* society, the government banned the organization. The murderers are said to have visited *Idiong* leaders to obtain a charm to protect them from discovery. Similarly, in the lion murders near Singida in Tanganyika, the victims were killed by men wearing lion skins with claws worn like gloves over the hands and feet. In many of the Singida murders, apparently, the murderers were hired from the sorcerers who controlled them by individuals whose motive was revenge. The type of fear which makes such atrocities possible hampers the authorities in suppressing them. In Nigeria, for example, actual witnesses of a crime, including mothers whose children were murdered, testified that a leopard, not a man, was the killer.

A more pleasant aspect of the traditional life of Africa is the extensive cultural heritage it has given us. Wood carving, music and dancing, mythology and folk tales, and the arts and crafts were more highly developed than is generally recognized. Students of African art now consider that the traditional sculpture or woodcarving of Africa has a high artistic quality. African masks, statuettes, and other carvings were used in the rituals of religion and magic. Being mainly of wood, these carvings have been largely destroyed. A missionary in the Belgian Congo is said to have boasted that he had burned over ten thousand woodcarvings.

African music and dancing are characterized by many kinds of songs and singing styles and a complex rhythm. Although drums are the best-known musical instrument, there are many others. Anyone who wants to learn to appreciate the intricacy and variety of African music might begin by listening to the fine 1954 prize recording of Baoulé and Malinké music made by the Institut Français d'Afrique Noire in collaboration with UNESCO. As for dancing, the tribal dances seen at the gold mines on Sunday mornings in Johannesburg are perhaps best known to Europeans, but there are many varieties, both ritual and recreational, throughout the continent.

Africans are also great tellers of folk tales, proverbs, and riddles, and they have a rich mythology, which is not surprising in a world where tribal history is transmitted orally. Slaves from Africa brought to the United States what have become perhaps the best-known American folk tales. Joel Chandler Harris (1848-1908) derived his Uncle Remus stories from this African inspiration.

Finally, mention should be made of the arts and crafts of western Africa, including the brass casting of Dahomey, the celebrated bronze heads of Ife and Benin, the "Morocco" leather that may have originated in northern Nigeria, and the silver and gold work and weaving of numerous areas.

The transition from the old Africa to the new began nearly five hundred years ago when a commercial revolution brought European trade out from the inland seas and rivers to the oceans of the world. Since the fall of Rome, a thousand years before, Europe had gradually worked its way out of a dark age of isolation in which life was similar in numerous respects to what has been described above in Africa. The traders, missionaries, administrators, settlers, and technicians who have entered Africa in successive and overlapping waves since the fifteenth century have taken much from Africa, but they have also made possible the process by which Africa is today entering the mainstream of world history.

When the new nation-states of Europe began to push their way around the west coast of Africa in search of trade and gold they established trading posts, and the local demand for European trade goods quickly developed. The simultaneous exploration and settlement of the Americas soon led to the demand for a new article of commerce—slaves to work the plantations of the New World. The resulting slave trade was the first great impact of the West on Africa. From the time it began in the sixteenth century until it ended in the nineteenth century, between 15 and 20 million slaves were landed in America, and it is estimated that 3 or 4 million others died in the slave ships. Including those killed in slave raids and in other ways as a direct result of the slave trade, this appalling loss of manpower may have totaled as much as 30 or 40 million—a bitter heritage of the Western impact. Although the average annual loss over this three-hundred-year period may have been less than 1 per cent of the population, the slaves were taken whenever possible from among the youngest and fittest Africans available, two-thirds men and one-third women. In addition to the actual loss of manpower, fear and uncertainty retarded the normal development of the area. African middlemen in dominant coastal tribes developed a monopoly of the slave-raiding and the selling of slaves to Europeans. They first sold their own domestic slaves and then began to raid other tribes. Kingdoms like those of Benin and Dahomey rose to power on the slave trade. Mention should also be made of the Arab slave trade with Africa, which began many centuries earlier and has not entirely ended even today.

It is an interesting fact, however, that some of the most advanced and densely populated parts of Africa today are areas where the slave trade was most active, the Gold and Slave Coasts and the Niger Delta—which suggests that the trade with Europe, even in slaves, must have been a considerable stimulus to certain kinds of development.

Not long after the trader brought his goods to Africa, thereby creating new wants and needs, Christian missionaries entered the continent. Aside from the Coptic Christians who entered Ethiopia from Egypt a thousand years earlier, Portuguese Catholics were the first to begin missionary enterprise. When the Protestants entered much later, the London Missionary Society launched David Livingstone on a famous career that was to help open the interior of Africa to science and commerce as well as Christianity. The success of Christian efforts is measured partly by the fact that Africa today has 21 million converts, about half Catholic and half Protestant. This is more than one finds in all the rest of the non-Western world.

In the early days, Christian missionary activity concentrated on saving the heathen from Hell. While evangelization is still the main emphasis, the missions have broadened their scope to education, medicine, and even agricultural and industrial development. It was the missionaries who translated parts of the Bible into about 250 of Africa's languages and began to teach Africans to read and write. Even today, 85 per cent of elementary education is given in mission schools, although governments now subsidize those schools that meet certain standards. The missionary, like the trader, brought to Africa something that people soon began to want, and the demand for education is strong today. The high standards of Christianity, including its insistence on the idea of equality and on improving the status of women, has stimulated African families to search for a better life. Christianity has thus been a powerful force in breaking down Africa's isolation and in accelerating its evolution.

On the negative side, the Christian contribution was marred by the confusing competition of Christian sects; the narrow-mindedness of certain missionaries and their inability to understand African customs; the occasional intrigues of missionaries who fostered the imperial designs of their governments; and the failure of Europeans, particularly the settlers in the multiracial areas, to practice the egalitarian ideas preached by the churchmen. These weaknesses, particularly Protestant sectarianism and the failure of Europeans to practice the Christian principle of the equality of man, have had startling results, particularly in South Africa, the main stronghold of the color bar. More than a thousand African separatist churches have been established after secession from the mission churches or splits among themselves. Some of them are anti-white, with theologies having reverse color bars in Heaven where whites are turned away at the Gate. They provide an outlet for the

African's urge for leadership and his desire for prestige and power. In Kenya, some of these anti-white religious sects were precursors of Mau Mau.

With the trader who brought goods, and the missionary who brought Christianity and Western education, came the administrator who introduced Western ideas and institutions of government. When the partitioning of Africa was completed, European administration spread throughout the continent, disrupting the indigenous political and legal systems and undermining the authority of chiefs and the peoples' respect for the old customs and laws. In areas of direct rule, chiefs became paid agents and subordinates of the administration. Under the system of indirect rule applied in certain British areas, local institutions and laws were preserved as far as possible and European administrators became advisers of the chiefs. In practice, however, an adviser was quite powerful because, as one of them has written, he could warn the chief that if he did not behave he would be reported to the governor or fined, or even deposed in favor of some other member of the dynasty. Or, if he were a good chief, he could be rewarded with money or honors.

In the early days, it was not uncommon for a young and inexperienced European university graduate, often with little knowledge or appreciation of the complexity of African life and customs, to serve as administrator, Jack-of-all-trades, and judge of final appeal over the traditional elders who ran tribal affairs on the basis of their long experience with local law and custom. Moreover, the European administrative system moves officers from post to post so rapidly, and piles so much paper work on them, that few have the opportunity to really get acquainted with their people. Nevertheless, many of them are doing fine work under these and other difficulties. Unfortunately, the authoritarianism of colonial rule seems inevitably to breed the attitude of paternalism that has become one of the main flaws of the colonial relationship. What educated Africans particularly resent, one of them told the United Nations Trusteeship Council in 1947, is the "Daddy knows best" attitude of their rulers.

When Western law was established, a fourth type of European, the white settlers, began to seek permanent homes on the Mediterranean and South African coasts and the temperate highlands of eastern and southern Africa. The economic skill and enterprise of these settlers and the capital they brought with them or attracted have contributed much to Africa. But the settlers take land that Africans need and want, and their political acumen does not match their economic skill. The white farmer's rural environment, his everyday dealings with Africans whose behavior exasperates him, his fear of being swamped by the natives and his inability to appreciate the political significance of powerful external pressures, makes him develop a myopic resistance to African advancement. As a result the areas of white settlement are generally the worst trouble spots in Africa, Southern Rhodesia being, at least for the moment, an interesting and notable exception. At the same time, it should be noted that in the Union of South Africa, where 2.5 million whites—or half of those in the whole continent—live, Africans have made more material gains than one usually finds elsewhere because they benefit from the by-products of living in the most heavily industrialized and Europeanized part of Africa. They are denied certain political rights and suffer from economic and social discrimination, but more than half the African children of school age are in school and about two hundred Africans are now graduating every year from South African universities, a record that compares favorably with that of other areas.

Finally, the number of technicians who have entered the continent since World War II is so large that they might be considered a fifth type among those who have made an impact on Africa. In the last decade several billion dollars have gone into Africa, mostly through the development and welfare programs of the European powers and South Africa. To this figure must be added several hundred million dollars from the economic aid and technical assistance of the United States, the technical assistance funds of the United Nations and its specialized agencies, and the loans of the International Bank for Reconstruction and Development, the most recent of which was an $80-million loan to the Federation of Rhodesia and Nyasaland for hydroelectric power in the Kariba Gorge on the Zambezi River, the largest loan for a single project the Bank has made thus far. Private investors have also put several hundred million dollars into mining, industrial, and agricultural projects in recent years. The piggy-bank financing that characterized pre-war economic development has been supplanted by money and technicians on a scale that has produced a real postwar boom and has increased Africa's importance as a supplier of raw materials to the free world. The base is being laid for an even greater expansion, but its success will depend to some extent on the intelligence and cooperation with which the different races take advantage of their good fortune.

These invaders, and the African reaction to them, have created a new Africa, or at least a continent in rapid transition from old ways to new. Economic development and the spread of education, the twin foundations of political advance, are doing away with the non-literate, non-machine characteristics of the old Africa in a few generations, a process that in Europe took many centuries.

What are the main economic, social, educational, and political trends in this changing world today? Perhaps the most obvious economic and social change is the startling growth of towns and increase in townsmen. Leopoldville, capital of the Belgian Congo, has jumped from a town of 35,000 before World War II to a teeming city of 300,000 Africans and 15,000 Europeans, and might ultimately reach the astounding total of one million. To a greater or lesser extent, similar boom towns are found all over the continent. Even the Bushmen in southwestern Africa, who are supposed to pine away if removed from their aboriginal habitat, are said to be beginning to feel the attraction of the towns. This process of urbanization is one of Africa's most significant trends and has repercussions in many fields. The accompanying introduction of a money economy tended to break down the old subsistence economy that provided a form of social security. It stimulated a demand for wages and the rise of migratory labor, which disrupted African households by the thousands as men left their villages for faraway mines or towns to obtain cash.

When workers quit their farms, agricultural production tended to decline. At the same time, congestion in the towns resulted in unsanitary living conditions, social insecurity, the breakdown of tribal discipline, prostitution, and other social evils which Alan Paton has vividly described in *Cry, the Beloved Country*. The consequences were not entirely negative, however, for urbanization tended to develop African skills, to stabilize the labor force in the urban areas, to put increasing pressure on the color ban, to develop a new attitude of Africans toward work and to enable them to make a bigger contribution toward the national income. On the whole it tended to improve the African standard of living.

A phenomenal rise in budgets accompanied this growth of towns. Until 1945 the development of Africa had been retarded by two world wars, a great depression, and a laissez-faire colonial policy with the cardinal principle that each colony must pay its own way. Out of World War II came a new philosophy of colonial development and welfare with financial assistance from the colonial power, along with aid from the United States and the United Nations. At the same time a sharp rise in the prices of agricultural and mineral exports from Africa brought new income and revenues and a great economic expansion from Tunis to Capetown, from Dakar to Djibouti. This wealth made possible new schools, hospitals, housing, roads, ports, and power, which in turn attracted new capital. The Federation of Rhodesia and Nyasaland, for example, has had an influx of £250 million of capital in the last five years, and has inaugurated a five-year development plan to invest £60 million in education, health, railways, roads, and water supplies.

Liberia is enjoying one of the biggest percentage increases in revenue, from $1 million a year before the war to $15 million in 1955. Thanks to copper, Northern Rhodesia had a fabulous rise from £1.6 million in 1938 to £33 million in 1955. In Nigeria, revenues rose from little more than £7 million before the war to more than £50 million today, and in South Africa from £44 million to £225 million in 1953. Although rising costs nullified some of the real value of rising revenue, the revenues of the central government of Nigeria, for example, still amount to three or four times as much as in the pre-war years. The report of a recent mission of the International Bank for Reconstruction and Development to Nigeria concludes that Nigeria as a whole, and the Nigerians as individuals, are better off now than ever before. An eightfold increase in currency circulation and the growth of post office savings banks are additional signs of this growing prosperity. Moreover, the development of the last few years can no longer be regarded as merely the transitory result of a postwar boom, because the productive capacity of the economy has risen and the index of the quantity of exports is now 50 per cent above the pre-war level. While adverse conditions outside and beyond Nigeria's control might temporarily slow down or interrupt the growth of income and wealth, the Bank mission thought that the rate of growth can be maintained and eventually increased if the human and financial resources now at Nigeria's disposal are used to the best advantage and are supplemented by the mobilization of new revenues.

A vital aspect of this flow of Africans into the towns is the rise of a volatile middle group of townsmen whose frustrations and desires make them a powerful force for change. From their upper ranks come the white-collar workers, traders, skilled craftsmen, and supervisors in industry and government. From the rank and file come most of the members of Africa's new political parties, labor unions, veterans' associations, and other action groups. Europeans in Africa point out frequently that Lagos is not Nigeria, or Kampala is not Uganda, or Leopoldville is not the Congo, but what may be more relevant is that the aggressive townsmen tend to carry the day sooner or later over the more complacent tribesmen who cling to the old regime.

The development of the middle class in tropical and subtropical countries was the theme of an interesting conference of the International Institute of Differing Civilizations in London in September, 1955. Africanists and other specialists present agreed that although there are few territories in which the middle classes are as much as 10 per cent of the population, they are beginning to have a mass as opposed to a purely personal influence. Their spirit of independence, the conference noted, made them an element of ferment, while the middle classes in Europe and North America are the main source of orderly progress in society. When the rising middle classes of the Western world were as small a proportion of the population as those of Africa, however, they too were a source of ferment. The conference concluded that as the growth of industry and commerce proceed, and as external tutelage diminishes, not only will the middle classes increase in size but their political characteristics will change.

Africa's impressive economic strides are matched by a notable expansion of education in the past decade, particularly in western Africa. Everywhere the number of children in school has increased, especially in the more developed areas. In the Gold Coast the number of children in school grew from 174,447 in 1946 to 521,989 in 1954, in the Belgian Congo from 885,038 to 1,138,700, in Nigeria from 614,173 to 1,114,985, and in French West Africa from 107,470 to 284,441. It is still rare, however, to find territories where even half the children of school age are in school. Educational "wastage" is high, moreover, which means that most children drop out of school after two, three, or four years.

The number of children who reach secondary schools is still only 1 to 3 per cent of the total, despite a similar expansion of secondary and technical education. Particularly important for the future is the remarkable progress of university education. Although Africa south of the Sahara is generally considered a huge void as far as university education is concerned, the fact is that it has about twenty-five universities and technical colleges, and a total of about 12,000 Africans doing university study either in Africa or overseas. Ten of these schools are in British territories, ten in the Union of South Africa (only five of which are open to Africans), three in Liberia, and one each in French and Belgian territories, with another scheduled to open in the Congo in 1956. In fact, several additional universities are in the planning stage. Since most of these new schools were founded within the past five years, they are still small and growing institutions with enrollments that should far more than double in the next decade. Even now, however, they have about 5,000 African students. More than 5,000 others are doing university work in England and France, 900 in the United States, and more than 100 in India which has recently inaugurated a government scholarship program for Africans. A few others are in Belgium, and there are several behind the Iron Curtain. When they graduate, these Africans will bring further pressure for political advance, because some of them will take up responsible administrative posts and others will become political agitators.

Contact with the West not only inspired new needs and demands for Western goods and education, but taught Africans new political ideas of freedom and equality, parliamentary government, and individual rights. The right of self-determination, enunciated in two world wars in which Africans fought alongside their European rulers, became the battle cry of nationalism, and the European powers are now having to choose between suppressing the agitators and making concessions to them. Those Western powers which practice democracy at home are finding it increasingly difficult to be autocratic overseas even in the interests of a benevolent paternalism. As a result African states are obtaining self-government before they have sufficiently viable economies and enough trained personnel to manage a modern state efficiently. The criterion of capacity for self-government seems to have become the ability of colonial peoples to force their rulers to grant it.

Already Libya, the Sudan, Tunisia, and Morocco have joined Egypt, Ethiopia, Liberia, and the Union of South Africa to raise the continent's list of independent states to eight, and the Gold Coast, Nigeria, and Italian Somaliland are on the threshold, with Uganda and the Federation of Rhodesia and Nyasaland not far behind. Eritrea has been federated with Ethiopia, and Algeria may soon acquire a new status.

The political map of Africa is thus in process of major revision and seems likely to become even more of a mixture than in the past. In addition to its eight independent states, Africa now contains seven trust territories, administered by Britain, France, and Belgium under the supervision of the United Nations Trusteeship Council, and more than thirty other territories under the rule of five European powers.

The rapid economic and educational developments since World War II will no doubt have a cumulative effect that will accelerate the pace of political change still further in the next ten years. Even in the Portuguese territories, which the outside world knows least about, economic developments in the past few years are certain to foster cultural changes that will have political repercussions. Faster political advance is inevitable in the Congo now that Belgium is beginning to give Africans political experience and higher education. France hopes to avoid what it considers to be the dead ends of nationalism and communism by persuading the inhabitants of French West and Equatorial Africa to remain willingly as autonomous states in a modified French Union, but the future of this experiment is uncertain. The French territories are affected both by what happens in turbulent North Africa and by the attraction of the independence movements in the Gold Coast and Nigeria. Moreover, the four northern territories in the eight-territory Federation of French West Africa are predominantly Muslim and might ultimately gravitate eastward, drawn by the pull of the expanding Islamic world. The future of some of the British territories in the eastern highlands of Africa is also obscure because of the presence of sizable communities of Europeans and Asians who are now engaged in an effort to develop these multiracial societies on the basis of what is loosely termed partnership. And in the Union of South Africa, whether some form of *apartheid* succeeds or fails, important political changes will occur sooner or later.

When the colonial relationship comes to an end the problems of Africa will not be solved; they will only change their form. Within a few decades colonialism, like the slave trade, will probably be a thing of the past, the memory of which will be occasionally recalled but largely overshadowed by new problems—economic weaknesses, political instability, irredentist movements, and communist and other intrigues. Democracy is unlikely to work well in the new Africa because the conditions under which it thrives will not exist. It is true that the system of tribal chiefs-in-council prevailing in much of the old Africa had its democratic aspects. But the political units of the new Africa will not be composed of small groups of tribesmen who know and understand each other; they will be relatively large states comprising many peoples of different customs, traditions, and languages. And it seems unlikely, on the whole, that these peoples will have the economic prosperity or security which, in the light of history, seems an essential condition for the successful operation of democracy.

The most that can be reasonably hoped for in the new Africa is political stability, and even this will be difficult to achieve. In the opportunity and excitement of new political activity, many a small duck in a big puddle will try to become a big duck in a small puddle, exploiting economic unrest and such factors as possible falls in the world market prices for Africa's exports. Like Latin America, Africa will not have the traditions and conditions that produce a stable two-party system, and voters will probably support personalities rather than principles, a practice that can foster political instability. Since the colonial governments which now suppress or curtail communism in Africa will no longer exist, Soviet activities will no doubt grow in many areas. And the spread of Islam, which has already made considerably more converts than Christianity south of the Sahara, may begin to have political repercussions—particularly now that Egypt is asserting its role in Africa as leader of the Muslim world.

Emerging Africa will pose many difficulties for the West in its efforts to retain African friendship and cooperation. Even if the colonial powers free colonial peoples rapidly and peacefully, Africa will still be affected by the suspicions and animosities that a relatively poor, black, and agricultural people can readily develop regarding a richer, white, and industrial people. There is hope, however, in the fact that Africans want material progress, which requires future cooperation with Europe and the United States. Another encouraging sign is the serious thinking about the future that is now under way among European and African leaders all over the continent. With patience and sympathy on both sides, mutual aid can be effective in overcoming some of Africa's problems. Under these circumstances, the best course for the West is to make every effort in the next decade to bring Africans nearer to European living and educational standards. If this effort is to succeed, however, Westerners will have to learn to regard Africans as people of a different rather than an inferior culture.

9

Latin America: Where Westernism Stopped

Situated in the Western Hemisphere; oriented to the United States in important ways; inheritor of the Roman Catholic religion, of European languages, and of many other aspects of Western culture, Latin America still shares so much with the non-Western world as to offer important lessons to anyone studying non-Western civilizations. Latin America's Westernism came initially from sixteenth-century Spain and Portugal, and many elements of that era of Iberian greatness remain today. Native Indian and imported African cultures are interwoven with varying results in different parts of Latin America. And recent influences from Europe and North America are noticeable in many aspects of life. The result is a Latin American civilization with enough basic homogeneity to be recognizable nearly everywhere south of the United States, but with important local variations in every facet of life.

This civilization is clearly different from that of the United States or other highly industrialized societies. The features that set Latin America apart from the mainstream of Western modernism are in many cases similar to features found in Asia and Africa. Latin America shares to a greater or lesser degree such elements as the yearnings and frustrations associated with poverty, past colonialism, weak and unstable national governments, severe economic instability, uncomfortably great dependence on the major industrial nations, and a strong desire to abstain from excessive involvement in international rivalries and problems that seem far from home. Latin America, for all the glamour of its music and its vacation spots, and despite the swelling tide of "North American" tourists, is not well understood in the United States. And United States thinking about foreign areas tends to take no more adequate account of Latin America than of Asia or Africa.

Most of the Latin American republics have had their independence for over a century and a quarter. Since gaining independence, each country has faced economic, social, political, military, and diplomatic problems on its own and has evolved institutions and methods that meet these problems with varying degrees of success. In virtually all areas of life, Latin American experience contains elements which at every turn suggest parallels with the newly independent, or not yet independent, areas of Asia and Africa. As Arnold Toynbee says, "Whatever their origin, those American civilizations are similar in style and type to the peasant civilizations of Eastern Asia. You could fancy yourself in Eastern Asia when you find yourself, as in the highlands of Peru and Southern Mexico or in the Peninsula of Yucatan, among a peasantry whose traditional way of life has more or less survived the disruptive effect of the Spanish conquest of Middle America and the Andes."

Latin America is commonly regarded as consisting of the twenty independent countries between the Mexican border of the United States and the southern tip of South America. For some purposes, one may add the small American dependencies of Western colonial powers, notably British and French Guiana, Surinam, British Honduras, Jamaica, Trinidad, Puerto Rico, and a number of smaller islands. With or without the dependent areas, Latin America has a total land area some two and a half times the size of the United States, and a total population slightly larger and growing more rapidly than ours. The production and income of Latin America are about one-eighth those of the United States. But production and income are very unevenly distributed in Latin America. This inequality is but one of the many aspects of its diversity.

Diversity is, in fact, a major theme of any serious study of Latin America. In size the independent countries vary from Brazil, which has an area somewhat larger than that of the United States, to Haiti, which is slightly larger than the state of Maryland. Populations vary from Brazil's nearly 60 million to the somewhat fewer than 1 million inhabitants each in Costa Rica and Panama. Temperature, rainfall, altitude, terrain, resources and other geographic features vary from one extreme to another. Peoples and customs also vary widely, from city to backlands, from rich to poor, and from one country to another. Even language varies, especially as between Spanish on the one hand and Portuguese, French, and Indian languages on the other.

Nature has endowed Latin America not only very unevenly,

but on the whole less richly than is often proclaimed. By contrast with the fortunate combinations of resources, climate, topography, and so on, found in the United States, most parts of Latin America have limited resources or can make only limited use of existing resources under present circumstances. There are, it is true, a number of very valuable mineral deposits, such as Chile's copper, Venezuela's iron and petroleum, and Brazil's thorium, iron and industrial diamonds. These and other known resources are being added to by new discoveries and by new technology. But grave problems of transportation combine with other difficulties to reduce severely the actual usefulness of these raw materials. Brazil's iron deposits are located far from any satisfactory source of coal, which is scarce in most of Latin America. Bolivia's tin mines are situated at extreme altitudes. Even the successful opening of major new iron mines in Venezuela since World War II has required the construction of difficult and expensive transportation facilities.

Besides mineral resources, there are in Latin America large areas of fertile land, forests of great immensity and wealth, and actual or potential sources of many materials needed in growing volume by the United States and other industrial countries. But here, again, nature's gifts have been limited. The greatest forests grow in the Amazon basin, the world's largest untamed jungle area. Development of this wilderness will be slow at best because of the equatorial climate, sparse population, and related factors making development difficult and expensive in this huge region.

The pampas of Argentina are one of the world's great agricultural and grazing areas. Elsewhere in Latin America, however, agriculture faces very great problems. The northeastern states of Brazil support a precarious agriculture that fails intermittently from recurrent droughts. In the Andean countries slope and altitude combine with problems of water supply to make agriculture extremely unrewarding for many cultivators under present conditions. Occasional earthquakes add an element of insecurity that affects the Andean peoples. In the West Indies hurricanes are an annual hazard and frequently cause great damage. Perhaps most serious of all these factors is the rugged terrain, which reaches extremes in the great barrier of the Andes Mountains, but is found also in Mexico, Central America, Brazil, and elsewhere. This terrain makes land transportation so difficult and expensive as to impose severe limitations on the possibilities for developing mass markets and mass production industries. Despite all these impediments, however, Latin American resources still provide a basis for rapid and continuing economic growth in the future, as we shall see in a moment.

Modern history for Latin America starts more than a century earlier than for the United States. Soon after Columbus's voyage of discovery in 1492, Spanish conquistadors subjugated and commenced to rule and exploit Mexico, Peru, and the other areas that now comprise the eighteen sovereign Spanish American countries, as well as Haiti, Puerto Rico, and parts of what is now the continental United States. The Portuguese established their rule in Brazil in 1500. With remarkable speed and thoroughness important aspects of Iberian culture were spread throughout these vast territories. Indigenous civilizations, which had reached high levels among the Aztecs and Mayas in what is now Mexico and Central America and among the Incas in Peru, were suppressed. Native rule was destroyed. Native religion was displaced by Roman Catholicism, although many native observances were continued within the new church by the adoption of varying degrees of Catholic modification of native practices. Racial changes began with the start of white migration from Europe and continue to the present day. Some 15 to 20 million African Negroes were brought to the West Indies, Brazil, and other parts of Latin America over a period of about three centuries. Whites intermingled at once and to a large extent with both Indians and Negroes, so that most Latin Americans today are of mixed blood.

With white rule firmly established, Spanish and Portuguese culture took hold very quickly. Cities were founded, their Hispanic origins evident in their layout and in their many great churches and other characteristic structures. The Spanish language displaced native tongues to such an extent that Spanish is the effective national language of eighteen countries today, without serious challenge from the various Indian and other languages and dialects that are still used in particular localities. The Portuguese language has the same command in Brazil, and French in Haiti, where French rule prevailed for a relatively short period before independence was achieved in 1804.

The Catholic Church not only cared for the religious needs of the Europeans and their descendants of varying color, but made a special effort to win the Indians and Negroes. Churches and schools were spread very widely, especially by the Jesuits and other orders, and today many churches more than four centuries old are still in use. Latin America soon became a Catholic area, and the church exercised great influence in all aspects of government and private affairs. The church was in effect an arm of the Spanish crown, through the king's power to appoint higher clergy. The Spanish Inquisition gave the church much added power in the colonies, reducing to negligible proportions any form of heresy or challenge.

Gold and silver were prime objects of Spanish conquest. With impressive thoroughness the conquistadors captured the treasures of the natives. Many gold and silver objects were melted down and sent to Spain as bullion. Mines were worked, and new ore bodies discovered. So thorough was Spanish prospecting that in Mexico, for instance, no major new gold or silver discoveries have been made in the century and a half since the end of Spanish rule. Agriculture was also mobilized to meet the purposes of the conquerors. In the early years Europeans did not come to Latin America as farmers. The conquistadors were soldiers, not tillers of the soil. They founded a ruling class that sought others to do the necessary manual labor. In most of Latin America Indians were present to dig in the mines, cultivate the fields, cook and sew in the houses of the Europeans and their offspring, and serve as artisans of all sorts. Their handiwork includes the building and decoration of many churches and other structures. In Brazil the Portuguese at first found neither bonanzas of precious metals nor an indigenous population that could be induced to do the colony's work. Getting along without so much treasure until later discoveries, the Portuguese early resorted to African slaves for their labor supply.

Independence from European colonial rule began when disruption in Napoleonic Europe weakened colonial ties to the New World. Growing economic power in the colonies combined with restiveness under static colonial rule to bring about separatist movements in one area after another. Between 1804 and 1825 all of the present independent Latin American countries were established, except three. The Dominican Republic and Cuba gained independence from Spain in 1844 and 1902 respectively. Panama was established out of peninsular Colombia in 1903. This wave of independence might have been pushed back again by European, especially Spanish, action, had not the United States with British acquiescence intervened from 1823 on with the Monroe Doctrine, proclaming its determination to prevent reimposition of European colonial control in the Western Hemisphere.

The leaders of the independence movements and of the new governments in Latin America were mostly whites born in the New World. These "Creoles" considered their role in colonial administration unjustly small. They seized on the ideas of individual liberty associated with the American and French Revolutions. English liberal thought strongly influenced some independence leaders. Yet the nature of Hispanic American society was such that these ideas did not penetrate very far into the new regimes. The masses of the people were not a significant factor in the independence movements, and governments have continued down to the present to be controlled by very small oligarchies in most Latin American countries. Without strong or deep popular roots or a tradition of government by law, Latin American governments have proved very unstable in the century and a half since colonial power was first thrown off. Constitutions have come and gone with passing regimes, while economic and social affairs showed only limited change from colonial patterns until recent years.

Colonial rule in Latin America had a retarding effect strikingly parallel to that resulting from the seclusion of Japan during the Tokugawa era. Spanish and Portuguese culture in 1492 was about as advanced as any in Europe, and this culture was transplanted to the New World with truly remarkable success. But the profound developments in economic, social, and political life that occurred in England and elsewhere between 1492 and 1825 had very little counterpart or imitation in Spain, Portugal, or Latin America. Japan in 1600 was in many respects comparable to European countries, but the Tokugawa Shogunate cut Japan off from contact with the rest of the world for some two and a half centuries, until Commodore Perry's visit in 1854. In fact, the situation in Japan when Perry arrived there was far more favorable to modernization than that which existed in Latin America when European control was thrown off.

The people of Latin America are a product of this history, and represent a mixture of European, Indian, and Negro blood and culture. The mixture varies from one area to another, but three major racial regions can be distinguished. The main racial combination is Indian and European along the mountainous western spine from Mexico through Central America, Colombia, Ecuador, Peru, Bolivia, and northern Chile. In this Indo-American region white people of pure European ancestry are a small minority (except in Costa Rica), while over a quarter of the population are pure Indian. The large majority are mestizo, of mixed white and Indian ancestry. Many persons continue to use Indian languages and follow Indian ways, which in some of the more remote areas are little changed from pre-Spanish times. The highly developed Indian civilizations of the past have left important remnants here.

A second great region is dominated by mixtures of African and European elements. This Afro-American area includes all of the West Indies, the lowland areas of Venezuela and Colombia, the Guianas, and much of Brazil. Here colonial plantations were worked by slaves from Africa. The Indian populations of these areas were smaller and less advanced than in the western mountains. European men mixed with African women very freely, especially in Brazil, where Portuguese traditions placed less stigma on black skin than existed in the English colonies.

The third great racial and cultural region is dominantly European. This Ibero-American area covers southern Brazil, Uruguay, Argentina, and most of Chile. Paraguay is considered culturally a part of this area, despite the survival of many Guarani Indians and wide use of the Guarani language. Here the sparse Indian population and the few African slaves who were brought in have been submerged in what is now in most parts of the region a predominantly Caucasoid population with European culture. Immigration from Europe has continued to the present day, bringing Spanish and Portuguese, many Italians, Germans, some Poles and others. Small numbers of immigrants have also come from Japan, particularly to Brazil.

Almost everywhere in Latin America the culture of the ruling class is deeply rooted in the Iberian Peninsula. Outside of Brazil, Haiti, and a few other areas, this dominant culture comes from Spain. Westerners familiar only with the United States, Canada, Britain, Germany and other highly industrialized countries will find much that is different in this Spanish American culture. It comes from the Spain of the sixteenth century. Spain was finally winning national unity and its long struggle against the Moors and Arabs when Columbus landed in Hispaniola (the island that now comprises Haiti and the Dominican Republic). The Spanish society that was carried to America contained strong Levantine elements, such as gestures and modes of expression that are quite alien to Anglo-Saxon society.

The conquistadors took with them an elemental nationalism

and a Christian faith whose forms, force, and even ferocity reflected this struggle against Islam. The Spanish Catholic Church was subject to royal control. No Reformation had tempered the single-minded and uncritical acceptance of the traditions and power of the church. The Spanish Inquisition was imported into the New World and sought, although not always with complete success, to prevent any deviation from approved dogma and Church decisions. No Spanish lords had ever gathered at a Spanish Runnymede to impose checks on the absolute power of their king. No emerging middle class or industrial revolution during the long centuries of Spanish rule in America worked to enforce a modification of the traditional authoritarian forms of Spain. No *habeas corpus* or English common law provided any check on, or appeal from, the acts of the Inquisition.

The Catholic Church continues to be a very powerful element of Latin American society. Although strongly opposed and strictly limited in Mexico and certain other countries where its association with the old colonial order brought upon it the hatred of the new leaders, the Church commands loyalty and respect everywhere. Even in Brazil, where many people profess to take it much less seriously than is customary in Spanish America, the Church's power remains sufficient to prevent the legalization of divorce. In general, educated Latin American men take their religion much more lightly than do farmers, laborers, and nearly all women. Education in most Latin American countries is very strongly influenced by the Church, which operates many schools and participates in many other educational activities and in policies regarding education. Most feast days and other great celebrations—such as the pre-Lenten Carnival in Rio de Janeiro—that punctuate the life of Latin Americans in all countries are either saints' days or otherwise related to the Church calendar.

Opposition to the Church has at certain times and places become bitter and violent. But this is not a theological opposition. Rather it is an anti-clericalism on the part of persons most of whom consider themselves good Catholics but object to Church influence or control in education, politics, and other matters deemed to be outside the realm of religion.

Family and personal loyalties in the Spanish and Portuguese traditions are so strong as to make difficult the development in Latin America of dependable large impersonal organizations like corporations or governments. A Latin American maintains close relations with cousins, aunts, uncles, and many others whom the circumstances of life in present-day United States have separated, and additional honorary but close ties are sought and maintained with godparents, who assume important obligations. Latin Americans tend to give confidence to relatives more than to outsiders, and there is a common tendency among government officials and business executives to seek relatives as subordinates. The preference for doing business through family and friends remains strong. Avoiding the impersonal procedures of "staff work" and other paraphernalia of modern United States society, the Latin American official or executive tends to delegate very little responsibility, scrutinizing in detail much that United States executives would consider trivial, and as a result often becoming bogged down in work and slowing affairs that may be of great urgency. Civic organizations and activities are relatively rare and weak. Latin Americans do not normally share much sense of obligation to the community outside of the family.

The economy of Latin America is as much the product of this Iberian cultural background as of the great economic forces that have shaken the whole world in modern times. The products of the soil and the mines, are, of course, determined in large part by existing resources and markets. But the organization of production, the economic institutions that have evolved, and the technology being applied are derived from Latin America's Iberian roots, which show in many places. Despite impressive development in recent years, only a small proportion of Latin Americans are yet living in the industrial twentieth century with its higher incomes and modern conveniences.

Most of Latin America must be considered as economically underdeveloped. Returns from economic activity are meager and undependable. Poverty, illiteracy, poor health, and other manifestations of underdevelopment are the lot of most people in most Latin American countries. The 1955 average production per person is estimated to have been $286, while per capita production the United States came to $2,343, nearly eight times as much. Economically, Latin America is far closer to Asia and Africa than to the industrialized countries of Europe and North America. It is little wonder that Mexico and other Latin American countries are acutely self-conscious in their relations with the United States and find an affinity with the Afro-Asian bloc in the United Nations on economic and social problems.

Extremes of poverty and wealth have characterized Latin America since the days of the conquistadors. On the one hand, ordinary people even today earn only the very poorest livelihood in many localities such as Brazil's Northeast and the Altiplano of Peru and Bolivia, as well as in remote Indian villages up and down the continent. Here life is harsh and short. On the other hand, Latin America also has a very wealthy class, usually in the cities such as Buenos Aires, Rio de Janeiro, and Mexico City. These cities rank with great cities anywhere in the world in architecture, fine arts, and some of the amenities for those who have wealth and power. But these cities also hold millions who are desperately poor.

From early colonial times, top officials and clergy lived in magnificence. Lesser persons enjoyed varying degrees of luxury. Indians or African slaves performed the necessary work under varying degrees of duress and for the most part received a very low level of food, housing and clothing—although escape was sometimes possible, for instance through the significant opportunities available to Negroes in Brazil for earnings and for the purchase or gift of freedom. There was almost no middle class or anything resembling a middle-class outlook in Latin America until fairly recent times, when the demands of bureaucracy, commerce, and industry have called into existence a small white-collar group that is exhibiting middle-class traits to a certain extent.

Agriculture in the colonies was largely carried on in *latifundios,* or landed estates. A "big house" for the master and his extensive family would serve as center and headquarters for the *fazenda, hacienda, estancia, fundo,* or *rancho,* depending on the local terminology. This rural estate might be huge and require the services of hundreds or even thousands of workmen. These and their families were controlled by the owner of the estate, who acted not only as employer, but for many purposes also as the local political chief. He provided a chapel and the services, at least part-time, of a priest. Many estate owners and other employers took their paternalistic role seriously and treated their Indian, African, or mixed-blood workers well. But because of urgent need for labor or for other reasons many employers, both on the farms and in the mines, failed to live up to such standards, and many rural Latin Americans have existed in peonage, literal and at times extreme. The Catholic Church early took the Indians under its special care and often succeeded in preventing or softening the harsher forms of treatment. The Spanish Crown also sought to protect the Indians, and the Laws of the Indies contain many provisions for this purpose.

This system of ownership and labor perpetuated inefficient and unproductive methods. Many landowners spent much of their time away from the land and in the capital or another city, to which flowed much of the product of the soil. The overseers who actually managed the farms were often persons of little technical or supervisory skill, who not infrequently served what they conceived to be their own interests, without much regard for either the workers or the owners. In spite of its shortcomings the system worked well enough to survive, and today landowners continue to be one of the major elements of the oligarchy of most countries, along with the Church and the military class. With the sanction of the Church and the support of the army, the "day" of the landowners in Latin America has lasted for over four centuries. Many estates, especially those producing sugar and other export crops, have come under foreign ownership. Foreign individual or corporate plantation owners have in some cases introduced high technical standards and treated workers better than native employers, but the foreigner has been a particular object of political attack on the part of groups seeking to change the existing system.

Land reform has been considered by many a necessary prerequisite to improving the lot of the peasant masses, to political reform, and to technical progress in agriculture. In recent years Guatemala and Bolivia have inaugurated far-reaching programs, and some land reform has taken place in Argentina and Chile. But Mexico has gone furthest in breaking up the large estates, having redistributed more than half the country's cultivated land since 1916. A traditional form of Mexican agricultural community, the *ejido*, has been re-established in large numbers in the redistributed areas. Some *ejidos* today are cooperative farms; in others, individual farmers receive specific plots of land and are permitted to cultivate more or less as they like. Financing has been provided by a special *Banco Ejidal*, and various national policies have been aimed at promoting the *ejidos*.

For millions of Mexicans the land reform has brought real improvement in economic and social status. Still, some *ejidos* yield no better income for their populations than did preceding arrangements. Agricultural techniques have at times been even below former standards, with no overseer or owner to provide guidance. Output has not kept pace with population growth in many *ejidos*, and many young people are without land to till.

Some of Mexico's surplus farm population, both from *ejidos* and elsewhere, find jobs in nearby towns or cities or go to Mexico City. Many cross the United States border to seek wage work, usually as migrant workers on large farms. Mexican farmers come to the United States for the most part only temporarily, returning after a season with their earnings. These Mexican *braceros,* who enter the United States legally, are provided certain protections under United States law. Many more Mexicans enter illegally, and such "wetbacks" lack this protection, and in fact are deported in large numbers on being discovered by United States authorities.

Latin American agriculture provides huge exports of several major products, as well as most of the food needed domestically. Coffee is the principal agricultural export, followed in order of value by sugar, wool, cotton, wheat, hides, cocoa, linseed oil, meat, and bananas. Among non-agricultural products, petroleum has recently reached first place in export value, displacing coffee. Other mineral products, despite their long history, their many problems, their economic importance to producing countries like Bolivia, Chile, and Mexico, and their strategic value to industrial nations, yield much smaller export proceeds today than do agricultural products. Copper, lead, tin, nitrates, and zinc lead the list. In 1950 exports of these five minerals totaled $442 million, compared with $1,327 million for petroleum and $3,367 million for the agricultural products mentioned above. Imports into Latin America include capital goods for economic development, other manufactured goods for consumption, certain raw materials, and significant quantities of fuel.

Fluctuations in Latin America's foreign trade are frequent and violent. The world depression of the 1930's lowered export volume and prices drastically and brought about such widespread economic disorder in Latin America that foreign obligations were dishonored in large volume, deep social unrest was felt nearly everywhere, and many governments fell. Then in World War II a submarine blockade caused large quantities of coffee, cotton, and other export products to pile up in useless surplus while urgently needed imports became unobtainable. Since 1945, world markets for primary products have continued to gyrate violently. Coffee prices rose from 13 cents a pound in 1946 to 88 cents in 1954 and then dropped to 58 cents in 1955. Cocoa prices went from 9 cents a pound in 1946 to 51 cents in 1947, 19 cents in 1949, 69 cents in 1954, and 27 cents early in 1956. Such instability has impeded

Latin American efforts to develop a more productive economy, a more stable society and government, and more effective foreign relations. Because of such fluctuations and for other reasons, many Latin Americans feel strongly that they are still living in a colonial economy. They are keenly aware that Latin Americans do not control these markets. Many feel that their efforts yield more value to foreigners than to Latin America itself.

Attempts to deal with this situation have included schemes of various kinds to control export prices, imports, foreign exchange, and domestic prices; measures to develop domestic sources of industrial products; various discriminations against foreign capital; and other nationalistic measures. Within the context of Latin American society and history it is not surprising that such policies and activities have not always been wisely conceived or effectively administered. Serious inefficiencies have characterized many controls. Import restrictions and other measures have proved very costly, for they have resulted in many local interest groups establishing high-cost enterprises and exploiting consumers and government far more thoroughly than had the fluctuations of foreign trade or the activities of foreign capitalists. Inflation has plagued Chile, Brazil, and other countries, partly as a result of the basic difficulties arising from shortages at home and market fluctuations abroad, but also because of grave inadequacies in domestic public and financial administration. In the textile industries of Mexico, Brazil, and other countries, both managers and labor are exacting behind tariff walls a toll that slows down economic development and puts a burden on all consumers. Brazil's hypernationalistic petroleum legislation is preventing foreign assistance in the discovery and production of crude oil from resources that are considered vast but will not be known with certainty until wells are actually drilled; and meanwhile Brazil's scarce foreign exchange resources are being poured out to meet a large and growing bill for imported petroleum.

Economic growth is, nevertheless, gathering momentum in Latin America. Stimulated by memories of the hardships of the 1930's and 1940's, assisted by balances of United States dollars accumulated during World War II when the proceeds of strategic materials exports could not be wholly spent, and spurred by increasing pressure from the voters, all Latin American governments have felt compelled to promote economic development. At the same time, a group of modern business managers has been emerging. United States private business investment has played a limited but important role, not only in bringing in capital, but also in training local labor and managers, in importing technology, in opening up remote areas and developing natural resources, and in providing some impressive examples of modern business methods. Sears, Roebuck and Co. and a number of other American firms have given significant demonstrations of these methods in their successful postwar ventures in Latin America. Other factors in economic growth have included United States government and international loans and technical assistance, and favorable prices for Latin America's export products.

The rate of economic development has been rapid, although varying from country to country and from year to year. While Argentina under Peron was hardly holding its own economically, the rest of Latin America has been increasing its gross national product per capita by more than 2 per cent a year during most of the period since World War II. This rate is comparable to the long-run growth rate of the United States and has been maintained despite population growth of some 2.5 per cent a year. An important element in Latin America's current economic expansion is a high rate of domestic saving and investment. By now development in Brazil, Mexico, Venezuela, and some other countries may have become self-perpetuating. If so, these countries have reached a stage not yet attained by most areas in Asia or Africa. Continuation of growth is supported by profitable operation of existing enterprises, including the large United States petroleum, iron, and other ventures in Venezuela and elsewhere. Recent overtures by the Soviet bloc toward Latin America may result in expanded trade with Communist areas, in some Communist technical aid, and perhaps in an increase of aid from the United States.

Government and politics reflect Latin America's traditional society and economy. Control has rested almost exclusively with a small oligarchy. Landowners have been the chief element in this controlling group, supported by the military forces and the Church hierarchy. Gradually the rank and file of voters have become a factor in politics, but so far they are generally no more than followers, not imposing a serious check on most regimes and seldom serving as a source of initiative. Political groups tend to be the personal followings of particular leaders and consequently do not adhere strongly to abstract principles. Leadership tends to be vigorous, often authoritarian. The leader of a political party or labor union often lives in the grand manner. Abstract honesty tends to be regarded less highly than an impressive appearance. Democratic principles and procedures have only a limited hold, and some outright dictators, notably Getulio Vargas in Brazil and Carlos Ibáñez in Chile, have, after losing power, been returned by popular vote.

Governments, therefore, tend to be governments of men, rather than of laws. Policies often aim more at making a show than at laying the groundwork for slow and quiet progress. An imposing party platform, laws that call for impossibly high labor standards or the latest in benefits for government employees, and constitutions more "modern" or "democratic" than those of the United States or other Western nations, are common in Latin America. Since political leaders tend to put their family and friends into government positions, the level of performance is often below what might be expected of a trained and experienced career civil service. And jobholders, many receiving salaries too low to provide their minimum needs, and knowing the likelihood of losing their jobs in any political overturn, often succumb to the temptation to supplement their salaries by illegal means. Meanwhile, supporters of opposition political leaders remain on the outside and attempt to unseat the government, accusing it of various shortcomings and making large promises. Under these circumstances Latin American governments have shown a marked tendency toward instability, or authoritarian methods, or both.

The army is a major force in most Latin American governments. Military leaders have had an honored place in society from the time of the conquistadors. The prestige of the military officer has tended to be higher than that of the businessman. Latin American armies and navies have at times been required for genuine military purposes, and some local wars have been fiercely fought. In World War II Latin American military forces contributed to the Allied effort, for example, through the Brazilian navy's extensive patrolling in the South Atlantic and the service of a Brazilian army division in Italy. Similarly, the Colombian army sent a small force to Korea following the Communist invasion of South Korea in 1950. But the principal continuing role of military forces in Latin America is political. Their support is necessary for the success of a government, and withdrawal of support usually leads to a government's downfall.

With economic development and growth of education a

small middle class is emerging and increasing numbers of people are becoming politically articulate. Labor unions are now a significant factor in politics. So far, however, political rivalries tend to remain within the oligarchy, and frequent so-called "revolutions" are in fact usually *coups d'état* in which only a small number of persons are involved and very few people hurt. Mexico has had a revolution with more profound effects. In this revolution, which started in 1910 and is referred to by Mexican leaders as still continuing, major economic and social changes have been brought about, and the common man now has a place in political life far superior to what he formerly endured. The programs of the Mexican government have changed from one administration to another, but a genuine interest in the general welfare seems to have motivated the regimes of the past thirty years, even though it would be exaggerating to say that popular pressure has determined the main course of political events. Three other countries—Uruguay, Chile, and Costa Rica—are commonly regarded as practicing effective democracy today. Others vary widely in political maturity and stability, just as they do in literacy and other related factors.

Gradual evolution from unstable, at times turbulent, authoritarian rule by one or another faction of an oligarchy may lead to more and more democratic government. But rising demands and increasing political participation by the common people are subjecting Latin American governments to greater pressure. There is no assurance that expectations will always be met. On the contrary, the deep frustrations and resentments of the millions may lead to occasional violence. In this situation, communism can be expected to make progress at times, as happened in Guatemala during the decade following World War II.

The foreign relations of Latin American countries have advanced in a century and a half from early fears of European reconquest, through a long period of local wars, deep suspicions of "Yankee imperialism," and a gradual development in international action in the Western Hemisphere, until today the Organization of American States (OAS) stands at the head of one of the world's most successful systems of international cooperation, and Latin American governments are making an important contribution in the United Nations and its specialized agencies. This evolution has taken place without any Latin American nation developing such strength as to be able to resist determined action by a great power unless some other great power intervened. British naval power and British forbearance protected Latin America in the nineteenth century. In the twentieth century, United States power has played a decisive role in this region.

Territorial disputes have punctuated Latin America's history ever since the achievement of independence. Even today several stretches of international boundaries remain undetermined, and dissatisfaction exists over a number of territorial matters, for instance Bolivia's lack of direct access to the sea. Brazil's boundaries were mostly settled by negotiation or arbitration—an important achievement because every South American country, except Chile and Ecuador, touches on Brazil.

Arbitration has been widely used by other countries, especially in territorial matters. But some rivalries have precipitated open warfare, of which the extreme case was Paraguay's war against Brazil, Uruguay, and Argentina in 1864-70. Hopelessly outnumbered, the Paraguayans continued to fight until most able-bodied men had been killed and their places in the army had been taken by boys and women. Before accepting defeat, Paraguay had lost half its population, and many more died of hunger and disease in the early years after the war. Paraguay remains today one of the least developed areas in Latin America.

Relations with the United States are the most important element in Latin American foreign affairs. The "Colossus of the North" was long feared and suspected by Latin Americans, who looked on unhappily as the United States made large territorial gains at the expense of Mexico in 1848, acquired Puerto Rico and important rights in Cuba as a result of the Spanish-American war in 1898, intervened in the 1903 revolt establishing Panama as a country independent of Colombia, and immediately signed a Panama Canal treaty favorable to the United States, and stationed Marines in the Dominican Republic, Nicaragua, and Haiti for long periods, ending only in 1933, when the last troops were withdrawn from Haiti. Meanwhile, United States economic and military power was growing far beyond the total of all Latin American countries combined. The importance of the United States as a market for Latin American exports and a source of many imports and of investment capital has grown through the years, especially as a result of the two world wars, which temporarily cut off most contacts with Europe and reduced Europe's capacity for trade and investment. Many Latin Americans look on their economic relationship with the United States as a colonial relationship, in which our tremendous power is used to extract advantages in unequal bargains.

In United States foreign relations, Latin America has always been a secondary element, subordinate traditionally to relations with Europe and recently also to relations with Asia and the Middle East. From the first expression by President Monroe in 1823 of United States determination to prevent further European colonial advances in the Western Hemisphere, the United States has tended to assume a paternalistic role toward Latin America. Still, interest in Latin America has been spasmodic right up to the present. At times force has been used or threatened, and this country's brief flirtation with old-fashioned imperialism was carried on mostly in Latin America—by the Spanish-American War, by various forms of intervention in Latin America, and by an arrogant attitude on the part of the United States government and of private businessmen alike toward United States private investment abroad. The last vestiges of this period of American history are not long past, if indeed they have fully disappeared.

The most successful United States effort to win Latin American confidence and cooperation has been the Good Neighbor policy, which came to flower under President Franklin D. Roosevelt after its roots had been planted in Herbert Hoover's administration. Friendliness, cooperation, and restraint are outstanding features of this policy. Formal United States treaty rights to intervene in Cuba and Panama were renounced, and in 1936 at Buenos Aires the United States joined all the Latin American governments in declaring "inadmissible the intervention of any one of them, directly or indirectly, and for whatever reason, in the internal or external affairs of any of the parties."

World War II brought shortages in the United States of strategic materials, many of which were actually or potentially available in Latin America. Along with procurement and other activity directly aimed at meeting such needs, the United States government sought to assist in meeting some of the felt needs of Latin America, and thus to attract more support for Washington's policy and for the war effort. Through the efforts of Nelson Rockefeller, Coordinator of Inter-American Affairs, a number of cultural and economic activities were initiated, notably technical assistance in health, agriculture, and education. These wartime activities proved so successful and so popular in Latin America that they were continued on a small scale after 1945, despite declining United States interest in the area.

In 1950, when President Truman's Point Four Program became a reality, interest on the part of the United States government in technical assistance became greater than ever, and Latin America has since shared in the program. The experience of more than ten years of technical assistance in Latin America has contributed much to the techniques now being used by the International Cooperation Administration all over the world.

Inter-American cooperation has developed progressively, although unevenly, during these different phases of relations between the United States on the one hand and Latin America on the other. As long ago as 1826 at the Congress of Panama, which was commemorated at the July, 1956, meeting of American heads of state, representatives of the newly independent states expressed a number of noble sentiments about collective security, a continuing organization, and the use of peaceful means for settling disputes among American states.

Such ideas were to be repeated often before the first Conference of American States met in Washington in 1890 and created a continuing organization. The ninth Conference of American States in Bogotá in 1948 gave this organization its present form, under the name Organization of American States. The OAS now oversees, through its various organs, execution of many inter-American agreements on economic, social, health, military, political, and other matters, including a treaty on pacific settlement and a treaty of reciprocal assistance. This latter, signed at Rio de Janeiro in 1947, is the basis for important actions to keep peace in the Western Hemisphere. Early in 1955, for instance, the OAS mediated a dispute that had caused open warfare in Costa Rica with forces which had entered from Nicaragua. This mediation was prompt, vigorous, and effective. Among the many aspects of the Inter-American System that have served as models for other international action, the Rio treaty was followed in large part in the formulation of the pact creating the North Atlantic Treaty Organization.

To succeed in multilateral diplomacy among a group of twenty-one very unequal participants has required more than a little learning on the part of all concerned. In this process forbearance and willingness to listen are necessary on the part of the United States. And every government in the OAS needs to show responsibility and realism. All these qualities have been demonstrated to a degree that seems to increase with the passing of time. With such an organization functioning effectively, the United States need not resort to unilateral intervention and can counteract much Latin American suspicion of North American "colonialism."

Progress in group action is being made. But the virtually universal belief that Washington intervened to remove the leftist government of Jacobo Arbenz in Guatemala in 1954 is evidence that foreign relations in the Americas, in spite of the progress to date, have not yet satisfied all the high hopes that lie behind the OAS. The largest area of disappointment, so far as the Latin Americans are concerned, is economic. Repeatedly their representatives have sought much greater United States assistance in tackling problems associated with fluctuations in prices of primary products, greater financial assistance for economic development, greater sympathy for their widespread wish to hasten development of heavy industry and other manufacturing facilities, and less readiness to preach to and prescribe for their governments.

10

Telescoped Revolutions

COLONIALISM—DEMOCRACY—COMMUNISM NATIONALISM

No issue in the relations between West and non-West, as already pointed out, is so difficult for Westerners to understand as the difference in the time element of their respective historical development. While the Western peoples have taken several centuries to go through the major revolutions of modern times—the rise of nationalism, the gradual development of democratic institutions, the challenges of nazism and communism, the impact of industrialization—the peoples of the non-Western areas covered in the preceding chapters have had to telescope these revolutions into the span of a few years or a few decades in the twentieth century. To use Stalin's phrase, which is applicable to Asia, the Middle East, and Africa as well as to Russia, the non-Western world, instead of accepting a slow gradual growth, is endeavoring to catch up rapidly with the West, knowing full well that the West, for its part, does not and will not stand still.

Because of this discrepancy in the timing and pace of the revolutions which have shaped both West and non-West in modern times, the two sectors understandably take profoundly different views of major issues in world affairs. For the West, which only yesterday ruled colonial areas, this period of its history is as if it had vanished into the past—in spite of the obvious fact that colonialism still exists, in a variety of forms, in Asia, the Middle East, and particularly Africa. For the non-Western peoples, colonialism is not just a memory to be laid aside and forgotten, but a vivid reality which it will take at least another generation or more to erase.

For the West democracy is the ideal form of government, the most satisfactory type of relationship between human beings, which has developed over centuries and is constantly being improved. For the non-Western peoples democracy is a theoretically desirable, but often unattainable, goal, and as practiced by the West in colonial areas often no more than a sad travesty of the principles symbolized by the slogan of the French Revolution, "liberty, equality, fraternity," and by the ideas of John Stuart Mill, Abraham Lincoln, Thomas Jefferson, and Franklin D. Roosevelt. For the West communism is an unmitigated evil, fostered by Russians and Chinese who are trying to impose it on helpless nations which must rely on American military might for their defense as the only deterrent to Communist aggression. For the non-West communism is a way of life unpalatable to non-Communists, but fraught with the promise of providing a short cut to the creation of a modern economy through industrialization. For the West nationalism is a completed process, which must now yield to the newer phase of internationalism—although few Western nations are ready to accept the practice, as distinguished from the theory, of genuine subordination of national sovereignty to international cooperation. For the non-Western peoples the achievement of national independence, the fulfillment of a national identity often obscured or suppressed in the past by colonial domination, is a deep-felt need which brooks no further delay and must take precedence over such objectives as military blocs, whether democratic or Communist.

This discrepancy in the sense of time causes non-Westerners to put more emphasis on their resentment of colonialism even where it has come to an end than on the current benefits which democratic nations of the West can and do bestow on underdeveloped nations. Such an attitude is particularly difficult for the United States to understand. Americans feel that this country has been traditionally anti-colonial because of the revolt of the American colonies against Britain, which at that time was the world's leading colonial power—and retained that role as late as the middle of the twentieth century. Having challenged and repelled colonialism in the 1770's, Americans subsequently opposed it in other parts of the world, with the result that the United States came to be regarded abroad, as well as at home, as the champion of anti-colonialism.

Why, then, we ask, are we suspected of colonialism by the newly independent peoples of Asia, accused of "Yankee imperialism" in Latin America, viewed with doubt in French North Africa? Is this due solely to Communist propaganda, or is there a deeper cause for this feeling?

First, of course, we must define what we mean by colonialism. The usual assumption is that colonialism represents political or military control of a territory which is not a geographic part of the colonial power—usually, although not always, an overseas territory. In this respect, the only colonies the United States has had in its history are the Philippines, to which we voluntarily granted independence, and Puerto Rico, which, although not an independent state, has in recent years gained a large degree of autonomy and acquired the title of commonwealth. By contrast, all the colonies of the European nations—Britain, France, the Netherlands, Portugal, Belgium, Spain—fitted or, where they still exist, fit into the colonial category.

There are, however, other forms of colonialism besides that most obvious form of political or military control. In essence, the colonial relationship is any relationship between an advanced country and a less advanced area, under which the advanced country succeeds in attaining a special position of influence by reason of its predominance—political, military, economic or ideological, or even spiritual—or a combination of some or all of these elements.

This relationship may be bad, harsh or benevolent, detrimental to the interests of the less advanced area or conducive to its development—all depending on existing circumstances in each case. The significant thing is that it is a relationship based on inequality between an advanced and a backward economy, between a people versed in the skills of modern technology and a people still dependent on primitive tools, weapons, and techniques. The ruling country assumes that it is superior, in one or more respects, to the area over which it rules, and bases its claims to special privileges on this assumption of superiority, about which no impartial judgment is allowed to be made by the ruled.

This claim to special privileges has taken and still takes diverse forms. For example, it may take the form of "capitulations," which assure the right of the advanced nation, specified by treaty, to have its nationals brought before special courts instead of native tribunals—a right enjoyed until World War I by the Western nations in Turkey and Egypt, and until 1956 by the United States in Morocco. Or it may take the form of spheres of influence arbitrarily established by great powers on the territory of small weak countries, such as the spheres Britain and Tsarist Russia established in Persia, now Iran, in 1907, with Britain claiming the south, where rich oil resources were subsequently discovered, and Russia the north, in terms of oil less desirable—leaving the middle of the country to the Persians. Or it may take the form of special trade or strategic advantages, such as the Western powers' arrangement about treaty ports in China; Russia's long-time leaseholds in Port Arthur and Dairen, in 1895, and again in 1945, terminated in 1955; or monopolies over local production and exports, such as are enjoyed by the United Fruit Company with respect to the banana output of Costa Rica and Guatemala. Or it may be just the feeling of satisfaction an insensitive Westerner experiences in treating a person of another color as inferior. In short, it is a relationship which a Western people would seldom impose on another Western people—except in time of war, as the Nazis did on the French.

Colonialism, painful as it was from the outset to the peoples on whom it was imposed, became intolerable when revolutionary aspirations began to stir the imagination of Asians, Middle Easterners, and Africans. Karl Marx and his principal exponent, Lenin, with their determinist view of history, regarded colonialism as an inevitable consequence of capitalism. They contended that, as capitalist countries developed, their industries would require more and more raw materials and ever larger markets for their manufactured goods, and that these could be found only in the underdeveloped areas of the world, which the capitalist governments would then proceed to conquer, rule, and exploit. This sequence, as described by Marx and Engels in the 1860's, was actually an accurate picture of what had been happening since the start of the age of exploration and colonization, and both the European colonial rulers and their increasingly rebellious charges could see it with their own eyes in the nineteenth and early twentieth centuries.

In fact, this is the picture that most Americans long thought they saw when they looked at colonialism. As late as World War II American writers and teachers expressed criticisms of European colonial powers which were essentially similar to those made by Marx and Engels in the 1860's and by Lenin in the 1920's. They did so not because they had become enslaved by Marxist doctrine or subject to the guidance of Moscow, but because they had been brought up in the tradition of anti-colonialism deeply rooted in the experience of the United States. This experience differed profoundly from that of the Asian, Middle Eastern, and African peoples who lived under the rule of Britain and other European powers. For the English-born inhabitants of the American colonies sprang from the same background, beliefs, and historical experience as their fellow citizens in England. They did not differ from the English in race, language, religion, or, up to the time of their exodus to the New World, stages of development, as has been true of the Indians with respect to the British, the Indonesians with respect to the Dutch, or the Indochinese and the North Africans with respect to the French.

The American colonists, it is true, had left their English homeland largely because of rebellion against political and religious practices to which they objected, and were determined to build for themselves a new home on the American continent. This passion for independence also shaped their decision to challenge England's attempts to impose on them economic restrictions which they regarded as onerous. But they were not animated, like the colonial peoples of Asia, the Middle East, and Africa in our own times, by feelings of discrimination or by resentment against Western civilization. The American colonists rejected interference in their affairs by England, whose jurisdiction they had voluntarily left. But they did not reject the ideas and practices, the language or the religious beliefs, of their former fellow citizens.

Yet as the United States, founded on Britain's former colonies in the new world, became a great industrial power with increasing interest in world affairs, Americans carried over their initial rejection of British colonialism into the young republic's foreign policy. Because Britain had once seemed the obstacle to the fulfillment of the colonists' dreams of economic as well as political independence, Americans who had not experienced colonial rule for a century or more continued to experience an automatic reflex of hostility toward any form of colonialism, wherever it occurred. Twisting of the British lion's tail remained a national pastime until 1945, when Britain, under the Laborites, in defiance of Winston Churchill's determination not to liquidate the British Empire, started the process of colonial disengagement which led from the relinquishment of India, Pakistan, Ceylon, and Burma in 1947 to the grant of self-government to the Gold Coast and Malaya in 1957.

During the decades when Americans, in and out of season, criticized colonialism without stopping to consider the contributions the colonial powers may have made to the territories over which they ruled, American commentators, like Communist spokesmen, emphasized the iniquities of colonialism and the exploitation of backward peoples by advanced nations for their own self-interest or the self-interest of their bankers and industrialists. So vigorous was this American criticism, and so powerful and widespread was its impact on the minds of colonial peoples, that the French historian André Siegfried has claimed that the United States, rather than the U.S.S.R., was the principal architect of colonial revolts against the western European nations.

These outward similarities between the attacks made on colonialism by Communist Russia and capitalist America, however, have led, in the twentieth century, to strikingly different policies. Lenin, basing his approach on the Marx-Engels theory that colonialism was the inevitable result of capitalism, took the view in 1917 that Russia itself was a colonial country—that is, a country which, while politically independent, was economically dependent on the advanced industrial nations of the West, exporting its food and raw materials—notably wheat and oil—to the Western nations, in return for their manufactured goods, without developing its own industrial production. In the light of this contention Lenin argued, first, that Russia, as a colonial nation, belonged in the camp of other colonial territories, not in that of the Western powers, and that its policy was thus both anti-capitalist and anti-colonial. He thereby repudiated on Russia's behalf its pre-1917 role as a member of the Western great powers club, and aligned it without qualifications on the side of the non-Western anti-colonial peoples—in spite of the fact that millions of Asians, within the administrative framework of the Tsarist Empire, remain today under the rule of the U.S.S.R. To symbolize this change in Russia's world role, the Soviet leaders, on coming to power, denounced the "unequal treaties" concluded by the Tsarist government with less advanced nations of the Middle East and Asia—notably Persia—which had given special advantages to Russia, as well as to Britain. Probably no other single aspect of Soviet policy had such an impact on the colonial world—both the rulers and the ruled—as the anti-colonial stand taken by Russia after the Bolshevik revolution of 1917.

This stand, which Stalin's successors continue to maintain and emphasize, has made it possible for the U.S.S.R. to present itself to India and Burma, to Egypt and Syria, and to the restive peoples of Africa, as the protagonist of the revolt against colonialism which they have either experienced in the past or are experiencing today. Russia's anti-colonial role, however, has been challenged by the Western powers on two grounds. First, they contend that while Western colonialism is in decline, a new Russian colonialism is in the ascendant. Not only have the Russians made no move to give independence to the Asians within their borders, as Britain, France, and the Netherlands have done in the arc from Pakistan to Indonesia, but, their Western critics point out, the U.S.S.R. has imposed a colonial status on once free nations of eastern Europe, from the Baltic to the Black Sea.

The Western attack on Russia's domination of its eastern European satellites finds support in the criticism of Soviet methods made by a Communist country, Yugoslavia. Tito, after expecting that a Russian Communist government would act differently from the governments of the "capitalist" West, was all the more disillusioned to discover through his own experience that Russia was not different from other great powers and, like them, wanted to obtain Yugoslav raw materials for its developing industry. It is significant that the financial arrangements made by the U.S.S.R. after 1945 with Rumania, Hungary, and Bulgaria, which sided with Nazi Germany in its war against Russia, were modeled until their discontinuance in 1955 on those made by Britain with oil-producing nations of the Middle East, for a 51-49 division of profits—with this important exception. Whereas British investors, with or without government aid, put capital into such enterprises as the Anglo-Iranian Company, the U.S.S.R. used so-called German assets (that is, local assets expropriated by the Nazis and then taken over by the Russians as war reparations) as their share of the "investment."

While it could be convincingly argued that the economies of most of the nations of eastern Europe, with the notable exception of highly industrialized and democratic Czechoslovakia, were in many respects comparable to those of Asia and the Middle East, not to those of western Europe, and were treated more or less as "colonial" by industrialized and westernized Germany before the advent of the U.S.S.R., this does not of itself relieve Moscow of the West's charge that it has resorted to a new form of colonialism. The eastern European nations now within Russia's orbit had, for shorter or longer periods, enjoyed a measure of political independence in modern times, and might have recovered it again after World War II had it not been for the intervention of Moscow. Among them, the Czechs and Poles were more closely linked with the West than with Russia, and in many respects had been more advanced than the Russians before 1945. In fact, the Czechs today occupy a position of leadership in the Soviet program of "competitive coexistence" with the West, their technical skills and industrial productivity being used as the spearhead of the Communist campaign to challenge the monopoly hitherto enjoyed by Western nations in the markets of non-Western areas.

The West's attack on Russia's treatment of the Asian peoples living within its borders—from the Uzbeks to the Kirghiz, from the Mongolians to the Turkmen—may not prove as convincing to the "uncommitted nations" as its criticism of Russia's domination over eastern Europe. From the point of view of Asia, the Middle East, and Africa, Russia's Asian subjects are not a "lesser breed without the law," dwelling far from the mother country in overseas territories under political, economic, and social conditions profoundly different from those enjoyed by the colonial rulers. For better or worse, they are an integral part of the Soviet system and therefore in a position to enjoy such benefits as it may dispense—even while enduring, along with the other peoples of the U.S.S.R., its hardships and disadvantages.

No other colonial power has taken the risk of integrating the peoples of its colonial territories within its own political, economic, and social structure. Given this attitude on the part of Western colonialists, Moscow can make a case which, while still unacceptable to Westerners, does impress non-Western areas, that by associating Asians on a more or less equal basis with other inhabitants of the U.S.S.R., it thereby speeds their development and opens to them opportunities for advancement which Asians and Africans outside Russia did not enjoy under former Western colonial rulers.

The second line of attack by the West against the U.S.S.R. on the issue of colonialism—based on the conclusions reached in the first—is that Russia's blandishments, its offers of economic and technical aid to Afghanistan and India, Egypt and Latin America, represent a serious danger to those independent nations of the "uncommitted" sector which might be tempted to accept them. These offers, the West contends, are comparable to the Trojan horse. No sooner do the Russians, in the guise of technicians, gain access to these nations than they try to subvert their existing governments and sooner or later bring them, helpless and deprived of all means of future resistance, into the Iron Curtain camp. While many of the leaders of the "uncommitted" group recognize the dangers of communism, and vigorously combat it at home, they have no desire to antagonize Russia or China by joining a Western military bloc, and believe, rightly or wrongly, that they can make use of Soviet aid without becoming slaves of Moscow.

But, one might point out, if Russia presents such a grim aspect to non-Western peoples, this should surely make the United States shine in the midst of darkness as an exemplary nation which is guilty neither of the nineteenth-century colonialism associated with the western European powers nor of the twentieth century colonialism associated with the U.S.S.R. Why, then, is the United States still viewed with distrust and suspicion in Asia, the Middle East, and Africa, and even among our neighbors in Latin America?

For this seemingly irrational attitude toward the United States, admittedly the first nation to rebel against Western imperialism, there are three main reasons which we need to examine carefully if we are to understand the way our country looks to non-Western peoples, both those which have recently achieved independence and those still living under various degrees of colonial rule.

First, the United States, since 1945, as viewed by many non-Westerners, has suffered from arrested anti-colonialism. The outlook of Americans, who once saw nothing but evil in the colonial policies of the Western European nations, has been profoundly altered by the revolutionary change in this country's international role during the past decade. On the one hand, as former colonial areas achieved independence and began to play their own part in the "cold war" which characterized that decade, our criticism of their Western rulers naturally faded away. Instead, we began to be critical of the course followed by the new nations, notably India, which had assumed that when we cheered from the sidelines their efforts to achieve independence we really meant that we would welcome untrammeled action on their part.

As our minds became increasingly focused on the struggle between the West and the U.S.S.R., between democracy and communism, we found it difficult to understand how the new nations could choose to stand aloof from both the United States and the U.S.S.R. and follow what they regarded as their own interests. We insisted that they had to make instant choices between Washington and Moscow, between ideological white and black. We asked them persistently, "Are you with us or against us?" Since one of the principal objectives of former colonial areas, notably India, had been to achieve the right to decide their fate according to their own ideas, our demand that they should without delay accept our lead was interpreted by some of them as the substitution of one form of Western domination for another, and was rejected outright, on the ground that there should be "no strings attached" to any relationship, economic, political, or just politely social, they might choose to establish with the United States.

Given our preoccupation with the danger of communism in the form of either military aggression or internal infiltration and subversion, some of us then began to wonder whether we had been wise to urge the Western powers' withdrawal from key areas of the world, such as the Indian subcontinent, Indonesia, or the Suez Canal. Where the situation was beyond recall, we limited ourselves to criticizing the erstwhile colonial peoples who had attained their own freedom of choice. But where the situation was still in flux, as in Tunisia or Morocco or Algeria, we often gave the impression that it might be in the interests of the "free world" to leave some peoples relatively unfree for the time being, so that their efforts to win freedom might not upset the common applecart, in which by that time we had acquired a significant stake.

This attitude was reinforced, on the other hand, by our reliance, new in our history, on the long-term political and military commitments we had made to our western European friends, notably through the North Atlantic Treaty Organization. For, obviously, if we wanted the loyal support of Britain, France, the Netherlands, Belgium, and Portugal in the collective security system we had sponsored in western Europe, we would have to be far more tolerant than in the past toward their remaining colonial possessions, whether France's Algeria or Portugal's Goa. The confused state of mind resulting from this two-edged policy—the attempt to reconcile our traditional anti-colonialism with our newly developed dependence on the colonial powers of western Europe—became particularly evident in the United Nations whenever the Afro-Asian bloc brought up issues disturbing to our Western allies, and therefore also to us, such as Tunisia, Morocco, or Algeria.

And third, areas once unimportant to Americans, which were "geographical expressions," have come to assume importance because of their strategic military value. We now have to consider bases in Morocco, in the Middle East, in Turkey, on Formosa, in the Philippines, in Japan. If internal changes occur in these areas, whether free of colonial rule or aspiring to achieve freedom, such bases may slip from American hands or, even more disturbing, pass under the influence or control of Moscow or Peiping. Under these circumstances, new in our national experience, even some Americans who had once been critical of Western colonialism began to wonder whether it would not be in our long-run interest to help maintain the status quo, instead of accepting or, as in the pre-1945 days, inciting changes.

Given this state of mind, we are likely to ask ourselves whether good colonialism is not, actually, preferable to inefficient native rule—a question which the British, French, Dutch, and other colonial powers often asked themselves in their heyday. The answer offered by experience is in the negative. Good government, as was often said of the British in India, is not a substitute for self-government. Continuance of government by the colonial power, no matter how benevolent and efficient, stifles the growth of democracy. For the Western rulers usually give their confidence to an upper-class native group which then tends to acquire a vested interest in the continuance of administration by the West and, in effect, becomes an obstacle to political, economic, and social change by peaceful means, leaving no alternative except resort to force, a situation which plays directly into the hands of extremists, be they Communists or Fascists. Thus, no matter how great our stake in the maintenance of the existing situation for the sake of avoiding disturbances which might redound to be the benefit of Moscow or Peiping, it remains in our long-range interest to further the transition from colonialism to self-government as rapidly as possible. This, in effect, the United States acknowledged during and after the crisis precipitated by the Anglo-French attack on Suez.

But now that we can watch colonialism at much closer range than we ever thought necessary in our anti-colonial period, we also ask ourselves whether we were right in assuming, as we once did, like the Marxists, that the colonial powers enrich themselves through the colonial relationship. Again, the answer given by experience is that colonialism seldom enriches the colonial nation as a nation, since colonial rule and the protection of the colonial territory require considerable expenditure by the mother country on military defense, internal security, administration, and at least a modicum of economic development. Private interests, however—traders, investors, bankers, and in the early stages, unscrupulous administrators—may and often do benefit financially by special privileges in colonial territories, which they do not always choose to share with their fellow citizens at home. To this extent the Marxist interpretation of colonialism contains at least an element of truth.

We have also been driven to ask ourselves whether the colonial subjects of western European powers did, in fact, feel the deep-seated hostility toward their rulers that the American colonies, presumably, felt when they rebelled against the British. The answer, surprisingly, does not give unqualified support to our anti-colonial assumptions. The moment the British left India, Pakistan, Ceylon, and Burma, these new nations, which might have been expected to turn their backs on Britain, instead chose either to join the Commonwealth outright or to cooperate closely with it through the Colombo plan for economic assistance. Even Morocco—which had seemed to have good reasons to resent the French—once it had achieved independence, declared its intention of retaining a link with France—to have "independence within interdependence"—although this decision was stalled by France's attempts to suppress the Algerian rebels.

Thus our black-and-white assumptions about colonialism, firmly held since 1776, have been challenged both by the colonial powers and by their former or current subjects in colonial territories. Chastened by this forced revision in our deeply rooted assumptions, we have given considerable thought to the alternative arrangement which might be substituted for the colonial relationship now, in any case, undergoing rapid erosion. We have begun to see that political independence, which we had at one time regarded as the be-all and end-all of freedom from colonial rule, does not automatically bring about economic independence in underdeveloped areas which perforce must at least for a time depend on some nation or nations for sources of goods unavailable at home, for capital, for export markets, for defense, and above all, today, for technical assistance in the modernization of their economies.

We have realized with a shock that these areas, once free of colonial rule, may turn for aid not only to the West, notably to the United States, but also to Russia, and may even find it advantageous to play off the West against the Soviet bloc in a novel form of struggle for an economic and technological balance of power, where the stake is not armed forces so much as nuclear reactors, outlets for one-crop economies such as the cotton of Egypt or the rice of Burma, and the building of essential industrial plants, such as a steel mill in India or a dam in Egypt.

We have become afraid that peoples who have just emerged

from the overlordship of the Western powers whom we harshly criticized for a century and a half may, through weakness, gullibility, or lack of internal stamina, fall under the even less desirable overlordship of Moscow and Peiping. And we have started to ponder whether the alternative to Western colonialism, which we have no desire to imitate, and the colonialism of Russia, should be sought in joint measures of aid to underdeveloped areas, either by channeling technical aid through the United Nations and affiliated agencies like the World Health and the Food and Agricultural organizations, or through regional security and economic arrangements such as the Southeast Asia Treaty Organization and the Baghdad pact. In considering these approaches we have gradually admitted to ourselves that our original dream of having colonial peoples pass rapidly and painlessly from Western colonialism to a Western-type democracy have not been justified by reality, and that we must not expect nations whose traditions and experience differ profoundly from those of the West to be transformed overnight, or even in the course of a century, into carbon copies of Britain or the United States.

Yet the West, and the United States in particular, has found it difficult to accept the possibility that termination of colonial rule, as in Pakistan or Indonesia, or of native authoritarianism, as in Russia and China, will not automatically be followed by the appearance, like Athena from the head of Zeus, of democracy armed with all the features familiar to Western countries, from a responsible middle class to a two-party system, from a literate electorate to equal justice for all. By a projection to other continents of an ideal not fully realized even in advanced Western nations, American observers have sometimes demanded perfection with an earnestness, even a fierceness, which gives the impression that we expect more from others just because we have been disappointed at the failure of the West to attain the heights of ideal human behavior. Editorial writers frequently inveigh against non-Western nations for failing to discard authoritarian institutions or to achieve tolerance between conflicting religious or national or economic groups—ideals which seldom, if ever, have been fully attained in the New World or in Western Europe.

If we could take time out from our criticism and exhortations about Russia and India, Egypt and Indonesia, we might realize that, judging by the experience of the West, the establishment of representative government was preceded, not followed, by economic and social change, the liquidation of feudalism, the growth of a money economy, the rise of a middle class and the decline of an authoritarian monarchy underpinned by an aristocracy; and that even in the twentieth century Western democracy has been hard-pressed in France and Italy, and well-nigh destroyed in Germany. To demand that peoples who are only now emerging from authoritarian administration, whether by foreign colonial powers or by native dictators, should promptly introduce the practices of Western democracy is to insist on a course of action which the Western democratic nations—Britain, France, the Netherlands, Belgium—found impossible or inadvisable to introduce in their overseas territories. For in the colonies—and this is one of the principal handicaps of democracy in non-Western areas today—democracy was Janus-like: in the mother country it wore the face of freedom and equality, but when it turned toward "the barbarians," as John Stuart Mill called Britain's non-English subjects, its face was that of domination and inequality.

The principal political task of the newly independent nations of the West, as we have seen, is not the immediate establishment of Western-type institutions, but the reorientation of the national fronts formed to oust colonial rulers—such as the Indian Congress, the Muslim League, and similar across-the-board groups in Burma, Indonesia, the Philippines, and so on—into parties which can effectively tackle the vast multitude of domestic problems created by the changeover from colonial status to nationhood. The first stages of this post-independence adjustment are fraught with controversies about the future of new nations, at home and abroad. Any artificial attempts to copy Western institutions for which adequate foundations have not yet been laid may dissipate the energies of men and women dedicated to freedom by a proliferation of clashing parties—as happened in Indonesia—or create in the West the false illusion of democracy through a façade built on sand, as was the case in pre-World War II Japan.

Disheartening as it may be for the West, far-reaching economic and social changes which may eventually produce conditions favorable to the development of freer political institutions have, for the most part, been introduced, in the first instance, by more or less authoritarian governments. This has been true of Japan between 1867 and 1941, of Turkey under Kemal Ataturk, of Russia under Lenin and Stalin, of China under Mao Tse-tung, of Egypt under Naguib and Nasser. Some of our best friends outside of western Europe, whom we describe as bulwarks of the free world, are ruled by civilian or military dictators—notably the majority of Latin American countries, as well as Pakistan and Thailand. It is only after twenty years of one-party rule that Turkey, whose economic advance we often praise, found it possible to move, not without many subsequent setbacks, toward a two-party system. And even India and the Philippines, which have come closer than any of the non-Western nations to our ideal of democracy, have depended for their inner strength and stability on the guidance of powerful individual leaders—Nehru and Magsaysay.

In history, as in other spheres, generalizations are dangerous. But the experience of the West itself indicates that the formation of the nation-state emerging from a welter of conflicting political, military, and religious loyalties, was due in Western Europe at the end of the Middle Ages, as it is today in non-Western areas, to the paramount role of strong individuals—England's Henry VIII and Queen Elizabeth, or France's Louis IX and Louis XIV. If we could draw counsel from this experience, and stop demanding greater speed and riper wisdom on the part of Asia, the Middle East, and Africa than the West was able to display, we might be better prepared than we now are to help them in their adjustment to the twentieth-century world.

The West, however, finds it not only difficult, but even dangerous, to view this process of change with equanimity when it sees the possibility that communism, rather than democracy, may benefit by the transition from colonialism to national independence in the non-Western areas. Why, we ask ourselves, does communism have such an appeal to the new nations or those still struggling to be born? Why is not democracy their primary goal?

While the democracies felt little compunction, at the outset, in creating colonial empires and in fact believed, often sincerely, that they were bestowing great benefits on the "children of darkness" in "heathen lands," democratic colonialism, by definition, was bound to prove self-liquidating. For no matter how outwardly ruthless the treatment of colonial peoples—and the record of the Western powers, in spite of post-World War II efforts at its rehabilitation, is by no means free from the stains of cruelty, mismanagement, and indifference to human values—the colonies were sooner or later affected by the democratic ideas held in the metropolitan country, in Britain and France, in Belgium and the Netherlands. The liberal or revolutionary ideas of Mazzini and Garibaldi, of Mill and

Bentham, of the French Revolution, inspired those who struggled for independence in the colonies. Here was a striking example of the power of ideas, which broke down military defenses, bureaucratic safeguards, and economic barriers.

Defenders of democracy in London and Paris, in Brussels and Amsterdam were vigilant in their attempts to emphasize the irreconcilability of democratic faith with authoritarian rule over colonial peoples. But no matter how great their good will or how lofty their ideals, they found it well-nigh impossible to dissociate themselves from their own environment, traditions, and customs, and to meet the colonial peoples without self-consciousness on a basis of genuine equality until these peoples had achieved independence. Moreover, they insisted that these peoples could be worthy of independence only if they showed the capacity to practice Western-type democracy and, since this goal was usually unattainable, rationalized by saying that the time for independence had not yet arrived. This, as Charles Issawi of Egypt has well said, set up a vicious circle, whereas what was needed was a "virtuous" circle of ideas which would start by admitting that democracy could not be the first step of backward peoples in their struggle to achieve independence, even if under favorable circumstances it might be the last.

This is why communism found it possible to play a role which made it appear as the champion of the poor, the downtrodden, the oppressed in the colonial world. Communism proclaimed its essential anti-colonialism and its solidarity with colonial areas, past or present. By contrast, capitalism was long identified with imperialism, and the democracies themselves believed that their way of life was not an export product.

Moreover, the impact of colonialism, aided by the efforts of Christian missionaries of all faiths to convert the non-Christians, had caused the disintegration of the pre-colonial social and economic order and had raised gnawing doubts about the adequacy of native religions without bringing new values in their place. The spiritual vacuum thus created was made to order for communism. The Communist party, militant by character, assumed the role of an international Robin Hood, the defender of the poor and the oppressed.

The past experience of the non-Western areas, whether under native rulers or colonial administrators, had been on the whole authoritarian in character. Communism, therefore, did not represent as violent a change for them as it would have been for the West. To give but one example, it was difficult to make a clear-cut choice between the authoritarian regime of Chiang

Kai-shek on Formosa, with its secret police, its arbitrary executions and its suppression of criticism, and the totalitarianism of the Communist regime on the mainland. Only in countries where the basic experience of the people has proved vastly different from communism over a long period of years, notably India, is there a possibility of genuine grass-roots resistance to Communist influence.

Communism also identified itself with the deep-seated aspirations of the non-Western peoples. It identified itself with the spirit of change in general, with land reform and industrialization, with the secular state, with literacy and adjustment to modern technology. Communism thus looked as if it were the modern, advanced ideology. The colonial powers, by contrast, were too often identified with resistance to change, with the desire to maintain the status quo with opposition to all new ideas which might spell disturbance of the existing order. Moreover, the tendency of the West to equate any agitation in favor of change with communism, even if this was well known locally not to be the case, cast doubts on the veracity and integrity of spokesmen for democracy.

The attraction of communism has been well described by Gabriel Almond in his book, *The Appeals of Communism*. He found in studying communism in France and Italy—and his conclusions hold even more true of non-Western areas—that men and women who abandoned the Communist party wanted to turn not to a conservative group but to a militant left movement. They rejected the authoritarianism of the Communists, their rigid discipline, their manipulations, and their subservience to the U.S.S.R. But they still sought a party which would fight vigorously for the interests of the working class, and of the poorer groups generally. In both France and Italy the existing Socialist movements were viewed as too weak, ineffective, and splintered to provide an adequate alternative. Despite this dissatisfaction, however, the largest proportion of deserters from communism gravitated to socialist parties—not to middle-of-the-road groups—and this conclusion, too, holds true for non-Western areas.

Paradoxically, the stage of development at which communism emerges in non-Western areas is the stage when they begin to see at least a faint hope of economic and social improvement. The West must therefore realistically face the prospect that the more aid we give to backward areas, the more rapidly they will, for a period at least, become interested in communism—not in being ruled by the U.S.S.R. or Communist China, but in the ideas and techniques which have enabled Moscow in less than half a century to catch up with the technical development of the West, up to and including A- and H-bombs and guided missiles. At that stage it is particularly important for the West not to become synonymous with reaction.

In assessing the relative strength of democracy and communism in their contest for the minds and hearts of the non-Western peoples, who are also for the most part the "uncommitted" peoples, the West must not confuse the influence and power of Russia or China as national states, or even as foci of communism, with the influence and power of Communist ideas. Whatever may be our justifiable objections to and our legitimate measures of defense against Russia or China, we shall make, to use Gandhi's phrase about one of his own decisions, a "Himalayan miscalculation" if we assume that the maladjustments, turmoil, and clashes we see in Asia or the Middle East or Africa are due, first and foremost, to intervention by Moscow or Peiping. The Communists of Russia and China capitalize on these conditions, turn them to their own advantage, and use them mercilessly to castigate the West. But they did not create them; nor will the democracies cure them merely by denouncing communism or even destroying the Russian and Chinese states.

The success of communism in the non-Western areas is due primarily to the perspicacity and skill of Communist leaders in understanding that the two objectives most urgently sought by peoples now emerging from colonial rule or still living under it are national identity and economic improvement. The Communists, in spite of their dedication to an international movement which is supposed to know no frontiers, have perceived that the phase of nationalism which characterized the development of Western states cannot be bypassed, or wished out of existence.

Yet this search for a "national personality," to use Premier Nasser's striking phrase about Egypt, is a craving as powerful as hunger in the individual, and is capable of overcoming a multiplicity of languages as in India, or abject poverty as in Egypt, or the complexities of a multiracial and multireligious society as in Israel or Malaya. By espousing the cause of nationalism, the Communists won a great asset. But they may also have forged the instrument of their own defeat. For, as Yugoslavia demonstrated by its defiance of Moscow's dictation, nationalism is no respecter of ideologies. It can fission international communism as it has fissioned democratic colonialism. Its explosive character indicates that the world is yet far from the stage when national sovereignty will bow to international considerations, and has forced the Soviet leaders to recognize, notably in their relations with Communist Marshal Tito and with Poland's Communist leader Gomulka (although not in anti-Communist Hungary), that there can be more than one variety of socialism, just as there is more than one variety of democracy.

The Communists have also shown perspicacity and skill in recognizing the urge of non-Western peoples to improve their economic conditions as rapidly as possible, and to do so not merely as recipients of charity from advanced nations, but through their own efforts, both by constructive enterprise at home and by trade with the rest of the world. This has been all the easier for the Communists because the Soviet bloc, from East Germany to China, needs a wide range of raw materials, foods, and consumer goods, which the non-Western areas now produce or could arrange to produce in the future. The Western nations, particularly the United States, have been generous in providing financial aid, technical assistance, and gifts in kind, but have not always been fully aware of the sense of pride—a concomitant of the spirit of national freedom—which animates the former colonial peoples, who, now that they have achieved political independence, want economic independence as well. Nor have Westerners been quick to understand that the underdeveloped nations cannot be expected to have the will to defend themselves against what Secretary of State John Foster Dulles described as the "predatory" character of Russia's offers of aid unless they already have, at home, economic and social achievements worth defending.

Thus, as the non-Western peoples gradually shed the constricting ties of colonialism, they use their new-won freedom to weigh the relative appeals of democracy and communism. As they telescope into a short period of time the several revolutions which made the West and Russia what they are in the twentieth century, they seek to discover their own ways of dealing with the vast political and social problems that confront them once they have crossed the threshold of independence.

11

Retooling for the Future

The overthrow by revolution of a native government or the achievement of national independence from colonial rule by a Western power, is only the first, if the most dramatic, act in the effort which a non-Western people must make to move from whatever age it is living in—neolithic, feudal, or early nineteenth century—into the nuclear age. It must then retool itself for the new tasks which it could foresee only dimly, if at all, in the period of ferment when its entire attention was focused on the immediate objective of revolution or nationalist struggle for independence.

Political Problems

In the wake of revolution or victory over a colonial ruler, three main political problems emerge. First the revolutionary or nationalist movement—or, as frequently happens in this era of telescoped changes, a combination of the two—must be reoriented into a responsible administration. This is a far from easy task. Usually the movement has been composed of many diverse elements rallied into a single organization (the Congress in India, the Muslim League for Pakistan, the independence movements in Burma and Indonesia, and so on). Political and economic groups which had little or nothing in common except the desire to end an intolerable situation may find that, once the struggle against a common enemy has been won, they no longer have any reason to stay together. They may drift apart, or even come to blows with each other in the endeavor to win power and satisfy group or individual ambitions. The once monolithic opposition to native tyranny or foreign domination may develop unexpected fissures—right and left wings discontented with a moderate center, Socialists who cannot put up with conservatives, and vice versa,

Communists who challenge religious and business authority, military leaders who question the soundness of civilians.

Once the first act of glorious achievement is over, the curtain rises again on sober and often somber scenes where the former leaders of a joint crusade must rapidly, and in full sight of the spectators who are about to become voters, take on new roles, learn fresh lines, and assume new responsibilities. Nor can they rely any more, as they did while the struggle for liberation was under way, on denunciation of an unpopular native ruler, such as King Farouk in Egypt or Emperor Bao Dai in Indochina, or of foreign "exploiters" such as the British in Egypt and the French in North Africa, as the one and only source of all trouble, as the universal scapegoat. Henceforth, if anything goes wrong, they may find themselves in the unaccustomed role of target for attack by new spokesmen of their peoples, held up to opprobrium for failures or alleged mistakes.

Second, without a moment's delay, they must undertake the political reorganization of the country they have freed from the rule of others, before a vacuum dangerous for their own survival can develop. Since the leaders of non-Western nations must usually deal with populations which are largely illiterate and for the most part unacquainted with democratic methods of government, they must promptly decide whether they should, as in a Western democracy, ascertain the will of the people through elections before they take political action or, using their own best judgment, shape the new polity in accordance with what they believe to be the interests of their fellow citizens.

This decision may have to be made at a time when the new nation is in the throes of civil strife—as, for instance, in Russia in 1917, shaken by a disastrous war and racked by revolution, or India, rent by bloody Hindu-Muslim riots in the wake of partition, or China, spent after nearly twenty years of internal conflicts and war with Japan. The most likely result, then, is resort by those in power to some form of authoritarianism, whether the totalitarian dictatorship of Communists in Russia or China, or the practically unchallenged personal rule of Nehru in India, U Nu in Burma, Sukarno in Indonesia. Quite apart from the dictatorial concepts and practices of communism, the overwhelming problems of the retooling period invite, if they do not necessarily justify, the application of the "father knows best" policy, or what Sukarno has called "guided democracy." Such a policy, whether or not this is recognized by its spokesmen, may not be fundamentally different from that of the native ruler or colonial power they have just overthrown except in its aspirations for ultimate liberalization.

Out of the turmoil of the post-revolutionary or post-liberation period there almost invariably emerges a leader who crystallizes in his own person the aspirations and hopes of his people. This leader may be a military man, like Kemal Ataturk in Turkey, Naguib, and then Nasser, in Egypt, Perón in Argentina, General Iskander Mirza, first president of the Islamic Republic of Pakistan, or Marshal Tito of Yugoslavia. Or he may be a civilian, like Nehru in India, U Nu in Burma, Sukarno in Indonesia, Lenin, and then Stalin, in Russia, Mao Tse-tung in China, or Dr. Syngman Rhee in South Korea. These leaders have one thing in common: each is a charismatic personality—a personality who, in the eyes of his people, has a more than human endowment, a touch of divine grace and special wisdom, which fits him in a way no one else in the country is fitted for the office to which God, or destiny, or the will of the people as he senses it has called him. Under these circumstances he would, as he sees it, be acting against God, destiny, or the will of the people if he should humbly reject the responsibility thrust upon him, or refuse, at a subsequent time, to persist in his efforts for the common good.

Nor is this charismatic aspect, which can easily transform the leader into a "father image" for his nation, merely a figment of his imagination or that of his fellow-citizens. During the period of transition, a powerful personality who enjoys widespread confidence can, and often does, succeed in creating the bases for what may eventually become a form of democracy. The democracy of India, or Russia, or Indonesia, or China may turn out to be very different from that of the United States, Britain, and France—but let us remember that by World War II advanced industrial nations like Germany and Japan had not yet achieved what the West describes as democracy.

Once political reorganization has been effected, the authoritarian ruler must face a third task—that of carrying out "the revolution of greater expectations" which he and his associates fostered during the preceding struggle and of fulfilling the promises of a better, richer, happier life they had held out as the guerdon of a new era. At this point, again, the leader must decide whether the eagerly anticipated economic and social changes are to be carried out by peaceful means, primarily through voluntary partnership between the state and the individual, with genuine respect for human rights and freedoms, or by force, through a system imposed on the individual from above, with little or no concern for his comfort, liberty, or desires. The Congress party of India, under the leadership of Nehru, has chosen the voluntary way. The Communist party in Russia and China has hitherto followed the way of dictatorship and force. In Turkey, Kemal Ataturk and in Egypt, Premier Nasser have used both the carrot and the stick.

But whatever the choice, the problem faced by the governments of all non-Western nations is to discover or to create, as rapidly as possible, a common ground on which conflicting elements can genuinely pursue the national interest without becoming engaged in political struggles that might rend the fabric of a society still in the process of formation and jeopardize its survival. Only once this common ground has been established, once the period of storm and stress has been traversed, is it possible for non-Western leaders to consider how they can broaden the base of political power, encourage free elections, afford unchallenged protection for civil rights, and foster a sense of community responsibility and dedication on the part of the individual citizen to the welfare of the country as a whole.

The process of retooling for change in non-Western nations proceeds, as it did in the West at a comparable stage of development, in all sectors of society. It involves profound psychological adjustments on the part of every individual tantamount to a personal revolution—a revolution in thought patterns, in habits of living, in the individual's relations to the state, to religion, to the family, and to the social group within which he was born and the professional group with which he works.

First—and most important in societies where one or at most a few political personalities set the example for their fellow citizens and direct their actions, with or without resort to force—the leader of the revolutionary or independence movement must adjust himself to the role of leader of a responsible, although not necessarily a representative, government. For example, in India, Nehru and Gandhi in their noncooperation movement against the British deprecated the use of force and advocated nonviolent methods to oust the foreign ruler—such as civil disobedience, which took the form of student nonattendance at universities, or the practice of having men, women, and children display passive resistance to the authorities by lying down on the tracks of railways and street cars, or long-term fasting as a form of pressure on British opinion.

Upon coming to power, however, they found that these methods, when used by their fellow citizens to defy the Republic of India, were detrimental to the security and stability of the newly independent state. Nehru has not hesitated to use troops or police to prevent Communist agitation, as in Hyderabad, or riots about linguistic reapportionment of India's component states, as in Bombay in 1956. He has deprecated the "lie-down" tactics of the Dravidians in the state of Madras, who chose this method to protest against New Delhi's insistence on the adoption of Hindi as an official language, which is resented by the South Indians with something of the same passion with which the American South has resented "damn Yankees." In 1953 he pleaded with one of his independence-movement collaborators to give up a fast initiated for the purpose of persuading the government to create a new state, Andhra, for the Telegu-speaking population. And he has eloquently urged the people of India to think in terms of national unity, not of language or geographic loyalties.

Second, the political leader may also find that the dominant religious organization, which was an asset in cementing the nationalist struggle against foreign rule, can become a liability after the objective of independence has been achieved. This is particularly true if the religious hierarchy resists social and economic change and demands the retention of traditional ways of life and thought which hamper post-independence reforms. The young officers who overthrew King Farouk in Egypt discovered that the Muslim Brotherhood, which had outdone political rebels in their attacks on the British before the Suez Canal base was relinquished in 1956, represented a threat to their reform program, and finally relegated its most outspoken leaders to the background after breaking the power of the king, of old-line parliamentary politicians, and of industrialists and bankers who had supported Farouk. In Guatemala the anti-Communist government of Colonel Armas, after ousting the pro-Communist regime of Jacobo Arbenz with the aid of the Catholic Church, then found that the Church intended to participate actively in political life—a course bitterly opposed by many of Armas' political supporters.

And, third, the political leadership can be greatly aided or dangerously hampered by the bureaucracy it has inherited from the past. The bureaucrat, familiar with the intricacies of administration, must face, perhaps at a relatively advanced stage in life, the often painful need to readjust his outlook to changed conditions. If he has become intimately linked with the regime which has been overthrown or persuaded to withdraw, he may find himself unable to work satisfactorily with the new masters, or may even be rejected by them as out of harmony with their purposes or as an alleged "stooge" of the Western ruler.

Even if he accepts the new order and is in turn found acceptable, he must still overcome the hurdle of changing from a bureaucrat who worked hand-in-glove with a vanished colonial ruling group exercising more or less authoritarian rule, into a servant of his own people, responsible to an elected government and a popular assembly. He will be tempted, as happened in the case of some able and upright members of the Indian Civil Service organized by the British, to assume the "father-knows-best" attitude for which nationalists have criticized the colonial rulers, to enjoy the privileges, emoluments, and fleshpots of power once reserved almost exclusively for the foreign rulers, and to resent public criticism or scrutiny of his actions.

Economic Problems

It is not enough, however, for political leader and bureaucrat to readjust their sights to the responsibilities of governing a state free of foreign domination. They must also, without delay, devise ways and means of reorganizing the nation's economy, which to a greater or lesser degree has become dependent on some form of assistance from the colonial power—military, or economic, or financial, or a combination of all these. The people have been encouraged by nationalists to believe that independence would bring not only freedom from foreign rule, but also improvement in living standards. Mere continuance of the past, at a moment when a nation has reached a turning-point in its history, may be regarded by the impatient, the idealistic, and the ambitious as unwarranted conservatism, or even denounced as reaction—a trend on which the Communists are quick to capitalize.

Yet the far-reaching economic and financial reforms which are required to set the nation on a new course are usually resisted, at this stage, by the landowners whose land in excess of a set maximum is being demanded for redistribution to the landless, and by the as yet small but often powerful group of entrepreneurs who have been creating the rudiments of industrialization. The landowner must be persuaded of the need to provide an improved standard of living for the peasants and to increase the agricultural productivity of the nation as a whole. The entrepreneur, who at this stage of development is likely to be a speculator in commodities, such as cotton, sugar, and jute, must be persuaded that both he and the nation will benefit over the long run if, instead of merely trying to speculate on the sale and purchase of commodities, he, in effect, becomes a capitalist, by investing capital in industry, and thereby accelerates his country's transition to a modern economy. The "financial expert," to quote the title of an Indian novel which has a wily moneylender as its central character, must be transformed from a man who lends money to poor peasants or townsmen at exorbitant rates (which sometimes reach 30 or 40 per cent), chiefly for consumer goods and celebrations such as weddings or burials, into a banker who lends money at reasonable rates for constructive purposes—house building, purchase of machinery and draft animals, establishment of small businesses, and so on. The foreign businessman who decides to remain after the achievement of independence must learn to train local personnel at all levels, not only clerks but managers and technicians; to share his profits more equitably with the government, as in the case of Western oil companies like Aramco in Saudi Arabia; to invite and encourage local investment; and to consider first of all the needs and interests of the country where he does business, not solely those of his own enterprise or nation.

Once this reorientation has taken place, the new nation, which usually has a small and relatively weak middle class, will be able to develop its own group of managers and technicians, instead of remaining indefinitely dependent on the technical knowledge and guidance of foreign powers. The importance of this readjustment is strikingly illustrated by the problems non-Western nations face in their efforts to harness atomic energy for their economic development. These nations—India and the Philippines, Pakistan and Indonesia, to mention only a few—are all eager to obtain atomic reactors from the three great powers which have made the greatest advances in atomic development—Britain, the United States, and the U.S.S.R. But with the exception of India, where Nehru has taken a personal interest in spurring the development of the Tata atomic energy project in Bombay, these countries have as yet few or no technicians of their own trained to operate atomic equipment, and are particularly reluctant to make use of foreign personnel. This desire to develop native technicians and managers as rapidly as possible is a challenge to the West, which belatedly recognized that the U.S.S.R., having emphasized scientific education for many years, is now ready to export technicians abroad in large numbers and train local people for the operation of modern machinery. By contrast the technicians of advanced Western nations, who enjoy remunerative employment at home under comfortable circumstances, are reluctant to go abroad for any length of time except at rates of pay which are exorbitant by non-Western standards.

The new managers and technicians of non-Western lands face a problem which did not exist to any significant extent in the Western nations at a comparable stage of retooling for industrialization. This problem is that workers, and to a lesser degree peasants as well, expect and demand human welfare conditions which the West attained only with the full flowering of modern industry in the twentieth century. Irrespective of whether a newly independent non-Western nation has the resources to fulfill these conditions, the spokesmen of peasants and workers, particularly those who have been organized into unions, press the government for immediate fulfillment of their demands. The government, already harassed by the many-faceted tasks of political and economic reorganization, must either satisfy these demands, at least in part, or run the danger of being undercut by the Communists, who make high-sounding promises, whether or not they deliver on them once they are in power.

The non-Western nations face another politico-social problem unknown to the West. Peasant and labor leaders who speak for the hitherto voiceless masses which in the past had little influence on either native or foreign rulers emerge on the scene more or less at the same time as the new middle class, instead of following it chronologically, as happened in Western countries. As a result the middle class cannot exert the stabilizing influence it might have wielded in an era of gradual social adjustments. Instead, the old pattern of a society dominated by the family group, as in China, or by the combination of family and caste, as in India, disintegrates with lightning rapidity under the impact of Western ideas, of industrialization, of scientific knowledge, of political change. The individual, who in the past enjoyed the economic protection of caste or family, which gave him a sense of stability within an accepted order, suddenly finds himself uprooted, often disoriented, and subject to all the pressures and frustrations familiar in the urban communities of the West. He becomes one of "the lonely crowd."

If he is not to fall prey to the enticements of the demagogue and find refuge in the disciplined ranks of a totalitarian movement—communism or religious fanaticism—the non-Western nation must discover ways and means of integrating him into the new order, and hold out to him the hope of gradual but steady improvement for himself and his family. And he, for his part, must learn to become not merely an object either of repression or benevolence by native autocrat or foreign ruler, or of demagogic pressure, but a human being who can stand on his own feet, can speak for himself, and can not only assert his rights but exercise his responsibilities in a newly free society.

Thus every element in the non-Western social order—the leader and the led, religion as well as politics and economics, ideas as well as machines—must be retooled for change if the nation is to tackle successfully the vast problems of independent existence. Population and food, land reform and industrialization, capital formation and technical assistance, education and employment, the reconciliation of human welfare with the stability and security of the state, the role the new nation is to play in world affairs—all these problems which once were in the hands of native rulers or Western colonial powers cry simultaneously for answers. And at the pace at which mankind is moving in the nuclear age, these answers must be found not in some distant future, but today.

Population and Food

In their arduous efforts to telescope into a few decades the economic and social revolutions which it took the nations of the West several centuries to achieve, the non-Western peoples face what at first sight seems an insuperable obstacle. This obstacle is not new. It was defined in 1798 by the English clergyman and economist Thomas Robert Malthus, who said in his *Essay on the Principle of Population* that all species of plants and animals, including man, tend to increase faster than the means of subsistence.

It was Malthus' belief that the utmost development of agriculture and industry cannot possibly keep pace with a population growth arising from a natural birth rate and a modern reduced death rate. He consequently argued that population growth must be controlled either by "positive checks," which increase the death rate—wars, pestilences, epidemics—or by "preventive checks," which reduce the birth rate. In short, as he saw it, mankind faced a perilous race between production and reproduction.

Was Malthus right? And if he was right about Europe on the eve of the nineteenth century, then what hope do the peoples of Asia and the Middle East, of Africa and Latin America, have of overcoming the current disproportion between their vast populations and their as yet limited production capacities?

Those who believe that Malthus may be proved wrong base their optimism primarily on the experience of the Western nations. During the century and a half, 1800 to 1950, which followed Malthus' prophecy, the population of Northwestern Europe, by an increase never before seen in history, doubled in size. Yet not only were food resources found for its sustenance through improved agriculture and expanded foreign trade, but Europe, and to an even greater degree North America, achieved the highest living standards known to man. In one important respect, however, Malthus was proved to be right. The population of the West, as it moved into urban centers, did adopt preventive checks in the form of family planning.

It should be noted, however, that the West had an initial advantage over the non-West when it entered the period of industrialization—an advantage which for the non-West is in the realm of fantasy—and that is a numerically small population. This made it possible for the Western nations to make their demograhic transition in a gradual way, without facing the anxiety about day-to-day survival which constantly haunts the political leaders of India, with 360 million, China with close to 600 million, or Japan with 90 million crowded in a cluster of small islands.

In this gradual process of adjustment, the Western peoples were also greatly aided by the advances they were able to make in agriculture, which, in turn, permitted them to increase their output of food and to release manpower from the land for work in industry. The most striking example of this changeover is the United States, where 10 per cent of the population provide ample food for the other 90 per cent, as compared with India, where 80 per cent of the population are engaged in primitive agriculture. Manpower thus released in turn accelerated the spread of industrialization, which not only provided machinery for agriculture, transportation, and communication, but also, by expanding urban life, created conditions favorable to the adoption of "preventive checks" on population growth. Industrial expansion, moreover, made it possible for the Western nations which could not supply their entire food needs—notably Britain, Germany, Belgium, and Italy—to export manufactured goods in payment for imported food and raw materials.

Even with this expansion in productivity, the experience of the Western nations might have proved Malthus right if at the peak of their population growth they had not found an outlet for increasing populations through emigration to overseas territories—in the New World, Australia, New Zealand, and South Africa—which together have absorbed 60 million Europeans since the beginning of the nineteenth century. During the period 1650-1950, the population of Europe (not including the U.S.S.R.) increased by about 300 million, but 400 million people of European descent now live outside Europe. One can only speculate as to what might have happened to Europe and its civilization if emigration outlets, sources of raw materials, and markets had not been opened up outside its confines by the explorers, administrators, and merchants of Britain, France, Spain, Portugal, and Italy. "Without this frontier," says Walter Prescott Webb in his article *Ended: Four Hundred Year Boom,* "modern Europe would have been so different from what it is today that it could hardly be considered modern at all."

The fulfillment of Malthus' dire prophecy, moreover, was postponed in the Western nations by the acquisition of colonial empires, whose food and raw materials supplemented the resources of the mother countries and thereby facilitated the maintenance of high living standards which would otherwise have proved impossible. Meanwhile, the increase in food supplies, which led to improvement of diets, and the development of modern medicine and public health, which gradually eliminated communicable diseases such as smallpox, tuberculosis, and typhoid and opened up the prospect of disease control through the use of antibiotics, cut down death rates from about 30 per thousand in the seventeenth century to less than 12 per thousand in 1950, and raised life expectancy to 70 years, as compared with 35 years during the Middle Ages in Europe and less than 20 years during the Bronze and Iron Ages in Greece.

The decline in death rates and the corollary rise in life expectancy, however, would have merely resulted in a sharp rise of population growth—as has hitherto proved true in the underdeveloped countries—had it not been for a decline in the birth rate during the century 1850-1950. Before World War II birth rates had declined to less than 16 per thousand in Britain, France, Germany, and the Scandinavian countries, and even the birth rate of heavily populated Italy had dropped to 17.6 in 1952. Yet death rates were still lower—about 12 per thousand—and as a result populations continued to grow even in countries of low birth rates, with a continuing increase in the old-age brackets. It is important to note that in the West the reduction in the birth rate tended to follow, rather than to precede, the decline in the death rate and the general rise in living standards. This decline is generally attributed to the altered pattern of life and the new motivations created by urban existence. The over-all process of adjustment, which took 150 years, ended rapid population growth and brought about a demographic equilibrium.

If the experience of the 20 per cent of the world's people—in Western Europe, the United States and Canada, Australia, and New Zealand—is a reliable guide, then the 80 per cent who have not yet achieved a comparable demographic transition face a frighteningly complex task. Starting in most cases with already vast populations, the countries of Asia, Africa, the Middle East, and Latin America, which contain nearly two-thirds of the world's inhabitants, must find ways and means of checking further growth while they still depend for their subsistence on backward agriculture and an industrialization that is as yet in its early stages. Compared to the United States with an average annual per capita income of $1,750 or even the U.S.S.R. with $300, these countries have incomes ranging from $23 to $75 and face a life expectancy less than half of that in the Western nations, with low levels of health due to inadequate nutrition.

In the underdeveloped countries, actual and potential population growth remains high, owing to the combination of high birth rates and reduced death rates. The tragic paradox, as can be seen in the case of India, is that the introduction of public health programs, while eventually beneficial to the population as a whole, has the result, in its initial stages, of sharply reducing death rates, thereby leading, along with the maintenance of a high birth rate, to a population growth of about 3 per cent annually in spite of low living standards. In Ceylon, to take another example, a successful anti-malaria campaign sharply reduced the death rate, but since no measures were taken to reduce the high birth rate, this public health achievement is expected to double Ceylon's population in twenty years—with no comparable increase in food production and commerce in sight.

Poverty, lack of privacy, and ignorance of modern science, moreover, make the introduction and application of preventive checks difficult, even in countries like India, Japan, and Egypt, where religion and custom do not block planned parenthood. The sad result of this situation is that positive checks—wars, pestilences, disease—would actually help to relieve grave population problems, and, as in earlier centuries in western Europe, do not create the sense of dismay and horror which would greet them today in Europe, the Commonwealth, and North America.

Of the remedies which were open to the West in the period between 1800 and 1950, emigration and colonization are not available to the underdeveloped countries except on an insignificant scale and under perilous risk of war, as Japan discovered when it attempted to colonize Manchuria in the 1930's and to conquer Southeast Asia in the 1940's. There are few areas today that are not already well populated, and in those few—such as Australia, which still has wide-open spaces for settlement—insistence on "white" immigration, which Australians share with South Africans, effectively precludes large-scale emigration from countries with vast populations, such as India, China, and Japan.

What the underdeveloped lands can and must do if their population growth is not to attain fantastic proportions, with "standing room only," is to develop their agriculture as rapidly as possible so as to expand their output of food, cut down on food imports, which divert resources of foreign currency from industrialization, and release manpower from farm labor for work in new industrial establishments. It is doubtful, however, as we shall see in a moment, whether most of the underdeveloped nations will find it advisable or feasible to undertake large-scale industrialization in the immediate future, since many of them lack the combination of iron and coal, or iron and oil and hydroelectric power, which made possible the development of Pittsburgh and Detroit, of the Ruhr and the Donbas, of the Urals and of Canada.

The more promising approach, both from the point of view of human welfare and of widespread even if modest improvement in living standards, may be the combination of small-scale industries meshed with village community development projects which is under way in India and is contemplated in

Egypt. The avoidance of rapid urbanization, however, could delay the adoption of preventive checks and thereby delay, also, the stabilization, let alone reduction, of population growth. This problem will be further complicated by a continuing decline in the death rate, made inevitable by the adoption of modern public health measures, enriched diets, and generally improved health conditions. In contrast to the West, the non-Western nations face the seemingly insuperable task of reducing their birth rate not *after* they have completed their changeover to modernized agriculture and to industrialization, but *parallel with* this process of adjustment.

It is the magnitude of this task which causes pessimists, both in West and non-West, to wonder whether Malthus, although proved not to be a prophet in his own country, may turn out to be right in the non-Western sector of the world. The populations of this sector have for the most part increased substantially during the century 1850-1950 which witnessed the gradual decline and stabilization of populations in Western nations. It is estimated that 100,000 people are being born every day, and at this rate the world's total population of two and a half billion may reach four billion in the year 2000. Experts believe that in the future the decline in the death rate may be more rapid, and less dependent than in the past on over-all economic progress. During the decade 1936-46, for example, death rate declines ranged from nearly 40 per cent in Puerto Rico to about 11 per cent in Guatemala.

Seen in this frame of reference, the population problem of most of the non-Western nations—there are some exceptions, notably Indonesia with its relatively more favorable ratio of population to resources, parts of Africa, and a few countries of Latin America—would seem to justify Malthus' grim prophecy. Production may not keep up with reproduction. The problem is enhanced in our times by the demand of non-Western peoples for a rapid rise in living standards which in Europe, at a comparable stage of development, were reserved for a tiny minority at the top of the social pyramid, and even then became available through a combination of circumstances most of which, as already pointed out, cannot be expected to recur in the case of the non-West.

Yet, quite aside from the basic fact that man, irrespective of color, race, or stage of development, finds it difficult to accept an answer dictated by despair, the West's own experience in the modern era points to some possibilities which over a period of years might at least alleviate the dire prospect of a world with more people than there are resources to keep them alive.

First, while positive checks on population growth are rapidly disappearing with the decline in contagious diseases, improvements in public health, and the well-nigh universal desire to avoid the ultimate catastrophe of nuclear war, preventive checks are becoming both more acceptable and more readily accessible than in any previous period of history. Today "birth prevention," or planned parenthood, is officially opposed only from two sharply contrasting quarters—the Vatican, and Communist Russia, where birth prevention is regarded as an "imperialist" device designed to reduce the manpower of underdeveloped lands and keep them indefinitely in subjection to the West. By contrast, most of the non-Western non-Catholic nations which face a rapid increase of population growth—notably India, Japan, and Egypt—are not only willing but eager to practice planned parenthood, and even Communist China, departing in this respect from the example of the U.S.S.R., apparently has among its leaders men and women who recommend preventive checks. Nor do the principal religions of the non-Western world—Hinduism, Buddhism, Islam, or Confucianism—present obstacles to planned parenthood, although devout followers of Gandhi tend to agree with those Catholic population experts who object to "birth prevention" and advocate the use of the "rhythm method." Thoughtful Catholics, too, are studying the problems of overpopulation which, they believe, play into the hands of the Communists—as indicated by the decision of the Catholic Institute of Social Research at Geneva to offer a substantial award for the best proposal by a Catholic or non-Catholic for checking population growth.

The main problem, then, is not how to win public acceptance of measures that would check fertility, as was long true in some countries of western Europe and of the New World. The problem is how to devise a method of fertility control which would be sufficiently simple, inexpensive, and harmless to be used by people living in conditions of poverty, illiteracy, and often complete lack of privacy. Medical experts, however, are hopeful that such a method will be discovered in the foreseeable future, possibly through research into the use of materials obtainable in the non-Western countries themselves. And the experience of India, where men and women in a population 80 per cent illiterate have shown a lively and comprehending interest in "family planning" not only in cities but also in rural areas, appears to indicate that informed leadership—in this case provided by Prime Minister Nehru and his associates—combined with a popular understanding of existing conditions and a growing desire to improve the lot of children, may bring about a change in public attitudes much more rapidly than might have been previously expected.

Second, the very fact—otherwise seemingly unfavorable—that the non-West, unlike the West, must try to check population growth simultaneously with its efforts to accelerate economic development may, over the long run, prove an asset rather than a liability. The non-Western nations, if they are to survive at all, are forced to plan the utilization of their often limited resources of food and industrial raw materials in relation to existing and potential population. And planning, which makes the development process far more visible and understandable to the people involved than was possible in Western countries, where economic and social transition was stretched over centuries, focuses attention on the advantages that development may bring in the lifetime of men and women now living. Instead of accepting poverty, disease, and ignorance as their predestined lot, and merely hoping that death will either bring a welcome release or a glimpse of better things in another world, the peoples of non-Western nations can now see, at least in token form, the advances in health, education, and modest amenities of life which they, and in even greater measure their children, can hope to enjoy on earth.

If this hope can be kept alive, and increasingly justified by practical achievements, the long time-span of population decline through urbanization which Western experience has assumed to be necessary may be considerably reduced, possibly without waiting for the spread of city life, provided modern improvements can be brought to rural areas—an approach used, in varying degrees and different forms, by India and Egypt, Russia and Israel. The necessity of fulfilling this hope if the world as a whole, and not only the non-West, is to avoid the population explosion predicted by some pessimistic experts, could be a far stronger motivation for increased long-term financial and technical aid by advanced Western nations than the negative fear of communism. This fear, in turn, will gradually diminish as greater well-being, brought about by population decline or at least stabilization, permits increasingly improved labor output by healthier and better-educated men and women who will be better prepared to compete in world markets for higher money incomes than they could dream of obtaining today.

And, third, it is not unreasonably optimistic to believe that the discoveries of modern science, which were not available to the West during its demographic transition, can be utilized to cancel, or at least shorten, the time factor which would otherwise seem to justify Malthus' prognostication. The non-Western nations which lack the natural resources that enabled western Europe, the United States, and the Commonwealth to expand industrialization and modernize agriculture may find alternatives in atomic energy and solar heat, in newly developed methods of conquering tropical desert and arctic wastes, in photosynthesis and other ways of creating edible nourishment in laboratories. Asia and the Middle East, Africa and Latin America, have already shown how twentieth-century techniques can cancel centuries by jumping, in many instances, over the railway age, from the burro or camel, from the ox-cart and the rickshaw, to the truck and automobile and, most dramatically, to the airplane used as a generally accepted mode of transcending the obstacles of vast distances, or, to cite another example, from the papyrus and the village story-tellers to radio and television used for educational purposes.

Can Science Cancel Time?

In the non-Western world science has today become a new form of faith, as it once was for the West during and after the Renaissance, when the belief in the perfectibility of man, often decried in our less optimistic times with its anxiety about the "decline of the West," became a cardinal feature of Western tradition. Now that we of the West, having gone through an era of nazism and Stalinism, of barbaric conduct and spiritual disenchantment, are sadder if not wiser, we are apt to look with the skepticism of adults at the pioneering ardor of peoples whose hope seems bright. But our skepticism, far from dampening the spirits of our contemporaries in other parts of the world, makes them wonder whether we may introduce a new form of imperialism by withholding from them the keys to a promised land of food, health, education, and technical achievements. This, they claim, leaves them no choice but to turn to the Communists for the aid they want and are determined to obtain—if necessary "from the devil himself," as some of their leaders do not hesitate to say.

This aid they need in three main sectors: expansion of food

resources, reduction and eventual elimination of disease, and acquisition of scientific skills to replace the industrial raw materials they do not possess on their own soil. These three sectors are, in fact, closely meshed. The hungry man lacks the strength to work and is not capable of resisting the inroads of disease. The hungry woman cannot bear a healthy child and nurture him or her to maturity. No human being who must scrounge for enough nourishment to provide a meal a day with an intake of 1,700 calories (compared with over 3,000 calories a day in the United States and western Europe), as millions do in India, has the vitality, even if the possibility were available, to become literate and thus start on the education which might give him a chance to learn how to operate, or, more difficult still, build modern machines. And without machines, either in the field or in the workshop, he cannot hope to diversify the production of his village, his district, his nation. He cannot hope to make goods which would sell in world markets and bring him the cash he needs in order, gradually, to improve his own conditions and those of his family, and thereby, cumulatively, raise the living standards of his country.

Yet in this age, when science, to use Keats' beautiful phrase, opens "magic casements on perilous seas forlorn," the desires of peoples in underdeveloped lands are pitifully modest and easily realizable. Medical teamwork, small supplies of antibiotics and DDT or insecticides, readiness on the part of recipients to cooperate in the fulfillment of simple instructions, have in the short span of a few years ended yaws in the jungles of Southeast Asia, practically wiped out malaria in India and Ceylon, arrested tuberculosis in Asia, Africa, and Latin America, and prevented many infections that sap energy and shorten life. Doctors, nurses, and medical technicians from many lands have pooled their talents with an impressive spirit of dedication to prevent or cure disease under the aegis of the World Health Organization and the United Nations Technical Assistance program. And they spend what amounts to pennies on the task of building sound bodies or rebuilding broken lives as compared with the billions spent on preparation to launch or withstand nuclear attacks which might wipe out vast areas of the globe.

Meanwhile other dedicated experts, spurred by national scientific organizations as well as by the World Food and Agriculture Organization, have sought to expand existing resources of food. They encourage more efficient production by reforestation to stop soil erosion, use of fertilizers, insecticides, machinery. They push the frontiers of cultivation into arctic wastes and torrid deserts. They marshal the inventiveness of laboratories for the creation of synthetic foodstuffs to supplement, if not yet to replace, the nutrition made available by nature. The talents of Japanese rice-growers have been utilized by India to double its output of rice. The experience of agricultural extension workers from the United States has been applied in Asia and the Middle East to the improvement of seeds, the raising of poultry, the improvement of livestock through selectivity and artificial insemination. Norwegians have come to India to teach its coastal inhabitants the art of deep-sea fishing, which can provide new sources of food for the Indian's protein-poor diet. American investors, headed by the Rockefeller brothers, have put capital into refrigeration plants in Venezuela for the storage of perishable foods such as fish, which might otherwise go to waste. The U.S.S.R. has joined Western nations in using planes to fight locusts in the Middle East.

Russian agronomists have devised new varieties of fruit trees which can grow in arctic wastes, with little sun and heavy snowfalls, battered by harsh winds which had hitherto stunted all growing things. In Israel and Egypt, experts on desert conditions, unknown to each other, have boldly experimented with vegetation which might flourish in sandy wastes with a minimum of irrigation and have revived, for modern application, the use of "dew," mentioned in the Old Testament, as a source of desperately needed moisture. Deep-plowing tractors from Britian have helped to uproot the deep-rooted kans grass in India, thereby clearing for cultivation tracts of land which had been abandoned as hopeless.

In laboratories around the world, from Germany to India, from Britain to Japan, scientists have labored to extract nutritive elements from wood, to create new carbohydrates through artificial photosynthesis—the approximation of plant development under man-made conditions—and, most promising of all, to utilize fungi and algae which could furnish fats, proteins, and vitamins. Of the algae which have already been tested, the single-celled chlorella is believed to be potentially the most valuable in its high protein content. So far, both photosynthesis and the output of algae which human beings would find palatable are still expensive in terms of available scientific talent and actual cost of production. Nor can these methods be readily used by peoples who lack literacy, education, and technical training.

When these are available, however, as in Japan, where various algae are widely used to supplement a limited natural diet, they may become increasingly valuable, particularly if the possibilities of expanding arable land or of intensifying the output of living plants through modernization of machinery, application of fertilizer, and other methods cannot be expanded in a proportion adequate to population growth. Hopeful observers believe that dietitians, by giving more attention to ways and means of improving the edibility of algae, could persuade ill-fed people to eat, without repugnance, algae puddings or jellies, or soups enriched with algae. Everyone who has tried to alter the food habits of human beings—as American relief experts tried to do by urging Italians not to depend primarily on spaghetti or Indians to eat wheat in preference to rice—know from harsh experience the difficulty of persuading people to accept items of food they find repugnant for one reason or another. Yet careful educational preparation, particularly of women, who in the non-Western lands play a key role in shaping the customs of the family, may eventually overcome this hurdle.

With the modernizing of agriculture, as fewer workers are needed to produce the required amount of food, underdeveloped nations find it is not only possible but urgently necessary to diversify their output through industrialization. In many cases they suffer bitter disappointment on discovering that their hopes for improvement are nipped in the bud by the lack of essential energy resources, such as coal, oil, natural gas, or water, which could furnish hydroelectric power. Unfortunately for mankind, the world's resources are unevenly distributed over the earth's surface. Only a few nations—notably the United States and the U.S.S.R.—possess the combination of food and raw materials which can assure a more or less balanced economy capable of meeting the varied and complex requirements of the atomic age. In a nonscientific era this might have meant that some lands—for example, India and Israel and Egypt—were doomed to a harsh existence at a low level of human welfare unless they succeeded in conquering better-equipped territories by force, as Japan tried to do when it invaded Manchuria in the 1930's and Southeast Asia in the 1940's.

For raw materials, however, as for agriculture, science now opens up possibilities undreamed of a decade or two ago. Modern industry cannot operate without fuel and power. The great achievement of Western civilization has been to make use of resources unknown to earlier civilizations, which had to rely primarily on human muscles as a source of energy. The availability of cheap and abundant fuel and power has made it possible for the West to attain high living standards.

If the non-Western nations are to approach the living standards even approximating those of the Western nations, they will have to obtain far greater resources of energy than they command today. Can they obtain such resources, and if they can, how will their increased consumption affect the total resources of energy now available for the entire world?

Experts estimate that at the present rate of consumption, even assuming that the non-Western lands do not consume additional energy, available energy resources from all sources —coal, oil, natural gas, sun and hydroelectric power—would last less than a hundred years. Under the circumstances, the discovery that a new source of energy—atomic energy—can be produced through the process of fission and fusion which generates nuclear fuels has come none too soon if the Western nations are to maintain the living standards to which they have become accustomed, and if the non-Western nations are to effect the transition they dream of from backward agriculture to modern industry. This explains the eagerness with which the underdeveloped countries have welcomed the prospect of obtaining the means of producing atomic energy and the hope—regarded by some Westerners as premature—with which they look to atomic energy as the means to close the gap which now separates their economy from that of the West. The hope is particularly heartening to those nations, like Japan and Israel, which lack other sources of power and fuel, notably coal and oil, or to nations like India, which, although they have coal, find that the cost of transporting it to areas where iron and other industrial raw materials are located is prohibitive.

Britain, which spearheaded the Industrial Revolution by utilizing its coal to create power for industry, shares the interest of India and other underdeveloped nations in atomic energy. As its coal resources become exhausted, coal output grows increasingly expensive, and Britain has even been forced to "carry coals to Newcastle" from the United States, Poland, and West Germany, at a cost which imposes a heavy burden on the already strained British economy. Oil, regarded as essential for Britain's survival, must be imported from the Middle East, from which the British were cut off by the hostility of oil-producing Arab countries following their attacks on Suez in October 1956.

Alarmed by its fuel shortage, Britain has forged ahead of the United States by deciding to build twelve atomic energy reactors for peacetime purposes, all of which are to be completed by 1975. Although the cost of producing atomic energy will still be high, it is expected to compare favorably with that of extracting or importing coal—and may also compare favorably in the future with the cost, not only financial but military and moral, of maintaining overseas bases such as Cyprus for the defense of Britain's access to the oil of the Middle East. By contrast, the United States, which has not only coal, but ample oil resources within its own territory as well as access to the oil of the Caribbean, and can expand its hydroelectric power as well as its use of natural gas, is far less interested than either Britain or the U.S.S.R. and other non-Western areas in developing atomic energy for agricultural and industrial uses. In fact, the panel of laymen which prepared a report on the impact of the peaceful uses of atomic energy for the Joint Committee on Atomic Energy of the United States Congress in 1956, frankly pointed out that the use of atomic energy for agriculture would merely increase the surpluses this country is struggling to reduce, and thus add to the headaches of the American farmer, the American government, and the American taxpayer.

The United States, however, according to this report, has "a dramatic opportunity to lead underdeveloped, undernourished nations to higher living standards" by helping them to utilize atomic energy in the field of agriculture. With atomic radiation "we can hope to develop many more [useful new plant varieties]—types adaptable to wider ranges of climate, rain and soil; more resistant to diseases and insects; tailored to mechanized cultivation and harvesting. . . . We may . . . expect higher farm output, more flexibility as to the crops and animals produced, and ultimately more varied diets at lower costs." The cumulative impact of the application of atomic energy "will be an increase in the farmers' ability to specialize, diversify, and better deal with their traditional worst foes—weather, pests, and diseases."

This hopeful prospect opened to the non-Western peoples by the miracles of modern science cannot, however, be achieved by the waving of a magic wand. The peaceful uses of atomic energy, the report points out, "are particularly the tools of an advanced and mature technological and industrial community." This means that, before the non-Western nations can hope to use atomic energy in agriculture, they must obtain the means of developing their knowledge of the industrial processes for creating atomic energy. As the panel report points out, high-cost or energy-short countries may find that atomic power, even as generated from present reactors which, although high in cost, have been proved technically feasible, can be competitive with non-existent or prohibitively expensive conventional fuels—provided that they can obtain reactors and trained personnel to operate them. The United States, the panel concluded, should bring atomic power to the free world, by installing atomic electric generating plants in specific countries, accelerating the training of foreign technicians in nuclear research in friendly power-short countries needing greater industrialization, and speeding up the training of foreign technicians in nuclear research, which is already provided under bilateral agreements being negotiated with twenty-seven nations. In line with these recommendations, Washington has offered reactors to a number of countries, including India, Pakistan, Japan, and Turkey, and is assisting the development of the European atomic project, Euratom. It has also decided to create a nuclear center in the Philippines for the use of Southeast Asia. Meanwhile, the U.S.S.R. has promised reactors to Communist China and Egypt, and has announced the creation in Moscow of a nuclear research institute to service the entire Soviet bloc.

It is not enough, however, for the non-Western nations to have reactors and technicians. They must also have access to the raw materials of atomic energy—uranium, thorium, and monazite sands. Like other raw materials, those which provide atomic energy through fission and fusion are unevenly distributed over the surface of the earth. Uranium in large quantities is found in Canada, the Belgian Congo, the Portuguese colonies of Africa, in East Germany, and probably in the Central Asian area of the U.S.S.R., and is a by-product of gold waste in the Union of South Africa. India is in a peculiarly favorable position because it has its own sources of thorium and monazite sands.

As in the case of other raw materials, the underdeveloped nations fear that the advanced industrial powers—the United States, the U.S.S.R., and Britain—might try to corner uranium for their own atomic energy development, particularly if the atomic weapons race continues, and thus condemn them to economic backwardness. Whether or not this fear is justified, the very fact that it exists threatens to create a new split between the haves and have-nots—this time between the nations which either possess uranium or can control sources outside their borders through political pressures, and those which neither have such sources nor can hope to obtain them by political pressures. The struggle which may shape itself around uranium, as it has developed in the past around the coal of the Saar, the Ruhr, Upper Silesia, and the Donets Basin, and around the oil of the Middle East and the Baku area, emerged into the open during negotiations in Washington in March, 1956, for the formation of the United Nations atomic agency proposed by President Eisenhower. Statesmanship of a high order and mutual understanding will be necessary to prevent the possibility that the atomic arms race, which the Western powers hope to avert through control and inspection of atomic armaments, might be replaced by an atomic materials race on the part of nations determined to let nothing stand in the way of their plans for using the new source of energy to bring the plenty coveted by their peoples.

When the world's nuclear fuels are exhausted, as may prove to be the case in a few hundred years, hydrogen, which is in ample supply, is expected to provide energy requirements for an indefinite period. Solar energy, too, may be more effectively utilized in the future to generate heat and power—although its low temperature strictly limits its use for industrial purposes—as well as to help create organic matter through photosynthesis. Indians, as well as Americans, have been working on the construction of a solar stove which could concentrate the rays of the sun and utilize them for cooking, thereby eliminating the need to use cow dung or other agricultural waste for this purpose. Solar heating is of particular interest to India, where age-long deforestation has made the use of wood increasingly difficult, and the diversion of cow dung to fuel has been detrimental for the soil, starved of natural fertilizer.

Thus science can cancel time for the non-Western nations—but only if these nations can rapidly modernize their agriculture, make maximum use of machinery and fertilizers, reduce diseases among the peasants by the use of antibiotics, lower the fertility of rural populations, divert manpower to industrial enterprises, diversify their output of food and manufactured goods, aquire scientific skills necessary for work in laboratories where synthetic foods can be developed, harness atomic energy to industrial uses with all possible speed, and correlate all existing resources and talents for the development of the economy and the improvement of human welfare. Science, in short, is not a universal panacea. It can be the key that opens doors to the future—but only if the underdeveloped nations are willing to make the tremendous effort necessary to pass through these doors.

Before they do this, Asia and the Middle East, Africa and Latin America, must decide whether they should concentrate their limited resources of money and technical skills on the development of agriculture to feed their growing populations, or should focus, instead, on rapid industrialization—even at the expense of the immediate satisfaction of their basic needs.

Land Versus Industry

The Western nations did not have to make this Solomon-like choice between land and industry. Their economic development, spread over several centuries, was so gradual in pace that the underpinning of then modern agriculture could be created before the onset of the Industrial Revolution—with the result that a relatively well-fed, moderate-sized population was able to produce the tools and acquire the techniques of industry without endangering the future of food production. Today the percentages of total population engaged in agriculture in the West range from 33 for Europe, 20 for North America, and 10 for the intensive farming areas of the United States, such as Iowa, as compared with 70 to 80 per cent in Africa, Asia, and the Middle East; and out of the world's total of 2.5 billion people, 1.3 billion depend upon agriculture, of whom 1 billion live in Asia, Africa, and Central and South America.

The non-Western nations, under these circumstances, feel that they cannot afford to wait for a century or two of gradual adjustment to modern economic conditions, but must make, here and now, the choice, fraught with far-reaching consequences, between emphasis on agrarianism and emphasis on industrialization. This choice is complicated for them by the belief, widely prevalent in the non-Western world, that agriculture and raw-material production, which were the principal occupations of colonial territories under Western rule, are somehow inferior to industrial pursuits, which are regarded as both a unique attribute of the West and as the principal reason for its success in peace and war.

The resulting preoccupation with what might be called national economic status, which in some cases amounts to an obsession, causes one non-Western nation after another, once it has achieved independence, to insist on a measure of immediate industrialization, irrespective of whether it possesses the requisite raw materials, such as coal, oil, and iron, or the administrative and technical skills essential for industrial development. Moreover, the impression that "industrialization" means the establishment of factories for the production of a wide range of manufactured goods, whether for consumption or for war purposes, tends to obscure the contribution that the introduction of modern industrial techniques may make to the development of agriculture, transportation, communications, and trade, all of which are essential for the ultimate fulfillment of any industrial program.

Nationalism, nurtured on dreams of economic as well as political advance, may fail to come to grips with the practical realities of economic life. A non-Western nation may then sacrifice the unspectacular gradual construction of a sound base for future development to the gratification of displaying immediate if often excessively costly results. In this the underdeveloped countries are often abetted by the eagerness of the United States, their chief source of financial and economic aid, to demonstrate the effectiveness of the American aid program by quick and dramatic results. Yet the experience of some of the non-Western nations, notably India, indicates that this historic debate about land versus industry need not be an "either-or" proposition, but instead could lead to a harmonizing of agrarian and industrial development on a relatively modest but conceivably more lasting basis.

The main problem of agriculture in a non-Western country is the urgent need to carry out simultaneously land reform, or change in the practices of land tenure, so as to redistribute soil owned by the few among the many who suffer from "land-hunger," and reform of land use, or change in the methods of cultivating the soil.

The prospect of land reform, usually seen as a way of wresting large tracts of arable soil from big landowners—not only from private individuals but also from the state and the church, and not only from those who actually cultivate the land but also from absentee owners who live in cities or in resorts abroad on what they earn without seeming effort—has been perhaps the most important single inducement held out by revolutionary leaders or leaders of anti-colonial movements in the non-Western world. From Lenin and Trotsky to Nehru and Gandhi, from Ho Chi-minh to Premier Diem, from MacArthur in Japan to Arbenz and his opponent Armas in Guatemala, the rulers of peoples recently emerged from landowner-dominated governments or from colonial overlordship have promised that, once victory had been won, possession of land by the landless would be the glittering reward. The World War I slogan of the Russian Communists—"land, peace, and bread"—taken over by reformers elsewhere, had an intoxicating impact on the poor, the frustrated, the restless of all lands. To the extent that this desire for landownership in disintegrating feudal societies was satisfied, to that extent ferment culminating in revolution was kept within bounds, as in Bolivia, Burma, India, Japan. But where, for whatever reason, it remained unheeded, explosions came thick and fast like discharges of dynamite, as in East Africa, in Russia, in China, in eastern Europe. And leaders ready to break up and distribute estates rode to victory on the promise that, at long last, after hundreds of years of landowner or foreign rule, the land would go into the hands of "the people."

It was only after the excitement of land redistribution had died down that leaders and led, irrespective of ideology, began to realize a harsh fact: that land reform in and of itself, no matter how skillfully carried out, with compensation to dispossessed landowners and careful arrangements for orderly transfer of titles, does not solve the rock-bottom problem of an underdeveloped country—the problem of making the most effective use of the land possible, so as to satisfy the rising requirements of a growing population. On the contrary, the break-up of large estates into small individual parcels has often had the effect of reducing productivity instead of increasing it, as the new owners, with only a few acres from which to gain a bare livelihood for themselves and their families, proved unable to obtain the improved seed, the fertilizer, or the simple tools needed for intensive cultivation of their small plots.

The result of this unsettling discovery is that no sooner has land been redistributed than the need is felt—not only by the nation as a whole, but by the new owners as well—for some form of integration of agriculture. This next step is then undertaken, either through collectivization, as in the U.S.S.R. and Communist China, or through a combination of collectivization and cooperatives, as in Yugoslavia after 1948, or through consolidation of small individual strips of land and joint use of machinery for their cultivation, as under the community development projects of India and Egypt, or the *kibbutz,* the collective farms of Israel.

While the collectivization practiced by Moscow and Peiping

has definite political objectives—the subordination of the peasants to the goals of the state and their separation from direct land ownership, except for small private parcels of land designated for private use—some form of joint effort to modernize agriculture as rapidly as possible is urgently needed in every non-Western nation. However, the manufacture of farm machinery, fertilizer, and other requisites of increased agrarian productivity is at this stage still low or nonexistent. Such resources as are available either through domestic output or through imports from abroad must be utilized to maximum capacity by collective or cooperative arrangements for machine and tractor stations, to use the Russian term, which enable the farmers, for a set fee, to use modern tools they cannot buy either because of their scarcity or because of their price.

Land reform and improved land use, however, do not give the peasants the key they need to enter the next phase of economic development—the phase where they can have some cash to purchase the manufactured goods they need or long to possess. This can be achieved only if the peasants have an opportunity to sell their products for cash, either through collective farm organizations to the state, as in the U.S.S.R., or to private purchasers, domestic or foreign, as in India, Japan, and Latin America, and then, with the money thus obtained, to purchase nonagricultural goods. Here a new problem arises. For in the past the prices of foodstuffs and raw materials have fluctuated widely in world markets, as compared with the relatively stable prices of the manufactured goods the peasant is trying to purchase. The resulting gap between farm prices and manufacturing prices, which haunts all countries, from the rich United States to poverty-stricken India, needs to be closed if the farmer is not to remain indefinitely inferior, in potential capacity to develop and rise in the economic scale, as compared with the factory worker or the professional man.

What the food and raw-material-producing nations, from Pakistan with its jute and cotton to Malaya with its rubber, Brazil with its coffee and Chile with its copper, constantly fear is that their one- or two-crop exports, which command high prices in time of war, may bring so little revenue in time of peace and abundant supplies as to wreck their economies and, as a result of economic stringency, imperil their already precarious political systems.

They therefore seek remedial action in two directions. First, they urge international commodity agreements to stabilize world prices at a level which would assure their internal stability over a given period of years. Such proposals are resisted by the United States, not only because this country, with an advanced industrial economy, benefits by the competitive lowering of prices of imported foods and raw materials but also, and perhaps more important, because many Americans regard international controls as a step toward restriction of free enterprise and, ultimately, totalitarianism. The second remedy sought by non-Western nations is industrialization, which, as they see it, would make them less dependent on the advanced Western countries for manufactured goods.

Assuming that all non-Western nations have the resources for large-scale industrialization—and this is an assumption which cannot be supported by facts, since the world's raw materials are unevenly distributed over the earth's surface—duplication of the major modern industries by every country on the globe would eventually create a network of more or less closed, autarchic economies, each trying to the best of its ability to exist on a self-sufficient basis, irrespective of the hardships this might impose on its own people. Yet at the present stage of nationalism, any doubts Westerners express about the possibility of industrializing Pakistan or Indonesia, Egypt or Brazil, are viewed with deep suspicion by the underdeveloped countries, which think the Western powers—particularly those with a colonial past—are purposely trying to keep them backward by blocking their plans for industrial development.

The economic problem is aggravated by the political aspects of the controversy about the relative merits of land versus industry. The owners of landed properties, whether the *pampas* of Argentina or the jute and cotton fields of Pakistan or the tea plantations of India or the rubber estates of Malaya, fear and often vigorously oppose any move toward industrialization. They fear that they might lose their workers to newly developed urban centers, and also sense, rightly, that the establishment of factories and the growth of cities will change their accustomed pattern of life and shift the center of political power from their hands into those of the rising groups of industrial workers and the middle class of business, banking, and professions. The natural conservatism of the agrarian community, which wants to preserve its economic and social values, thus comes into conflict with the new ambitions of the city dwellers, whom the landowners regard as "radical" (conservative as the middle class may be in our terms), because of their desire for change, even if this change may be modest and limited by comparison with the standards of Britain and the United States.

If, under these circumstances, the foreigner enters the picture as an owner of food- and raw-material-producing properties—the coffee and bananas of Central America, the oil of the Middle East, or the copper of Chile—he may find himself regarded as "reactionary," even if he actually does his best to give his employees living conditions far superior to those prevailing in the country in which he works. If, however, he appears on the scene to invest capital in industry, and becomes associated with local leaders who are eager to build modern factories, he may be denounced by the landowners as the spearhead of economic and social revolution, and the derogatory term "capitalist" may be hurled at him both from the political right and the political left.

These conflicts and controversies are symptoms of the painful internal readjustments through which the non-Western nations are passing as they make the transition from agrarian feudalism to the industrial requirements of the nuclear age. In the midst of this transition, pessimists of both West and non-West are inclined to believe that countries which lag fifty, or a hundred, or even several hundred years behind the nations of the Atlantic community will have to take a long time to close the gap between backward agriculture and twentieth-century industry, and may never catch up with the West, which meanwhile, of course, is not standing still. The pessimists assume that economic backwardness is a liability which the non-Western peoples will find it difficult, perhaps impossible, to overcome.

Yet, without making falsely rosy predictions about the future, it is not unreasonable to ask whether this liability could be transformed into an asset through the very fact that the non-Western peoples have been forced by events to telescope into a short time the several revolutions which have shaped the Western world. We have already seen that it would be dangerous for the non-Western nations to wait for the gradual development and slow adjustment to new conditions which characterized the history of the West, in the hope that the shift from an agrarian to an industrial economy will bring about reduction in population, political stabilization, and widespread prosperity. Instead, the governments of the non-Western nations have an opportunity to take a course which was not open to the West several centuries ago. They can synchronize the modernization of agriculture with the creation of industry, by learning from advanced industrial nations, the U.S.S.R. as well as the United States, Britain, Germany, Japan, and others, the short cuts devised by twentieth-century science and technology. They can thereby get the best of both worlds —agriculture and industry—and avoid the tug of war that is precipitated whenever a choice has to be made between the two. And they can perhaps save their peoples from the more extreme hardships of the early Industrial Revolution which defaced the English countryside with slums and child labor amid what the poet William Blake called "these dark Satanic Mills."

This does not mean, however, that the non-Western nations must try to produce a carbon copy of the West's industrialization process, by first diverting the agrarian population to new urban centers and then trying to reverse the trend by decentralizing industry. The non-Western governments are in a position, if they wish, to start where the West left off. They can devise a new pattern of modernizing their villages by helping them obtain electricity and water, schools and hospitals, and thus give the peasant what he might otherwise be tempted to seek by migration to the city. They can anchor him and his family to the countryside by holding out the hope of improved life for their children. And they can offer him diversified sources of cash income by establishing small-scale industries—shoes and cutlery, tools and soap, furniture and cement—right at his door, within a walk or a bus ride of his agrarian community. He can then become either a full-time worker in a factory who at night returns to the village which he will have new incentive to improve, or he can remain a tiller of the soil, vastly aided by new implements and techniques learned from agricultural extension experts, who supplements the income derived from the sale of his crops with seasonal work in a nearby industrial establishment.

In either case, he will have some cash to spend, new wants which he will be able to satisfy in a modest way, access to medical aid, education, and technical knowledge, all of which will add up to expansion of his horizon without the need of uprooting him from his family and the community in which he was born, without the physical and spiritual dislocations that in the past have undermined existing institutions, leaving a vacuum in which communism, as in China, has proved the most powerful element of reintegration. This process of simultaneous land and small-scale industry development would not preclude the establishment of selected large-scale industries for which native raw materials are available—thereby satisfying understandable national pride—but it could facilitate the social, as well as technological, adaptation of non-Western peoples to modern life through a synthesis of agrarianism and atomic-age techniques.

Such a synthesis will not be brought about by haphazard, unregulated development. It will require planning and general direction by the state, even if detailed operations are left to private enterprise by individuals or groups concerned with agriculture and industry. This is important for Americans to understand, for all too often upon first coming in contact with non-Western nations, we feel troubled or repelled by planned economies and socialist forms of government. Yet we are also critical of unplanned and unregulated economies where limited local resources we help to develop or to supplement are dissipated or misused through lack of coherent programs.

The choice is not "either-or" between agriculture and industry. The choice is between leaving an underdeveloped economy to develop as the interests and concerns of various individuals and groups may dictate, in spite of the urgency of bridging the gap of centuries between non-Western and Western nations, or discovering a way to combine the growth of agriculture with that of industry in a form acceptable to the population. Agriculture and industry are not incompatible. They are complementary, as Eugene Staley has pointed out in *The Future of Underdeveloped Countries* (New York: Harper & Brothers for the Council on Foreign Relations, 1954) "Improvement in the productivity of agriculture is one of the most solid means of promoting industrialization; in fact, unless agriculture does modernize substantially, industrial expansion in most underdeveloped countries is likely to be cut short by lack of markets, for the great majority of the population will not have the necessary purchasing power. Conversely, agricultural improvements cannot go very far unless there is industrial development to take up the released manpower and to provide a solid technical base for the equipment and services essential to modernized agriculture."

It is, of course, possible that during the transition period a country may find it impossible to produce sufficient food for a population which is still growing, even if, as in the case of India, it does not remove substantial numbers of people from the land for allocation to distant industrial establishments. Or, as in the case of Russia, Hungary, and Poland, which before World War II were exporters of food, it may no longer be able to satisfy the food wants of its own people, let alone have a genuine surplus for export.

This situation, however, may be adjusted in the future through far-reaching changes in the character of world trade. The most notable of these changes is that the advanced industrial countries, notably the United States and Canada, are now also the world's principal exporters of food and agricultural raw materials, of which they have surpluses burdensome for their own economies. Judging by the efforts of the U.S.S.R. and the eastern European countries since 1955 to obtain wheat from Canada, cotton from Egypt and other cotton-producing countries, sugar from Cuba, and so on, it may turn out that in a world free from the fear of atomic holocaust, the most efficient trade exchanges will be triangular arrangements. The United States, Canada, Australia, and New Zealand could then export wheat, cotton, tobacco, wool, and other foods and agricultural raw materials to the less developed non-Western nations, and either buy from them raw materials needed by their industries, or machinery and manufactured goods produced by these nations for distribution or sale to other non-Western nations which have few or no industries of their own.

While this readjustment may seem far-fetched at the present time, the United States has already proposed a triangular arrangement along these lines to Japan, offering to sell cotton to Tokyo, which would pay in its own currency, the yen, and would use the resulting funds to produce manufactured goods which the United States would then purchase from the Japanese and give, as part of its aid program, to other non-Western nations receiving American aid.

Who Pays for What?

Whatever method is adopted to develop the underdeveloped nations, the next problem which confronts their governments is that of financing—of who is to pay for what. For the non-Western nations must somehow obtain the sinews of war on poverty, disease, malnutrition, and illiteracy. These sinews are: capital to finance development; technical assistance to provide new skills; and training of native entrepreneurs and managers to start and operate new enterprises.

The first of these sinews—capital—can be obtained from two main sources: internal and external. Internal capital can be accumulated or, to use the technical term, "formed," through two principal methods: taxation by the government;

and private savings, either voluntary, or forced on the individual by the state, as in the U.S.S.R. and Communist China. Both these methods, familiar to Western nations since the break-up of the manor, the rise of towns with their money economy, their merchants and bankers, and the spread of the Industrial Revolution, sparked by science, present grave difficulties for non-Western nations, which, as we have seen, often start under the handicap of large and still growing populations that live at a bare subsistence level. While taxes—on incomes, or as in Russia on trade turnover—may be high, the number of large incomes, and the extent of internal trade, are extremely small compared to the situation we find in advanced Western nations. Nor are savings, however modest, always readily available to the government because of the tendency of the poor, as well as the rich, in predominantly agrarian societies to use surplus income in non-productive ways. They may use it for various kinds of conspicuous consumption such as weddings, funerals, and other traditional feasts, or the purchase of jewelry, or expenditure on pleasure trips abroad—as Russian landowners spent their money before 1917 on taking the cure in Wiesbaden or a gay whirl in Paris, and well-to-do Indians or Argentines spend money today on visits to France or Britain.

Moreover, where banking and credit facilities are not yet adequately developed, the poor who need to purchase a bullock or a plough, or celebrate a family occasion, often become hopelessly indebted to moneylenders who charge as high as 30 to 40 per cent on loans; while the rich are apt to use their money to speculate for high returns on commodities—sugar, jute, coffee, rubber, and so on—rather than invest it on a long-term basis for less spectacular returns in industrial enterprises. And even the most responsible and public-spirited among the business community have neither the inclination nor the resources to invest in the creation of some basic forms of real capital—dams and railways, roads and irrigation projects—on which no profit can be expected, yet without which economic development is impossible.

Because of these conditions, the government leaders of non-Western nations, whatever their personal philosophy, find it necessary to prime the pump of economic development, at least in its early stages, and to direct the investment of such resources as are available through taxes and savings in those projects which, according to over-all plans drawn up by their experts, should have the highest priority at a given time. The government thereby withholds funds, both public and private, as much as possible from being dissipated on what it regards as nonessentials. A democratic government like that of India or the Philippines, however, is not in a position to impose its development program on the people in a manner comparable to that of totalitarian regimes such as those of the U.S.S.R. and Communist China today or Japan in the Meiji era, which can use coercion, postpone the satisfaction of consumer demands, and resist expenditures on social welfare. Yet, as we have seen, in the twentieth century, such expenditures are expected from rulers committed to social as well as political democracy.

As a result, the percentage of the total output of goods and services which goes into investment in the non-Communist countries of the non-West is low as compared with the advanced Western nations, on the one hand, and Russia and mainland China, on the other. For example, in India and Pakistan gross investment is roughly 6 to 7 per cent and in Indonesia only about 5 per cent of the gross national product, as compared with 16 or 17 per cent in the United States, Canada, and Western Europe, 15 per cent in Communist China, and a reported 20 per cent in the U.S.S.R. The present rate of investment in India and Pakistan is regarded by American economic experts—notably in a 1956 study by the Committee on Economic Development (CED)—as only just sufficient, and in Indonesia probably insufficient, to keep national income growing a little faster than population. The situation appears more favorable in Latin America, where per capita income is much higher than in Asia and more foreign, primarily United States, capital has been available—with the rate of gross investment averaging about 14 per cent of gross national product in recent years. Population growth, however, has risen more rapidly in Latin America than in most of the Middle East and Southeast Asia, and therefore a larger part of the capital invested "makes no contribution to raising the people's productivity and living standards," but merely helps to hold the line.

Given these circumstances, all underdeveloped areas—Latin America as well as Asia, Africa, and the Middle East—need more capital for economic development and improved living standards than is at present obtainable through internal capital formation. A group of international experts appointed by the United Nations estimated in 1951 that out of a total of $19 billion a year needed for the development of all underdeveloped countries of Asia, Africa, the Middle East, and Latin America, only $5 billion could be obtained from taxes and savings, leaving $14 billion a year to be obtained from external sources. Keenly aware of this need, some of the non-Western governments have made additional efforts to mobilize the savings of their citizens. Japan has already demonstrated the importance of accumulating savings through rural credit banks. India, after studying its own problems as well as the experience of Japan and other countries, decided in 1955 to create a network of rural credit banks, with the two-fold purpose of facilitating and encouraging small savings and substituting credit resources at low rates of interest for the exorbitantly priced loans of moneylenders.

The experience of Japan and India demonstrates that the ethics of thrift, often associated in Western minds with the Puritan philosophy or the French propensity to put surplus money in a sock or under the mattress—a procedure hardly favorable to industrial investment—are readily accepted by Buddhists and Hindus. They must be convinced, however, through practical experience that what they save will not be snatched away from them by the government but, on the contrary, will directly improve their own lives and, what is even more important, the health, education, and employment prospects of their children. This awareness makes even the poorest peasant—as has been amply shown in India's community development projects—willing to save his meager earnings and, what is more, to make savings in kind, through non-monetary contributions to capital development such as volunteer labor on roads and dams, or gifts of materials for building schools.

Great and devoted as may be the efforts of non-Western peoples in forming the capital required for their economic development, it is agreed by both West and non-West that additional capital must be provided from external sources if the newly independent nations are to maintain the momentum of economic expansion they have achieved without resort to the coercive measures of Communist regimes. Opinion differs, however, on three main points: 1) the amount of capital the non-Western nations can in practice absorb; 2) the form in which capital should be made available to the non-West by the developed Western industrial nations; and 3) the internal conditions in non-Western nations which would be most favorable to effective use of foreign capital.

As of 1956 the underdeveloped countries (excluding

colonial territories directly ruled by Western powers) were receiving long-term capital investment funds from the United States and other industrial countries at the rate of approximately $1.1 billion net a year. While there is considerable controversy among Western experts about the rate at which these countries could rapidly absorb additional foreign capital, the CED states that according to "conservative estimates" the independent underdeveloped countries of the non-Communist world as a group might be able to use effectively as much as $500 million to $1,500 million of new foreign capital each year during the next few years above what they are now receiving. "These amounts," says the CED, "if effectively used, would make possible a level of gross capital formation in the underdeveloped countries roughly 5 to 15 per cent higher than the present level."

This figure falls considerably short of the minimum $7 billion a year suggested by the UN experts in 1951. While the figure of $7 billion, said the experts, seems large, it would represent only 2 per cent of the annual national income of the major developed nations—Western Europe, Australasia, the United States, and Canada. Nor would this percentage be excessive, the experts contended, when it is realized that in the period of 1905-13 Britain exported capital to the extent of 7 per cent of its annual national income, and that United States loans and grants had been running at over 3 per cent of this country's national income over the period 1946-51. The UN experts' estimate, however, was criticized by some American economists as unrealistically high given the presumed capacity of non-Western economies to absorb foreign capital.

Assuming that agreement can be reached by West and non-West on the amount of foreign capital which could be supplied by the West and absorbed by the underdeveloped countries, several crucial questions then arise. Should such capital as well as the other two kinds of development sinews—technical skills and managerial know-how needed to make the best possible use of new capital resources—be provided from public or private sources? If from private sources, should they be in the form of repayable loans or outright grants and gifts? If public, should aid be channeled through bilateral, nation-to-nation arrangements, as between the United States and India or the U.S.S.R. and Egypt, or through some international agency—the United Nations, the specialized agencies (Food and Agricultural Organization, World Health

Organization, and so on), regional bodies like that established by the Commonwealth with American aid under the Colombo Plan, and international financial institutions, such as the World Bank and the International Finance Corporation?

To these questions many divergent answers have been given, depending on whether the answer comes from an advanced industrial nation whose aid is being requested, from an underdeveloped country seeking foreign aid, or from spokesmen for international agencies—and also on whether the views are those of investors or government officials in Western countries.

It is unlikely that American private investment in underdeveloped countries will be substantially increased in the visible future—even assuming that these countries, animated by strong nationalist sentiments, are willing to create conditions more favorable to private foreign investors—unless a far-reaching depression here forces investors to look abroad for profitable opportunities to invest capital. Meanwhile some of the underdeveloped nations, notably India, have begun to seek private investment capital in Western European countries rather than the United States on the ground that European investors would be less hesitant than Americans about using their capital to help develop "socialist economies."

In any case it is doubtful that even under the most favorable circumstances private foreign capital will be invested in the basic economic facilities urgently needed by underdeveloped countries in such fields as electric power, irrigation, atomic energy, transportation, and communications—partly because such projects yield no direct monetary return, and partly because in newly independent countries these projects are owned, operated, and controlled by the state, and therefore offer no room for private participation except in the limited form of employing foreign technicians. This Russia did in the construction of the Dneprostroy dam in the 1930's, and India has done the same during the 1950's in the building of dams, steel mills, and other enterprises.

Some additional financing, however, is made available through loans to private firms in underdeveloped countries by American governmental agencies. The Export-Import Bank, established for the purpose of promoting American exports and imports, often lends money to a foreign country when United States exports are involved—for example, the sale of machinery to Brazil and Japan—and will try to stimulate production abroad, particularly when the product involved is imported by the United States. The International Cooperation Administration (ICA), which administers the Point Four program inaugurated by President Harry S. Truman in 1949, as well as other aid measures, also makes development loans or grants to private firms in underdeveloped countries—but only on condition that the government of the country guarantees the loan or grant, since the United States cannot sue a private firm in India or Brazil as it can sue a private firm here.

In speaking of private aid, we should not forget the grants which Christian missions of the United States and other Western countries have been making for years—in their own version of what we call Point Four—by establishing schools, creating medical facilities, and providing other forms of assistance to underdeveloped areas. Private aid has also been furnished through CARE, with the United States government paying all transportation costs involved, the United Jewish Appeal, which gives substantial sums to Israel, and other philanthropic, educational, and medical agencies.

In addition to private capital from individual nations, international capital is provided to underdeveloped countries through the International Bank for Reconstruction and Development (IBRD), commonly known as the World Bank, established by forty-four nations at the Bretton Woods conference of 1944, before the end of World War II, and capitalized at $9.1 billion. Each member's subscription is roughly based on its national income and trade. Over a period of ten years the World Bank has made development loans totaling $1.8 billion, or approximately $180 million a year. Among non-Western areas which have received World Bank loans are Mexico (for modernization of railways); Kenya, Uganda, and Tanganyika (rail, port, and other transportation); Colombia (acquisition of farm machinery); Ceylon, India, Pakistan, and Colombia (power projects, along with three European countries); and Peru (irrigation program).

The World Bank, necessarily limited by its modest resources, has so far made loans largely for the development of enterprises which could meet a banker's test as to their feasibility and future prospects. This has given rise to criticism on the part of underdeveloped countries, which feel the need for an international lending institution that would be ready to supply venture capital for new and at the outset perhaps experimental and risky undertakings. For this purpose the World Bank has encouraged the establishment of the International Finance

Corporation, recommended in the United States by a committee headed by Nelson Rockefeller in a report entitled *Partners in Progress.* This corporation, an affiliate of the World Bank, would provide funds for productive private enterprise out of a modest capital of $100 million (the United States has pledged $35 million when other participants contribute sufficient funds to make it a going concern). Its most important function, however, would be to help recruit private investment capital and assist in locating experienced managers. The underdeveloped countries have been slow to sign up for the IFC. Up to now, the total of all loans made by the World Bank, representing international private capital, remains very small as compared with the known needs of the underdeveloped countries.

Since private capital investment from the advanced Western nations, siphoned either through private firms or government-supported institutions, is recognized to be insufficient for the acknowledged foreign capital needs of the underdeveloped countries, the question gets back to the prospects for public, governmental, or intergovernmental assistance and to the form such assistance could or should take. Up to 1956 the United States, principal source of capital in the free world, had concentrated its aid program primarily on the already industrially developed countries of western Europe under the Marshall Plan launched in 1947 and had paid relatively little attention to the foreign capital requirements of the non-Western nations. This was particularly notable in the case of Southeast Asia, which, with a population of more than 600 million, had been receiving from United States government agencies and from the World Bank only about $90 million a year of investment funds, compared with the $16 billion in Marshall Plan funds the United States expended in western Europe over a decade.

American public aid to underdeveloped countries has taken three main forms: 1) technical assistance through Point Four, which involves relatively modest expenditures to furnish the services of American technicians, as well as some direct financial aid; 2) direct grants under bilateral agreements with individual countries, which have often been linked with conditions about political, military, or economic cooperation that critical recipients describe as "strings attached"; and 3) repayable loans, as suggested by Secretary of the Treasury George M. Humphrey.

The Soviet bloc's competition in the field of foreign aid in the post-Stalin period caused some thoughtful Americans to weigh more seriously than in the past the possibility of creating an international fund for economic development, on the lines of the Special United Nations Fund for Economic Development (SUNFED) which has been strongly urged by some of the underdeveloped countries—Latin American as well as Afro-Asian. French Foreign Minister Christian Pineau proposed an international development fund in 1956; and President Eisenhower had indicated earlier that, if disarmament were achieved, money previously expended on armaments might be set aside for increased aid to underdeveloped areas—although in view of the snaillike pace of disarmament negotiations this suggestion, in the opinion of the non-Western nations, was tantamount to relegating large-scale aid to the Greek calends.

Prominent Americans opposed proposals for an international aid fund on the ground that the United States, as under previous aid arrangements, would have to furnish the bulk of the money. Others, however, believed that such a fund would test the willingness of the U.S.S.R. to cooperate with the West on the economic development front and would avert ruinous foreign-aid competition between the two great-power blocs, such as seemed to be in prospect for Egypt, which at one time received offers from both the West and the Soviet bloc to build the High Aswan Dam.

While the Eisenhower Administration was unwilling to engage in a dollar-for-dollar or dam-for-dam competition with the U.S.S.R. for the good will of the non-Western nations, some Americans pointed out the need of reviewing American foreign-aid policy in the framework of world changes precipitated by the Geneva "Summit" conference of 1955. This conference had indicated that, as the danger of nuclear war receded, economic competition between the West and the U.S.S.R. would take the center of the world stage.

At stake in this competition would be not only the role of the United States as leader of the non-Communist world but the need of our Western allies, less favored than we are with natural resources, for some of the principal raw materials required by their industries and available in underdeveloped areas—oil in the Middle East, rubber and tin in Malaya, uranium in the Belgian Congo, and so on. Expanded American aid on a long-term basis was therefore urged not only as a weapon in the struggle against communism (aid, it was pointed out, would be needed even if Lenin and Stalin had never existed), or only on grounds of humanitarianism (the recipient countries are aware that the motives of all human beings, including Americans, are mixed), or in the hope of obtaining strategic bases in non-Western areas such as Morocco and Saudi Arabia (intercontinental ballistic missiles may sharply reduce the need for air bases along the periphery of Russia and Communist China), but on the ground that in a fast-changing world the very survival of the United States, whose security depends on its allies, hangs in the balance.

Because of the crucial issues at stake, American opinion in 1956, to an extent which could not have been foreseen a year earlier, tended to accept competitive coexistence, and even the possibility of economic cooperation with the U.S.S.R. in the development of non-Western nations, as a fact of international life. Americans no longer insisted as vigorously as in the past on commitment by the non-Western countries, such as India and Indonesia, to the anti-Communist cause. They faced with relatively little dismay the prospect that the ranks of the uncommitted nations would continue to grow in the future, to the point where these nations might hold the balance of power in the UN. Some Americans went so far as to believe that "non-alignment" of the non-West, far from representing a danger for the West, and for the United States in particular, might become an asset for the free world by cushioning relations between the two superpowers that had emerged from the havoc of World War II—the United States and the U.S.S.R.—and preventing the bipolarization of the globe around these two power centers.

12

West and Non-West: The Heart of the Matter

In Jordan, whose army, the Arab Legion, was financed by Britain to the tune of over thirty million dollars a year and until his sudden expulsion in 1956 was led by a British officer with the storybook name of Glubb Pasha, crowds riot against the Baghdad pact, attack British and American offices, and tear down the Stars and Stripes. Saudi Arabia, made wealthy by the West's purchases of its only important product, oil, supports Egypt against Britain and France over Suez at the risk of losing its sole source of revenue.

Arab spokesmen contend that they can never lay down the sword until Israel, accused of being a Western intruder in their midst, has been pushed into the sea; yet an adventurous young Egyptian reporter who visited Israel, hitherto enemy territory, tells his Premier, Colonel Nasser, that Israel, once a British League mandate, agrees with Egypt in resisting Britain's return to the Middle East. Burma prefers to take aid from Israel rather than from Britain and the United States. Algerian rebels win Cairo's support in their struggle to end French rule. A leader of Brazil's ruling party accuses Washington of "imperialism." Asian statesmen like Nehru of India and U Nu of Burma who firmly oppose communism at home listen without dismay to charges of Western colonialism made on their soil by Russia's touring statesmen, Bulganin and Khrushchev. Egyptian patriots welcome Czech arms and heave a sigh of relief as they watch British troops leave the Suez Canal. Latin American diplomats castigate the United States for its reluctance to join a pact regulating the world price of coffee, one of their principal exports, and in spite of Catholic hostility to communism look for new trade connections with the Soviet bloc.

Have all these people—devout Muslims like the Arab leaders, Western-trained sophisticates like Nehru, Latin Americans educated in Catholic doctrines—become victims of Communist propaganda? Has a strong draught of Marxism-Leninism-Stalinism poisoned their minds, are they paid agents of Moscow, or must they be regarded, more in pity than in anger, as naïve stooges of Kremlin confidence men? How else can we explain their otherwise inexplicable ill-feeling against the West which has given them so generously of its own resources—such as Britain's contribution to India in terms of administrative experience and judicial practice, American grants of military and economic aid to Asia, the Middle East, and Latin America, and Western purchases of Arab oil?

So deeply is the West imbued with the sense of the benefits it has conferred on the non-Western areas in the past and is ready to confer in the future, that we find it difficult to believe anti-Westernism can exist and flourish without the help of communism. Yet this is the harsh reality we must face in Asia, the Middle East, and Africa if we are not to fall prey to perilous illusions.

The Russians did not need to lift a finger, fire a gun, or spend a single ruble to foment anti-Westernism in Egypt or Saudi Arabia, in Indonesia or Jordan. It's in the air. It is deeply imbedded in the consciousness of peoples who have lived under the rule of Britain, France, or the Netherlands, not of Russia. True, the Russians capitalize with marked success on a sentiment against the West which corresponds to their own; but they did not in the first place create it. This sentiment can exist and has existed apart from communism—just as some plants need no soil or fertilizer to remain alive. In fact, anti-Westernism was a sturdy plant in Russia itself during the nineteenth century under the Tsars, long before the Bolsheviks came on the scene.

As Hans Kohn has well put it in his book, *The Mind of Modern Russia,* "all the problems which Westernization later brought to India and China were adumbrated in Russia, the first non-Western society to come under the impact of modern Western civilization." Russia at that time, like Egypt or Indonesia today, felt both attracted to an repelled by the West, of which it did not form a part. By contrast to the Western nations, with their advanced technology, their rising middle class, their high living standards, their democratic institutions, their international power and prestige, Russia felt backward, lacking the advantages offered by the West, and vulnerable to military as well as economic pressures from the Western world. Russia's reaction to contact with the West during and after the Napoleonic wars took two sharply differing forms, which can be found today in the nations of Asia, the Middle East, Africa, and Latin America: a desire for Westernization, and rejection of the West in favor of a nationalist solution—the solution of Slavophilism, which in essence is Russian nationalism.

Advocates of Westernization—Peter Chadayev, Nikolai Danilevsky, and Alexander Herzen—wanted Russia to cooperate with Europe, to learn by Europe's experience, and to reject those elements of its past which it had inherited from its period of subjection to the Tartars—in short, its Asian experience. These men, in the 1830's, carried on the tradition of Peter the Great, who two centuries earlier had feverishly worked to transform Russia by force into a Western secular state with a modern economy.

At the opposite pole from the Westernizers were men like Dostoyevsky, a nationalist true to the Russian Orthodox faith, who opposed the West and extolled the Slav character of Russia, which he regarded as superior to that of Europe. To Dostoyevsky, the two worlds of Russia and Europe were incompatible. He foresaw a struggle between these two worlds, which would end with the victory of Russia and the regeneration, by the Russians, of decadent Europe. To him the West stood for force, violence, materialism; Russia for universal goodness and brotherhood. Against the Western imperialism, which he saw in terms of greed and conquest, he pitted, without benefit of Marxism, Russia's "imperialism of love." Leo Tolstoy, unlike Dostoyevsky, was not a nationalist. He thought in terms of the world, not of Russia alone. But, like the author of *Brothers Karamazov*, Tolstoy rejected Western civilization and found his ideal in the Russian peasant, in the village life which he idyllized. It is not an accident that he discovered a kindred spirit in Gandhi, spearhead of India's national struggle against British rule, who like Tolstoy believed that salvation would come from the village and urged a simple life within the framework of India's own traditional social order.

Viewed against this background, Russia's Communist leaders, from Lenin to Khrushchev, appear not as rebels against a deeply rooted tradition of Russian cooperation with the West and acceptance of Western values, but as successors to the anti-Western Slavophiles, the Russian nationalists, in the struggle between Westernization and rejection of the West which profoundly affected nineteenth century Russia and is still at work today not only within Russia, but within individual Russians. The men of the Kremlin used anti-Western sentiment to renew Russia's historic isolation from the West and to press for its transformation from a relatively backward agrarian country into a modern industrial state commanding the technical means to wage twentieth-century warfare, up to and including atomic and hydrogen bombs. Their anti-Westernism did not prevent them from making use of the West—the better to challenge it.

Paradoxically, their first objective was one opposed by the Slavophiles—adoption of the outward features of the West, at least so far as economic development is concerned; and to achieve this end they used the strong-arm methods of Peter the Great, a hero in the U.S.S.R. Yet their secret weapon was a direct inheritance from Dostoyevsky and his fellow-Slavophiles—the belief that Russia should reject the West, that a clash between Russia and the West was inevitable, and that Russia, rallying to its standard all the Slav peoples, would ultimately dominate the world and make all men brothers.

But if these manifestations of anti-Westernism in Russia were not initially a product of communism, were they, it might be asked, an exclusive product of Russia's historical development? Is the anti-Westernism we see today in other areas of the world just a carbon copy of that practiced in Russia? Would it vanish if the West could discover some magic formula for eliminating Russia or sealing it off from the rest of the world?

The answer, disappointing as it is for the West, must be in the negative. From New Delhi to Cairo, from Jakarta to Karachi and Nairobi, men and women who have never read Marx, Lenin, or Stalin and who often abhor what they know of Russia, are in the grip of the same emotions and ideas which fan the as yet unfinished controversy between Westernizers and Slavophiles in Russia. Their anti-Westernism, like that of the Russians, is an explosive mixture of contradictory reactions to the West inspired by rising nationalism.

The non-Westerners admire the material achievements of the Western nations—the fruits of modern science and technology. They long to have their own peoples benefit by these fruits, to which they feel entitled by reason of living in the twentieth century: this is the essence of what has been well called "the revolution of rising expectations." But they realize, with a poignancy which no Westerner, however, sympathetic, can possibly understand—because like intense fear or joy it cannot be expressed in rational terms but must be experienced to be known—that their own countries are poor and retarded, ridden with disease and ignorance. The contrast between what they see around them, in Egypt or Indonesia, and what they painfully wish to achieve for their peoples is so staggering as to fill them with a sense of hopelessness and frustration. Instead of trying to escape from this state of mind by tackling the nearest practical job, no matter how modest it may be, they are likely to vent their feelings of disappointment against the West, making it the scapegoat for all the ills from which they and their countrymen suffer.

This general revolt of the non-Western peoples against "white supremacy" and Western control—lumped together under the phrase "colonialism"—also hits at Christianity of all denominations, both Protestant and Catholic, which is often regarded as inextricably associated with Western interests. In fact, anti-Westernism, paradoxical as it may seem, has been crystallized by the teachings of democracy and Christianity. As a 1956 *New York Times* survey of the role of church missions in non-Western countries pointed out, Christians are now "paying a price, not for their teaching, but for not consistently practicing what they preach." Even those non-Westerners like Nehru who are willing to permit the continued operation of Christian missions—which the Communist Chinese have barred from their territory—see no reason why Western missions, any more than Western business enterprises, should keep on using Western personnel in top positions, and expect them, instead, to appoint native Christians.

The situation becomes all the more painful—for non-Western peoples and for the West—where the rulers, today or in the recent past, are or have been Westerners, who may well have concentrated on their own interests, such as the building of strategic facilities or the development of resources needed by Western industry, rather than on improvement of the economic, social, and political conditions in the areas under their control. Then the anti-Westernism which is found even in independent non-Western nations such as Japan becomes dangerously aggravated by anti-colonialism and, since the foreign rulers are representatives of white nations, also by racialism. To all these feelings must be added the fear of some who want to maintain ancient political and religious customs that the impact of the West will destroy the fabric of the nation's traditional life, and who want to oust all Westerners before this horrifying prospect has come to pass.

Anti-Westernism can thus bring together such diverse elements as the reformers who want to use Western experience to strengthen their peoples against the West, and the reactionaries who want no part of Western experience lest it contaminate their nations. It then becomes difficult for the Westerner to distinguish on the one hand between Mossadegh in Iran or Egypt's Muslim Brotherhood fanatics, who seek to overthrow not only the foreigners, but also the native leaders interested in learning from the West, and men like Premier Nasser of Egypt, who wants to modernize his country with aid from the West, but hopes to use his strengthened position to challenge the West in the Muslim world, from French North Africa to Kenya. It is a rare non-Western nation which, like India, is fortunate enough to possess a leader who has confidence in the capacity of his people to accept Westernism yet retain its national identity and meet the stupendous problems of adjustment of an underdeveloped land to the rapidly changing conditions of the nuclear age.

This inner conflict, familiar to every sensitive non-Westerner, between the desire to cherish and preserve traditional values and yet live in harmony with twentieth-century conditions is poignantly reflected in novels and plays portraying life among peoples of the non-West. The humble yet strong-minded peasant woman of *Nectar in a Sieve* by Kamala Markandaya of South India, who is torn between the advantages offered her sons through employment in the new cement factory of the nearby town and her attachment to her poor but familiar village life is sister to the Chinese farmers made memorable by Pearl Buck in *The Good Earth.* The troubled yet appealing Jay, scion of a maharajah family threatened by India's new social system, skillfully depicted by Santha Rama Rau in her novel of Bombay, *Remember the House,* would find much in common with the vacillating, well-meaning characters of Anton Chekov, who in *The Cherry Orchard* wonder out loud how they can reconcile themselves to the chopping down of the beloved cherry trees and the intrusion of a commercialism they regard as crude into their quiet and refined lives—and finds ready sympathy among dispossessed Japanese aristocrats. The detribalized, disoriented hero of Alan Paton's *Cry, the Beloved Country,* torn between old morality and new wants and emotions, is akin to the Japanese protagonists of Tanazaki's *Some Prefer Nettles* and Osumi Dazai's *The Setting Sun,* who, while impressed and tempted by Western ways, cannot bring themselves to accept what seems alien to their tradition, and seek a solution either through return to ancient customs or through suicide.

Nor should this seem strange to Americans. For in our own South we can see a comparable conflict between those who are moved by nostalgia for a disappearing agrarianism with its remnants of a slaveholder's mentality and the new social outlook brought by industrializers from the North. It is not surprising that Joshua Logan was able to transpose *The Cherry Orchard* into a Southern setting as *The Wistaria Trees.* What non-Westerners—as well as some of our Southerners—seek, on occasion through violent outbursts against the new, is a way of integrating themselves into the modern era by measures which will not violate their human personality as defined by historical circumstances peculiar to the non-West—or to our South.

The West, however, is particularly puzzled by the tendency of the non-Western nations to denounce Western colonialism yet say little or nothing about the colonialism of the U.S.S.R. Here, again, Russia's past experience is much closer to that which Asia, the Middle East, and Africa are now undergoing than is the experience of the Western nations. Russia itself was a relatively backward nation as late as the 1920's. It, too, both wanted to learn from the West yet feared the impact of the West on its institutions and on its national security.

This does not mean, and should not be interpreted to mean, that the Asian and African countries accept Russia without criticisms or qualms. They are aware of the dangers of eventual pressure from Moscow. They are not enthusiastic about Russian dictatorship—although, being often accustomed to authoritarianism at home, they are less repelled by it abroad than the nations of the Atlantic community, where democracy is —more or less—an old story. Russia was not invited to the Afro-Asian conference at Bandung in 1955, presumably because it is a Eurasian, not an Asian or African country. But Russia's experience in modernizing its economy and in making the difficult transition from ancient times to the nuclear age within a third of a century is of intense interest to all non-Western areas, which feel that they have more to learn, in a practical way, from a country far closer to their current problems and experiences than from such advanced nations as the United States and Britain. This sense of affinity with Russia—economic and social if not always political—on the part of non-Western peoples of diverse religious faiths, political traditions, and international aspirations constitutes the most difficult hurdle for the West in its efforts to find a cure for anti-Westernism.

This cure cannot be found by denouncing communism, by demanding that the non-Western nations abandon all contacts with Russia and Communist China, or by threatening to cut off aid unless they agree to join our side. Such moves would merely reinforce their hostility to and suspicion of the West, and cause them to strengthen rather than weaken their still tenuous bonds with Moscow.

As in the case of some other troubles, the most promising remedy is the hair of the dog. The cure for anti-Westernism is Westernization. But Westernization cannot be forced on non-Western peoples by military pressure or financial handouts. Nasser in Egypt or Nehru in India, like the Japanese after 1867 or the Russians after 1917, must be free to take the initiative in accepting or rejecting what the West has to offer. They must be free to pick and choose those features of Western development which they think best adapted to their own particular needs. Professor Arnold J. Toynbee has eloquently—although not necessarily validly—argued that a non-Western people cannot accept just a part of Western experience—it must take all or nothing. To a Westerner this position sounds logical, yet it has already been challenged in practice by the experience of Russia, Japan, and India, which have selected what they wanted among Western offerings, and rejected what they regarded as unsuitable.

The essence of anti-Westernism, in Tsarist Russia as in the U.S.S.R. and other non-Western areas, is resistance to the assumption, which the West makes as a matter of course, that our civilization is superior to the civilizations of other regions, and represents a norm which should be the ideal goal of Asians, Arabs, and Africans. When Glubb Pasha, upon reaching London after his expulsion from Jordan, was asked what it was the West had done wrong, he said that while the West had committed mistakes it had also done much good—but that its main error is its "superciliousness" toward the non-West. If the West is to succeed, it must learn to restrain its natural feeling of pride in its own achievements—a feeling which, when transposed to non-Western lands, looks and sounds like arrogance—and display modesty in offering to improve the conditions of Egyptians or Indians.

We must, moreover, constantly bear in mind that, as a matter of historical fact, many of these today economically underdeveloped countries had achieved a high type of civilization and culture when our own ancestors were still relative savages. It is no wonder, then, that they think they have something to preserve.

We think that our lack of communication with Russia is due solely to the Iron Curtain and the malevolence of the Soviet rulers. But how well are we doing about communicating with countries where the only existing curtain is woven out of their doubts and suspicions about the motives of the West, and of our own indifference to the religious and cultural interests of other peoples? Not only do we speak to each other at cross-purposes, but we also often look at each other as if we were cross-eyed. This is particularly noticeable in three areas of disputation between West and non-West: spiritual, political, and economic.

First, the non-West likes to believe the West is overly materialistic and bereft of spiritual values. The West contends that the non-West neglects human welfare while extolling the human spirit, and will not successfully develop its economy and carry out urgently needed social reforms until it has acquired Western material techniques which the non-West claims to despise.

Second, the non-West sometimes takes the view that the West is inherently imperialistic and bent on domination of weaker, less developed peoples, which it has hitherto achieved through its possession of superior weapons—most recently the A- and H-bombs. The West either denies current imperialist aspirations, pointing to its recent liberation of many former colonial territories, or justifies such domination as it still exercises by the need to assure its security or to preserve law and order for the benefit of multiracial populations—as on Cyprus or in Singapore—which might otherwise clash with each other in mortal combat—a justification, it should be noted invoked by the U.S.S.R. as well as by the leaders of the Atlantic community. It also points out that non-Western nations are not necessarily free of expansionist designs, notably Japan since the 1890's or, South Africa's white leaders say, India in Africa.

And third, the non-West argues that the West is reluctant to give it financial aid for rapid economic development commensurate in scale and amount to that readily given to Western Europe under the Marshall Plan—yet hesitates to accept such aid as is proferred for fear that it will come with "strings attached," on conditions unacceptable to nations which are determined to maintain their newly won independence. The West, particularly the United States, takes the view that the non-West cannot absorb financial aid as readily as the already developed countries of Western Europe, that its political situation, still in a state of ferment, discourages private investment, which has played an important role in the development of the West, and that it has shown little or no gratitude for such aid as has been given until now.

As is so often the case in all such dialogues between nations, none of the propositions advanced are either wholly true or wholly false. While the industrialized West places great emphasis on technology and the material results it can achieve, the Industrial Revolution has not prevented the flowering of art and literature, of music and philosophy, nor has science, in spite of qualms in the Western countries themselves, destroyed religious belief. On the contrary, technology has provided the material means to assure, in the West, the social improvements which all religions, at their most compassionate, have promised the poor and the humble on earth. And by creating and constantly broadening the economic foundation of modern society, technology has made possible the growth and continued expansion of political democracy, advancing mankind toward an equality undreamed of by Marx and Engels.

The non-West, for its part, is neither intrinsically opposed to technology, as some of its spokesmen occasionally seem to suggest, nor does it need to learn solely from the West the incentives necessary to spark industrialization, as Westerners somewhat arrogantly imagine. On the contrary, we have seen that such diverse civilizations as those of Russia and Japan have shown an impressive capacity for learning modern techniques and for adapting what they have learned to the conditions created by their own historical development, traditions, and national character.

Neither religious belief nor, as thought by some Westerners, preoccupation with arts and crafts, with literature or the theater, has prevented Russians and Japanese, Chinese and Latin Americans, Africans and Burmese, from learning how to operate steel mills, drill oil wells, build railroads or submarines, construct dams, run automobiles and diesel engines, or manufacture hydrogen bombs. And even Gandhi, who is often cited by Westerners as an example of the ascetic "spiritualism" of the non-West which might block material development, emerges, on closer study, as a leader who, while he opposed the impact of British industrialization on the as yet underdeveloped economy of India, found it possible to reconcile the ideals of the *Bhagavad Gita,* which he translated into his native Gujerati, with the creation of a modern economy in which agrarianism, industry, and the welfare state are combined in a society based on democratic socialism.

Nor is the West as blatantly and irrevocably imperialist as its non-Western critics—joining Western critics of colonialism—contend. Both the West and Russia, as we have seen, have resorted to expansion during a stage of their national development. This common experience has tended to be obscured only by the fact that Russia was able to expand overland, encountering little or no resistance in sparsely settled territories—an experience comparable to the opening of the American frontier by immigrants from Europe who founded the United States—while the Western peoples expanded overseas to Asia and the Middle East, Africa and Oceania. It would be futile, as it would be dishonest, to gloss over the record of cruelty and oppression, of exploitation and discrimination, which the West as well as Russia chalked up in the course of expansion—most recently in the Anglo-French attack on Suez and Moscow's suppression of Hungary. But it would also be dishonest, as it would be unfair, to disregard the contributions which the West—and Russia as well— have made to the development of underdeveloped peoples, long before Americans had thought of Point Four.

Nor were these contributions restricted to material achievements—to irrigation projects and hospitals, trading posts, mines, oilfields, railways, ports. There was, side by side, what the French accurately call a *mission civilisatrice*—an attempt not merely to confer the blessings of Western education and Christian religion on "the children of darkness" in a manner understandably resented by the recipients—who, however, were thereby prepared for the responsibilities they sought to achieve through independence. There was an effort also to discover and preserve the achievements of indigenous civilizations, as the British did in India and the French in Indochina, and to disseminate the fruits of this new knowledge in the Western world, whose literature, art, music, and philosophy have thereby been profoundly enriched.

And while most of the non-Western nations in our time have maintained a posture of nonaggression and conciliation in world affairs, Japan's conquests between 1932 and 1945, the Arab states' invasion of Israel in 1947 and their subsequent refusal to negotiate with the Israelis, Communist China's invasion of Korea and acquisition of Tibet, and the unresolved conflict between India and Pakistan about Kashmir, indicate that non-Westernism is not of itself a guarantee against imperialism and expansionism which the non-West is inclined to regard as peculiar attributes of the West. The non-West can be as ambiguous as the West about the issue of colonialism: witness Prime Minister Iskander Mirza of Pakistan, who in 1956 assured Turkey he opposed self-determination for Cyprus while proclaiming his anti-colonial sentiments. Moreover, the establishment of Indians and Pakistanis in South and East Africa, where they often achieve an economic and social status superior to that of the indigenous peoples and competitive with that of the white settlers, has caused some Western critics to claim that immigrants from the Indian subcontinent, who turn to their home governments whenever their interests are threatened, represent a form of "imperialism" in Africa. Nor does the ruthlessness displayed by both sides during the Hindu-Muslim riots which followed in the wake of India's partition in 1947—powerfully depicted by Khushwant Singh in the Indian novel *Mano Majra*—give the Westerner the impression that man's cruelty to man has geographic, or racial, or religious limitations. As India's ambassador to Washington, G. L. Mehta, has pointed out, the East has had Buddha and Christ as well as Xerxes and Genghis Khan, the West has had Hitler as well as Einstein and Schweitzer.

When it comes to the crucial question of economic relations between West and non-West, again the record cannot be painted all black or all white. As has already been pointed out, the West has done a good deal to assist the economic development of the non-Western peoples, but where so much needs to be done so fast if the non-West is to close the gap now separating it from the West, what seems a good deal to Westerners may legitimately look far from enough to non-Western leaders concerned with the welfare of their nations. Nor is it always possible to agree on a common yardstick of how much capital, technical assistance and imported food, raw materials, or machinery a given underdeveloped nation can absorb. For the West often uses the yardstick of a banker, or technologist, or politician who must persuade his constituents to make any contribution at all to peoples overseas, while the non-West uses the yardstick of overwhelming need, of fervent aspirations for improvement which political leadership fears to disappoint, and of anxiety lest failure to fulfill by democratic methods the dreams the West itself has aroused by its faith in technology and science may cause the frustrated and the disappointed to turn to dictatorship as the way out.

Because of this understandable divergence in outlook, it seems not only desirable, but imperative, that both the Western givers of aid and the non-Western recipients pool their offerings and their needs not through bilateral arrangements which create an often oversensitive relationship between the benefactor and the beneficiary, but through the United Nations and its constellation of specialized agencies, where both sides are represented on an equal basis, and suspicion of each other's motives can be reduced to a minimum. The success of the Colombo Plan, whose financial resources are modest compared to the over-all aid given directly to individual nations by the United States, is due primarily to the cooperative character of its operations, which bring giver and recipient together in the planning and fulfillment of what then becomes a common enterprise. The channeling of all available aid through the United Nations, moreover, would open up the possibility that the West and the U.S.S.R., instead of engaging in an economic competition for the favors of underdeveloped nations, might work together for the common good.

It is in the United Nations that the West and the non-West, profoundly different as they may seem today, find a common meeting-ground. The UN, in spite of its weaknesses —and these weaknesses are inherent not in the idea of international cooperation but in the reluctance, hitherto, of sovereign nations to entrust greater authority to the international organization—is a prototype of what Alfred Lord Tennyson envisaged as "the parliament of man." In its glass skyscraper facing the East River in a port city which has long symbolized a welcome from the Statue of Liberty to the world's weary and oppressed, the UN brings together, on a basis of an equal vote for each state, all religious faiths, all ideologies, all races and colors of mankind in a way that has not been, and cannot be, attained in the parliament of any national state, no matter how multiracial its population. Here the great powers of the West, which, in the international community, once played the role of overlords, saying to this colonial people "go, and he goeth," or that other, "come, and he cometh," can now be questioned, challenged, opposed, and even overruled by the weak and the small, whenever the weak and small cooperate with each other for a common objective.

Here the vast changes that have taken place since World War II in the relationships between West and non-West are made evident in a way that may escape us elsewhere. What was once, in various eras of history, the Concert of Powers, or the Holy Alliance, or the Big Four or the Big Three—and what is still, through an arrangement which some day will seem as atavistic as the appendix, the veto-wielding Big Five in the Security Council—can no longer determine the destiny of the more than half of the world's population who live in Asia and eastern Europe, the Middle East, Africa, and Latin America.

The majority of the world's peoples, as one can see at a glance in the UN, are nonwhite. But it is not color which reduces the Western nations to a minority in the UN forum. It is the community of political experience, of economic aspirations and social struggle, that creates a common denominator between the Afro-Asian bloc, which at Bandung held the first conference in history of nations from the eastern Mediterranean to the Pacific without the presence of white men, and the countries of Latin America, settled for the most part, like the United States, by immigrants from Europe, who found there indigenous Indians and brought there African slaves.

When working together the non-Western nations can, and as the threat of nuclear war which caused some of them to support the West against U.S.S.R. recedes they increasingly will, influence the decisions of the UN. They do not aspire to conquer the West. They are not engaged in a crusade against Western ideas. There is no indication, as Bandung amply demonstrated, of the "rising tide of color" or "the yellow peril," which was a bugaboo of the early twentieth century. What non-Westerners ask of the West is freedom to shape their own destinies as they see fit, and assistance in liberating themselves as rapidly as possible from the shackles of hunger, poverty, disease, and illiteracy. They want to be free to decide whether or not to join Western military alliances—SEATO and the Baghdad pact—or not to join them; whether or not to accept arms and trade with the Soviet bloc. Once they have achieved independence they may choose interdependence with the West—through the British Commonwealth or the French Union. What they insist on is the right to choose for themselves. And this, as they see it, is the fundamental right promised by democracy.

Because of their preoccupation with economic and social

problems, and particularly because of their hope that atomic energy will speed the modernization of their agriculture and the industrialization of their economy, the non-Western nations will enhance the importance of the Economic and Social Council, as well as of the Trusteeship Council dealing with territories which are not as yet self-governing. By relentlessly holding up to the Western powers and to the U.S.S.R., now also a great power through its achievement of industrialization, the promises they have made in the past, the non-Western peoples will, as the weak and humble have often done in history, win victories by the sheer weight of their moral appeal. And by seeing themselves as mirrored in the minds of the non-West, the Western powers will achieve greater understanding both of their own strengths and their own weaknesses—and of ways in which they can increase the first and reduce the second.

For the heart of the matter is that while there is, and it must be hoped there always will be, great diversity between the many civilizations of the earth, there are no basic differences between the human beings who compose them. Black and white, and brown and yellow, Muslim, Hindu, Buddhist, Christian, Jew, pagan, or atheist, men and women of West and non-West are moved by the same hopes and fears, the same aspirations and anxieties. There is no real differential between West and non-West except that created by the West's chronologically earlier acquisition of technology. This differential is being rapidly reduced, and will be eventually eliminated, as technology becomes increasingly available to non-Western peoples. The Industrial Revolution is a great leveler. It knows nothing of differentiation by race and color. It can serve with equal efficiency democracy and communism. It can erase the disparity between the advanced and the backward.

The Industrial Revolution can also produce the ultimate equalizer for all mankind—the knowledge that any future war would have to be waged with nuclear weapons, and that the resulting havoc, even if it did not destroy all life on earth, could destroy the means of future industrialization which we would no longer have the raw materials to replace. This prospect deprives the great powers of the advantage they have had for centuries over the non-Western peoples—the advantage of superior weapons—and gives the weaker underdeveloped nations the opportunity to use the weapon Gandhi made his own—the weapon of nonviolent moral suasion.

Selected Readings

1. Many Centuries in One

Brinton, Clarence Crane. *Ideas and Men: The Story of Western Thought*. New York: Prentice-Hall, Inc., 1950.

———. *The Shaping of the Modern Mind* (Concluding half of *Ideas and Men*). New York: New American Library (Mentor Books, No. MD 173), 1953.

Clough, Shepard B., and Cole, Charles W. *Economic History of Europe* (3rd ed.). Boston: D. C. Heath & Company, 1952.

Hammond, John L., and Hammond, Barbara B. *The Rise of Modern Industry* (8th ed.). New York: British Book Centre, Inc., 1953.

Rowland, Benjamin. *Art in East and West*. Cambridge, Massachusetts: Harvard University Press, 1955.

Toynbee, Arnold J. *The World and the West*. New York and London: Oxford University Press, Inc., 1953.

Zinkin, Maurice. *Asia and the West* (new rev. ed.). New York: Institute of Pacific Relations, 1953.

2. Russia: Non-Western Communism

Hammond, Thomas T. "Yugoslavia Between East and West." *Headline Series* No. 108. New York: Foreign Policy Association, November-December 1954.

Mosely, Philip E. "Russia After Stalin." *Headline Series* No. 111. New York: Foreign Policy Association, May-June 1955.

Roberts, Henry L. *Russia and America: Dangers and Prospects*. New York: Harper & Brothers for the Council on Foreign Relations, 1956; New American Library (Mentor Books, No. MD 182), 1956.

Salisbury, Harrison E. *American in Russia*. New York: Harper & Brothers, 1955.

Stevens, Leslie C. *Russian Assignment*. Boston: Little, Brown & Co., 1953.

Sumner, Benedict H. *A Short History of Russia* (rev. ed.). New York: Harcourt, Brace & Co., 1949.

Novels and Plays

Chekhov, Anton P. *The Cherry Orchard.*
Dostoevski, Fedor M. *The Brothers Karamazov.*
———. *The Possessed.*
Ehrenburg, Ilya G. *The Thaw.* Chicago: Henry Regnery Co., 1955.
Gorki, Maksim. *The Lower Depths.*
Sholokhov, Mikhail A. *And Quiet Flows the Don.*
Tolstoi, Count Lev N. *The Resurrection.*
Turgenev, Ivan S. *Fathers and Sons.*

3. Middle East: Islam versus Westernism

Badeau, John S., and Nolte, Richard H. "The Emergence of Modern Egypt." *Headline Series* No. 98. New York: Foreign Policy Association, March-April 1953.
Gibb, H. A. R. *Mohammedanism.* New York: New American Library (Mentor Books, No. M 136), 1955.
Lehrman, Harold A. *Israel.* New York: William Sloane Associates, Inc., 1952.
The Meaning of the Glorious Koran, trans. by Marmaduke Pickthall. New York: New American Library (Mentor Books, No. MD 94), 1953.
Nasser, Gamal A. *Egypt's Liberation: The Philosophy of Revolution.* Washington, D. C.: Public Affairs Press, 1955.
Polk, William R., and Butler, W. Jack. "What the Arabs Think." *Headline Series* No. 96. New York: Foreign Policy Association, November-December 1952.
Thomas, Lewis V., and Frye, Richard N. *The United States and Turkey and Iran.* Cambridge, Massachusetts: Harvard University Press, 1951.

4. India and Pakistan: Anglo-Asian Synthesis

Bouquet, Alan C. *Hinduism.* New York: Longmans, Green & Co., Inc., 1950.
Bowles, Chester. *Ambassador's Report.* New York: Harper & Brothers, 1954.
Gandhi, Mohandas K. *Gandhi's Autobiography.* Washington, D. C.: Public Affairs Press, 1948.

Nehru, Jawaharlal. *Independence and After*. New York: The John Day Company, 1950.

———. *Toward Freedom: The Autobiography of Jawaharlal Nehru*. New York: The John Day Company, 1941.

Rowland, Benjamin. *The Art and Architecture of India: Buddhist, Hindu, Jain*. Pelican History and Art Series. Baltimore: Penguin Books, Inc., 1953.

The Song of God: Bhagavad-Gita, trans. by Swami Prabhavananda and Christopher Isherwood. New York: New American Library (Mentor Books, No. M 103), 1954.

Spear, T. G. Percival. *India, Pakistan, and the West* (2nd ed.). New York and London: Oxford University Press, Inc., 1949.

Symonds, Richard. *The Making of Pakistan*. Hollywood-by-the-Sea, Fla.: Transatlantic Arts, Inc., 1950.

Novels and Plays

Kalidasa. *Sakuntala*, trans. by Arthur Ryder. New York: E. P. Dutton & Co., Inc. (Everyman's Library, No. 629).

Markandaya, Kamala. *Nectar in a Sieve*. New York: The John Day Company, 1954; New American Library (Signet Books No. S1336), 1956.

Narayan, R. K. *The Financial Expert*. East Lansing, Michigan: Michigan State College Press, 1953.

Rama Rau, Santha. *Remember the House*. New York: Harper & Brothers, 1956.

5. China: Confucius and the Commissars

Fairbank, John K. *The United States and China*. Cambridge, Massachusetts: Harvard University Press, 1948.

Fitzgerald, Charles P. *Revolution in China*. New York: Frederick A. Praeger, Inc., 1952.

Goodrich, L. Carrington. *A Short History of the Chinese People* (rev. ed.). New York: Harper & Brothers, 1951.

Latourette, Kenneth S. *The Chinese: Their History and Culture* (3rd ed. rev.). 2 vols. New York: The Macmillan Company, 1946.

———. *A History of Modern China*. Harmondsworth, England: Penguin Books, 1954.

Rostow, Walt W., and Others. *The Prospects for Communist China*. New York: John Wiley & Sons, Inc., 1954.

Walker, Richard L. *China Under Communism: The First Five*

Years. New Haven, Connecticut: Yale University Press, 1955.

Novels

Buck, Pearl. *The Good Earth.*
Hersey, John. *A Single Pebble*. New York: Alfred A. Knopf, Inc., 1956.

6. Japan: Asian Westernism

Borton, Hugh. *Japan's Modern Century*. New York: The Ronald Press Company, 1955.
Lockwood, William W. *The Economic Development of Japan: Growth and Structural Change, 1868-1938*. Princeton, N. J.: Princeton University Press, 1954; London: Oxford University Press, Inc., 1955.
Quigley, Harold S., and Turner, John E. *The New Japan: Government and Politics*. Minneapolis: University of Minnesota Press, 1956.
Sansom, George B. *Japan: A Short Cultural History* (rev. ed.). New York: Appleton-Century-Crofts, Inc., 1943.
———. *The Western World and Japan: A Study in the Interaction of European and Asiatic Cultures*. New York: Alfred A. Knopf, Inc., 1950; London: Cresset Press, Ltd., 1950.
Webb, Herschel. *An Introduction to Japan*. New York: Columbia University Press, 1955.

Novels

Dazai, Osumi. *The Setting Sun*, trans. by Donald Keene. New York: New Directions, 1956.
Tanizaki, Junichiro. *Some Prefer Nettles*, trans. by Edward G. Seidensticker. New York: Alfred A. Knopf, Inc., 1955.

7. Southeast Asia: Non-Western Pluralism in Transition

Emerson, Rupert. *Representative Government in Southeast Asia*. Cambridge, Massachusetts: Harvard University Press, 1955.
Harrison, Brian. *South-East Asia: A Short History*. New York: St. Martin's Press, Inc., 1954. London: Macmillan & Co., Ltd., 1954.
Mende, Tibor. *Southeast Asia Between Two Worlds*. New York: Library Publishers, 1955.

Mills, Lennox A., and Associates. *The New World of Southeast Asia.* Minneapolis: University of Minnesota Press, 1949; London: Oxford University Press, Inc., 1950.

Sjahrir, Soetan. *Out of Exile,* trans. by Charles E. Wolf, Jr. New York: The John Day Company, 1949.

Thompson, Virginia M., and Adloff, Richard. *Minority Problems in Southeast Asia.* Stanford, Calif.: Stanford University Press, 1955.

8. Africa: The Impact of the West

Bartlett, Vernon. *Struggle for Africa.* New York: Frederick A. Praeger, Inc., 1953. London: Frederick Muller, Ltd., 1953.

Carter, Gwendolen M. "South Africa." *Headline Series* No. 109. New York: Foreign Policy Association, January-February 1955.

Macmillan, William M. *Africa Emergent.* Toronto: Ryerson Press, 1938. London: Faber & Faber, Ltd., 1938.

Segy, Ladislas. *African Sculpture Speaks* (2nd ptg.). New York: A. A. Wyn, Inc., 1955.

Westermann, Diedrich. *Africa Today and Tomorrow* (3rd ed.). New York and London: Oxford University Press, Inc., 1949.

Novels

Abrahams, Peter. *Mine Boy.* New York: Alfred A. Knopf, Inc., 1955. London: Faber & Faber, Ltd., 1954.

———. *A Wreath for Udomo.* New York: Alfred A. Knopf, Inc., 1956.

Cary, Joyce. *Mr. Johnson.* New York: Harper & Brothers, 1951.

Paton, Alan. *Cry, the Beloved Country.* New York: Charles Scribner's Sons, 1950.

9. Latin America: Where Westernism Stopped

Hanson, Simon G. *Economic Development in Latin America.* Washington, D. C.: Inter-American Affairs Press, 1951.

Herring, Hubert C. *A History of Latin America: From the Beginnings to the Present.* New York: Alfred A. Knopf, Inc., 1955.

Humphreys, Robin A. *The Evolution of Modern Latin America.* New York: Oxford University Press, Inc., 1946.

Schurz, William L. *This New World: The Civilization of Latin America.* New York: E. P. Dutton & Co., Inc., 1954.

Williams, Mary W., Bartlett, Ruhl J., and Miller, Russell E. *The People and Politics of Latin America* (4th ed.). Boston: Ginn & Company, 1955.

10. Telescoped Revolutions: Colonialism—Democracy—Communism—Nationalism

Bingham, Jonathan B. *Shirt-Sleeve Diplomacy: Point Four in Action.* New York: The John Day Co., 1954.

Kohn, Hans. *The Idea of Nationalism.* New York: The Macmillan Co., 1944.

Shafer, Boyd C. *Nationalism: Myth and Reality.* New York: Harcourt, Brace & Co., 1955. London: Victor Gollancz, Ltd., 1955.

Staley, Eugene. *The Future of Underdeveloped Countries.* New York: Harper & Brothers for the Council on Foreign Relations, 1954. London: Royal Institute of International Affairs, 1954.

11. Retooling for the Future

Dean, Vera M. "New Patterns of Democracy in India." *Yale Review,* Vol. 43, No. 2 (Winter 1953), pp. 161-76.

Fainsod, Merle. *How Russia Is Ruled.* Cambridge, Massachusetts: Harvard University Press, 1953; London: Oxford University Press, Inc., 1954.

Laqueur, Walter Z. "The Appeal of Communism in the Middle East," *The Middle East Journal,* Vol. 9, No. 1 (Winter 1955), pp. 17-27.

Mead, Margaret (ed.). *Cultural Patterns and Technical Change.* New York: United Nations Educational, Scientific and Cultural Organization, 1953. Distributed by International Documents Service of Columbia University Press, New York. New American Library (Mentor Books, No. MD 134), 1955.

Murphy, Gardner. *In the Minds of Men: The Study of Human Behavior and Social Tensions in India.* New York: Basic Books, Inc., 1953.

Population and Food

Osborn, Fairfield. *Our Plundered Planet.* Boston: Little, Brown & Co., 1948. London: Faber & Faber, Ltd., 1948.
Population Bulletin. Published eight times a year by Population Reference Bureau, Washington, D. C.
Sax, Karl. *Standing Room Only: The Challenge of Overpopulation.* Boston: Beacon Press, 1955.
"Scientists Vision New Civilization for 21st Century." *The New York Times,* May 21, 1956, p. 1, col. 1, and all of p. 19. This article summarizes a study, entitled *Resources of the World: A Speculative Projection,* made by faculty members of the California Institute of Technology for major American corporations. At present the study itself is not available to the public.
Vogt, William. *Road to Survival.* New York: William Sloane Associates, 1948. London: Victor Gollancz, Ltd., 1949.

Can Science Cancel Time?

Bowles, Chester. *The New Dimensions of Peace.* New York: Harper & Brothers, 1955.
Calder, P. Ritchie. *Science in Our Lives.* East Lansing, Michigan: Michigan State College Press, 1955. New York: New American Library (Signet Key Books, No. Ks 320), 1955.
Kaempffert, Waldemar. "The Many Uses of the Atom." *Headline Series* No. 117. New York: Foreign Policy Association, May-June 1956.
President's Materials Policy Commission. *Resources for Freedom* (A report to the President). 5 vols. Washington, D. C.: United States Government Printing Office, June 1952.
Putnam, Palmer C. *Energy in the Future.* Princeton, N. J.: D. Van Nostrand Co., Inc., 1953. London: Macmillan & Co., Ltd., 1954.
"Scientists Vision New Civilization for 21st Century." (*See* above).

Land versus Industry

Buchanan, Norman S., and Ellis, Howard S. *Approaches to Economic Development.* New York: The Twentieth Century Fund, 1955.
Cressey, George B. *Asia's Lands and Peoples* (2nd ed.). New York: McGraw-Hill Book Co., 1951.
Goodfriend, Arthur. *What Can a Man Do?* New York: Farrar, Straus & Cudahy, Inc., 1953.
United States Business Abroad Case Studies. Various titles published irregularly by National Planning Association, Washington, D. C.

Zinkin, Maurice. *Problems of Economic Development in Asia* (rev. ed.). New York: Institute of Pacific Relations, 1954.

Who Pays for What?

Buchanan, Norman S., and Ellis, Howard S. *Approaches to Economic Development.* New York: The Twentieth Century Fund, 1955.
Committee for Economic Development, Research and Policy Committee. *Economic Development and the Role of American Foreign Investment* (A statement on national policy). New York: CED, February 1956.
International Development Advisory Board. *Partners in Progress* (A report to the President). New York: Simon & Schuster, Inc., 1951.
Myrdal, Gunnar. *An International Economy: Problems and Prospects.* New York: Harper & Brothers, 1956.
Staley, Eugene. *The Future of Underdeveloped Countries.* New York: Harper & Brothers for the Council on Foreign Relations, 1954. London: Royal Institute of International Affairs, 1954.
United Nations Department of Economic Affairs. *Commodity Trade and Economic Development.* New York: United Nations, 1953. Publication Sales No.: 1954.II.B.1. Distributed by International Documents Service of Columbia University Press, New York.

12. West and Non-West: The Heart of the Matter

Arnold, G. L. *The Pattern of World Conflict.* New York: Dial Press, 1955.
Kahin, George McTurnan. *The Asian-African Conference, Bandung, Indonesia, April 1955.* Ithaca, N.Y.: Cornell University Press, 1956.
Panikkar, Kavalam M. *Asia and Western Dominance.* New York: The John Day Co., 1954. London: George Allen & Unwin, Ltd., 1953.
Reischauer, Edwin O. *Wanted: An Asian Policy.* New York: Alfred A. Knopf, Inc., 1955.
Steadman, John. "The Myth of Asia." *The American Scholar,* Vol. 25, No. 2 (Spring 1956), pp. 163-175.
Sukarno. "Speech by His Excellency President Sukarno to the Foreign Policy Association in New York on 24 May 1956." New York: Information Office of the Consulate General of the Republic of Indonesia.

Index

Abdullah, Sheikh 90
Adaptation of Marxism 27-28
Adenauer, Konrad 69
Administration 25
Advocates of Westernization 256
Afghanistan 22
Africa 13, 14, 17, 19, 21, 154-72, Agriculture Rights 159, Cultures 158, 162, Democracy 171, Development 88, 167-69, Economic Life 160-67, Education 165-66, 169, Gold 156, Government 157, *Idiong* Society 161, Languages 154-57, Major Revision 171, Origin of Man 156, Political Structure 157-58, Production Efficiency 155-56, Projects 166, Religion 159-65, Ritual Murders 161, Self-Determination 170, Slave Trade 162-63, Social Security 167, Soviet Activities 172, Territories 154, Transition 162-63, University Education 170, Use of Cattle 159
Age of Exploration 18
Agriculture 159, 184, 228, 231, 232
Akbar 18
Algeria 28, Parliament Representation 28, Population 28
Almond, Gabriel 209
American Revolution 15, 19, 32, 178
Anglo-Iranian Co. 199
Anti-Colonial Rule 198-99
Anti-Greek Riots 55
Anti-Westernism 48, 190
Aramco 218
Arbenz, Jacobo 192, 216, 238
Argentinia 21, 22
  Peron 21, 214
Armas, Colonel 216, 238
Asia, Southeast 13-14, 19, 21, 26, 28, 30, 131-53, Communism 150-52, Crop Enterprises to World Market 133-34, Democracy 152, Economic Factors 131, 133, 146, 147, 148, 149, Education 140, Employment Possibilities 140, Gateway to Indian and Pacific Oceans 131, Hindu Caste System 134, Hostility to Western Rule 190, Independent Nationhood 131, Industrialization 147, Japanese Conquest 141, 149, Natural Resources 131, New Fields 141, Opening to Trade 134, Organized Labor 148, Political Democracy 149, 152-53, Resources 147-48, Western Influence 132
Asoka 18
Ataturk, Mustafa Kemal 50-53, 55, 59, 206, 214, 215, Communist 52, Abolishes Caliphate 52, Destroys Religion of Islam 51, Economic Reforms 52, Political Democratization 53
Atomic Development 218-19, 228, 233-35, 262, 268
Atomic Energy 19, 27, 30, 31, 166, 210, 229, 233, 234, 235, 252
Attitude in World Affairs 86-87
Awasi League 85

Baghdad Pact 68
Balfour Declaration 62

Bandungia, The Land of 13-16, Conference 61, 131, 146, 260, Creating Economy 15, Development of 14-16, Financial and Technical Assistance 15-16, Knowledge Accumulated by West 14, Rediscovering 16, Transition Period 16
Ben-Gurion 65, 69
Beria, Lavrenti 37
Bhave, Vinoba 81-82
Bolshevik Revolution 26, 34-36, 139, 198
Boycott, 67, 69
British Colonies 29, Cyprus 29, Malta 29
Buck, Pearl 259
Buddhism 23, 24, 73, 96, 132, 226, 247
Buell, Raymond Leslie 154
Buenos Aires 17, 34
Bulganin, Nikolai A. 44, 83
Bureaucracy 95

Capital to Finance Development 244-54
CARE 250
Caste System 75-79, 134
Catherine the Great 32-33
Catholics 50, 52, 132, 136, 164, 173, 176-77, 180, 216, 226, 255, 258
Chadayev, Peter 256
Changes in Western World 19
Changing Africa 156
Chekov, Anton 259
China 22, 23, 92-112, Administration 25, Bureaucracy 95, Changes within 102, Civilization 92-101, Communism 22, 110, Confucian Ethics 95-97, Downfall of Empire 100-101, Government 98-99, Inflation 107, Invasion 105, Japanese Aggression 104-05, Japanese Surrender 107, Manchuria 104, Nationalists vs Communists 108, Rebellions 106, Recognition as New Republic 102, Recovering Ice-free Harbors 30, Soviet Cooperation 102-04, "Soviet Republic" 104, Three People's Principles 102, Unification 103, War with Japan 105, Western Influence 99-102
Ching-wei, Wang 105
Christianity 19, 25, 49, 72, 139, 160, 164, 172, 180, 258
Christian Missions 250
Christian Crusaders 74
Churchill, Winston 23, 197
Civilization 92-101, 173
"Collective Leadership" 42
Colombo Plan 91
Colonialism 49, 133, 138, 192, 193-211, 238, 260, Africa 155, 171-72, Denouncement 260, Latin America 172, 178, 192, Middle East 48-49, Revolts Against 198, 200, Russian 199, Southeast Asia 133-145
Colonial Powers 28, 145, 209, 220
Colonial Rule 170, 177, 178, 205-06
Colonies 28, 194
"Colossus of the North" 189
Colson, Elizabeth 158
Communism vs Democracy 201-204
Communist Influence 15, 68-69, 82-83, 90, 109, 130
Communist Rise to Power 29-30
Communists and Communism 15-16, 18, 193-214, 238, Comes to Power 36-38, Control in Japan 128, *Manifesto* 20, Dictatorship in Yugoslavia 46, Establish Rule 27, Gaining Influence 15, In India 82-83, Victory in China 109
"Competitive Co-Existence" 27
Conference of American States 192
Confucianism 23, 24, 95, 100, 110, 111, 226
Congress of Panama 191
Conquistadors 176, 179
"Containment" of Russia 29-30
Control of Population 226-27
Cornut-Gentille, High Commissioner 154
Creation of Pakistan 72
Creative Years 19

Cultivation 19, 24, 46, 54, 133, 140-41, Agricultural Rights 159, Techniques 20, 24-25, 123, 133-34, 146, 155, 175, 176, 182-84, 205, 218, Atomic Energy 233, Aviation and Desert 19, Irrigation 25, 89-90, Opening New Lands 41-42, Modernizing Agriculture 228, 231-32
Culture 50, 113-14
Cyprus 54, Cypriotes 55
Czechoslovakia 60, Leadership in Soviet Program 199-200, Skoda Armaments 60

Dai, Emperor Bao 213
"Damn Yankees" Resentment 216
Danger of Communism 202
Danielevsky, Nikolai 256
Dazai, Osumi 259
Democracy 121-22, 140, 171, 193-211
Democratic Socialism 46
Denunciation of Native Rulers 213
Development 14-16, 53-54, 59, 61, 67, 70, 88, 152, 167-69, 186-88, 224-26, Between Land and Industry 236, Different Stages 18-19, of Western Countries 52
Development of Modern Weapons 30
Diem, Premier 238
Djilas, Milovan 46
Discrimination 77
Dostoyevsky 33
Dulles, John Foster 211

Economic and Financial Reforms 217-18
Economic Problem 217-20, 240-244
Economic and Social Changes 131, 133, 146, 147, 148, 206-207, 217-18, 220, 240-244
Economic Strangulation 69
Education 170
Egypt 21, 23, 55-61, Arms Purchasing 60-61, Community Development Projects 59, Developing National Personality 61, Facing Handicaps 56, Economic and Social Reform 58-59, Financial Resources 60, Intervention of Western Powers 64, 68, Limited Financial Resources 60, Military Government 56, Naguib 21, Nasser 21, New Constitution 60, Purchases Armament 68, Population 58, Policy 57-58, Revolution 55, Trading 60, Welcomes Return to Russia 68-69
Egyptian Invasion 69
Eisenhower, Pres. 23, 235, 252, Administration 252
Emancipation of Serfs 20, 35
Engels, Friedrich 27, 196, 198, 263
England 29, 32, Containment of Russia 29-30
English Revolution 15, 21, 32, 34
Enterprise, Private and Individual 23
Eurasians 145
Euratom 234
European Administration System 164
European Atomic Project 234
Export-Import Bank 249

Failure to Understand 114
Fascists 20
Federation of French West Africa 171
Federation of Rhodesia and Nyasaland 166, 168
Financial Assistance 15-16, 166, 168, 217-18, 244-54, 250-51
Five-Year Plan 39
Forced Labor 17, 19, 21, 32, 178, 194, 206
Foreign Trade 184
Fuel Shortage 233

Gandhi, Mahatma 34, 72, 81, 84, 88, 263
Gateway to Indian and Pacific Oceans 131
Germany 20, 51, Arab Boycott 69, Nazi Era 26
Ghulam, Bakshi Mohammed 90
Gomulka 211

Good Neighbor Policy 190
Gorky, Maxim 35
Government 98-99, 215-17
Grand Council 154
Great Zimbabwe Ruins 156

Harris, Joel Chandler 162
Height of Japanese Power 113
Henry VIII 18, 207
Herzen, Alexander 33, 256
Hinduism 23, 24, 51, 71-75, 132, 226, 247
Hindu-Muslim Riots 213, 265
Hitler 37, 63, 265
Hoover, Herbert 190
Hostility to Western Rule 190
Hydroelectric Power 166

IBRD 166, 168, 250-51
ICA 250
IFC 251
Independent Nationhood 131, 174, 177-78
Independent States 170
India 13, 17, 25, 71-91, Achieves Independence 82, Criticism of Indian System 81, Caste System 75-79, 134, Division with Pakistan 71, 79, Eisenhower Talks 83, Economic Development 81-82, Communist Influence 90, Riots 89-90, Five-Year Plan 39, Foreign Policy 83, Gandhi Policy 84, Language Barrier 78-80, Independence from Britain 72, Population 78-79, Prohibits Discrimination 77, Religion 72-75, Repressing Communism 83, Social Revolution 78, State Reorganization 80-83
Indian Civil Service 217
Indian Congress 206
Indian National Congress 82
Indirect Rule Imposed by Dutch 136-37
Industrial Expansion 222
Industrialization 30, 38-39, 121, 123, 147, 185
Industry 18
Inflation 124-25
Institut Français d'Afrique 162
Inter-American Cooperation 191
Inter-American System 191
Internal Problems 54, 150-53
International Bank for Reconstruction and Development 166, 168, 250-51
International Cooperation Administration 191, 250
International Finance Corporation 251
International Institute of Differing Civilizations 169
Intervention 67-68
Invasion of India 71
Iraq 57, 68, Britain's Ally 57, Rival of Egypt 68
Iron Curtain Camp 170, 200, 262
Islam 23, 24-25, 72-75, 160, 172, A Monotheistic Faith 73
Islam vs Westernism 48-70
Israel 49, Absorbing Jews 62, Competing in West 67, Boycott 67, Creation of New State 49, Dilemma 61, 66, Economy 65-67, "Economic Strangulation" 67, Export Trade 67, Future Development 69-70, Histradut 65, 67, Influx of Immigrants 65, Intervention of Western Powers 67-68, Invasion of Egypt 69, Palestine War 56, "Promised Land" 48-49, Population 62, 65, Target for Anti-Western Feeling 48, "War of Liberation" 62-63, War with Arabs 63
Issawi, Charles 208

Jamal-ud-Din al-Afghani 61
Japan 23, 31, 39, 101, Aggression in China 113, Attack on Pearl Harbor 105, 113-14, 125, Banking System 120, Communism 130, Culture 113-14, Earthquake 114-15, 124, Economic Development 122, 124, 125-26, 128, 129, Education 121-22, Failure to Understand West 114, Financial Policies 124, Foreign Relations 129, Industry 121, Industrialization 38-39, 123, Inflation 124-25, Meiji Era

119-22, Manchuria 104, 124, Manners and Customs 122-23, Occupation 126, 133, Recognition of Russian Rights 30, Recovery 126, Religion 116-119, Traditions 113-14, Treaty with United States 127, War with China 105-09
Japanese Conquest 113, 141, 149, 104-107, Occupation 126, 133
Jefferson, Thomas 194
Jinnah, Mohammed Ali 72, 85
Joint Committee on Atomic Energy 233
Judaism 25, 49

Kai-shek, Chiang 103-05, 108, 208-09
Karachi Government 85
Kashmir 89-91, Plebiscite 90, Population 89, Riots 89
Key Problem, Middle East 48-70
Khan, Kublai 114
Khrushchev, Nikita S. 44, 45, 85
King Farouk 52, 55-56, 213, 216
King of Siam 17
Kohn, Hans 254
Koran 49-50, 72, 84-85
Korean War 127-30, 147, 187
Kuomintang Military Academy 102-05

Labor, Forced 17, 23-24
Land Redistribution 20-21, 58, 238
Land Reform 58, 183, 239
Lands to be Discovered 13-14
Land vs Industry 236-44
Languages 53, 79-80, 154-57, 176-77
Laws of the Indies 182
Latin America 13, 17, 19, 21, 173-92, Agriculture 184, Civilization 173, Colonialism 173, 178, Conquistadors 176, 179, Cultures 173, Economic Development 186-88, Foreign Trade 184, Independence 174, 177-178, Industries 184, Land Reform 182-83, Language 176-77, Point Four Program 191, Politics 17, 186-87, Population 176-82, 186, Production 181, Resources 175, 184-185, Territorial Disputes 189, "Yankee Imperialism" 194
Leaders Emerge 213-15
Leaders, Soviet 39, 46, 211
League of Nations 48, 104
Lease on Ice-free Harbors 30
Lenin 35, 43, 46, 110, 196, 198, 206, 214, 237, 253, 254, 257
"Liberation" of Southeast Asia claimed 142-43
Lincoln, Abraham 194
Livingstone, David 164
Logan, Joshua 260
London Missionary Society 164
Louis XIV 207
Lyautey, Marshal 61

MacArthur, Gen. Douglas 125, 238
Magna Charta 24, 33, 34
Magsaysay 153
Major Revision in Africa 171
Makarios, Archbishop 55
Malthus, Thomas Robert 220-222, 228
Manchuria, 104, 105, 107, 109
Markandaya, Kamala 259
Marshall, Gen. George C. 108
Marshall Plan 250, 262
Marx, Karl 27, 31, 35, 46, 109, 110, 196, 198, 203, 255, 257, 263
Mau Mau 165
Meek, C. K. 159
Mehta, G. L. 265
Meiji Era 39, 119-23
Menderes, Premier Adnan 54
Mendés-France Pierre 28
Middle-East, Key Problem 48-70, Anti-Westernism feeling 48, Modern Way of Life 49, Rejection of Infidels 48-59
Military Campaigns, Anti-Communist 107-08
Mill, John Stuart 194, 206
Mindzenty, Cardinal 23
Minh, Ho Chi 149, 238
Mirza, General Iskander 214, 265
Modern Way of Life 49

Modernization 55, 58, 112, Turkey 55, Egypt 58, China 112
Mollett, Guy 28
Molotov, Vyacheslav M. 36
Monroe Doctrine 177, 190
More, Sir Thomas 23
Mossadegh 259
Mulk, Anand 89
Muslim Brotherhood 50, 52, 59, 216, 259, Accepting fellowship 70, Adapting to Modern Life 51, Culture 50, Establishment of State 72, Invasion of India 71, League 85, 206, 212, Dilemma 50-51, Religion 72-76, 132, Use of Violence 74

Naguib, General 55, 56, 60, 206, 214
Nasser, Colonel Gamal Abdel 47, 49, 55, 56, 57, 60, 61, 67, 210, 214, 215, 254, 259, 261
Nazi Era 26, 193, 196, 199, 228
Nazism 193, 228
Nationalists in China 106-08, 111
NATO 55
Nehru 47, 72, 79, 81-84, 90, 213, 214, 216, 237, 254, 261
New Inventions 19, Atomic Energy 19, A and H Bombs 30, Photosynthesis 19
Nigeria 28
Nkrumah 47
Non-Western Communism 26-47
North Atlantic Treaty Organization 191, 202
Nuclear Energy 27, A and H Bombs 30-31, 210, 252, Attacks 229, Center 234, Fuels 235, Guided Missiles 210, Nuclear Research Institute 234, Warfare 31, 125, 252

OAS 188, 191-92
Occupation in Japan 126
Occupation Policies 143-44
Opening of Southeast Asia to Western Trade 134-36
Organization of American States 188, 191-92
Organized Labor 148
Origin of Man 156
Ottoman Empire 48, 50, 51, 54, 56, 57, 61, 62

Pakistan 71-91, Attitude in World Affairs 86-87, Awami League 85, Church and State 72, Colombo Plan 91, Creation of 72, Devaluation of Currency 87-89, Division with India 71, Economic Development 87-88, Effect of Partition 87, Hindu-Muslem Riots 90, Kashmir 86-87, 89, 91, Political Problems 85, Population 85, Religion 73-75
Palestine 62-64, Immigration of Jews, 63-64, Mandate to Britain 62, Partition of 63
Partition Hardship 87
Pasha, Glubb 261
Patel, S. V. 79
Paton, Alan 259
Perón, Colonel Juan 36
Perry, Commodore Matthew 113, 115, 116, 118, 119, 178
Peter the Great 18, 33, 52
Pilsudski, Marshal 30
Pineau, Christian 252
Point Four Program 191, 250, 264
Political Changes 145
Political Problems 212-17, 219-220
Politics 17, 52-53, 57-58, 149, 152-53, 157-58, 186-87
Polo, Marco 13, 92, 95 *The Travels of,* 13
Population 20, 58, 62, 65, 72, 78-79, 89, 132-34, 176-82, 186, 220-28, Control 226-227, and Food 220-28, Egypt 58, India 72, 78-79, Japan 115, 128, Latin America 186, Pakistan 72, Southeast Asia 132-34, Western Nations 20
Primitive States 157
Problems faced by Governments 215-17
Problems of Agriculture 237-38

Purging of Leaders 37-38
Production 181

Rau, Santha Rama 259
Reformation The, 15, 32, 91, 92, In Egypt 58, Europe 50, Latin America 183
Rejection of Infidels 48-59
Religion 72-75, 110, 116-19, 159-65
Renaissance 15, 19, 32
Reorientation 218-19
Reparation Paid 69
Resistance to Foreign Rule 139-40
Retooling for Future 212-17
Revolutions 15, 17, 19, 55, 193-211, 238, American 15, 19, 32, 178, Bolshevik 36, English 15, 21, 32, 34, French 15, 19, 21, 32, 178, 194, 208, Hindu-Muslim 213, 265, Results which occur 21, Industrial 15, 19, 23, 32-33, 232, 236, 263, 268
Rhee, Dr. Syngman 214
Riots Fanned by Communists 55
Ritual Murders 161
Rockefeller, Nelson 190, 230, 251
Roberts, Prof. Henry L. 40
Roosevelt, Franklin D. 190, 194
Russia 17, 19, 21-23, Adaptation of Marxism 27-28, Autocracy of State and Church 34, Bolshevik Revolution 26, Collectivization 40, Collective Leadership 37, 44, Communist rise to Power 29-30, Concepts of Religion 31-33, Contacts 21-22, Development of Modern Weapons 30, Domination 199, *Duma* first Parliament 34, Economy 34-35, Emancipation of Serfs 20, Forced Labor Development 17, Freed Serfs 35, Geographic Description 29-30, Industrialization 30, Lease on Ice-free Harbors 30, Living Standards 22, Leaders 27-28, Leaders' Decision 39, Non-Western Communism 26-47, Parliament Representation 34, Period of Transition 35-36, Political Changes 38, Population 26, Purging of Top Leaders 37-38, Security 30, State Controlled 40-42, Strategical Weakness 30, System Established by Stalin 21, West's Judgment 26
Russo-Japanese War 30

SCAP 125-26
Science 288-36
SEATO 86, 151, 267
Separation of Church and State 17
Sharrett, Moshe 65, 69
Shinto 116
Siegfried, André 198
Singh, Maharajah 89
Sino-Japanese War 30
Smith, Edwin W. 160
Social Revolution 78
Southeast Asia 131-53, Colonial Rule 135, Communist Challenge 151, Democracy 153, Independent Nationhood 131, Japanese Conquest 141-42, Labor 148, Mineral Resources 147-48, Population 133, Religion 132, Social Structure 134, Western Education 138
Southeast Asia Treaty Organization 86, 151, 205
Soviet Union, Character of 28
Stabilizing World Prices 240
Stalin 37-38, 40-43, 46, 193, 214, 228, 253, 254, 257, Successors 198
State of Israel 62
State Planning Commission 38
States Reorganization Committee 79
Stepinac, Archbishop 23
Strategic Bases 253
Strategical Weakness 30
Suffrage, Universal 22-23
Sukarno 47, 153, 213, 214
SUNFED 252
Supreme Commander for the Allied Powers 125-26

Tanazaki 259
Teh, Chu 104
Tito, Marshal 45-47, 211, 214

Tokugawa Clan 118, 178
Tolstoy, Leo 34
Toynbee, Arnold 174, 261
Transformation of the West 19
Transition Period 16, 35-36, 45
Treaty of Kanagawa 113, 119
Trotsky 35, 43, 237
Truman, President 191, 250
Tse-tung, Mao 104, 206, 214
Turgenev 59
Turkey 13, 17, 31, 49-56, Anti-Greek Riots 55, Economic Problems 54, Emerges as Modern Western Way of Life 49, Gateway to the Middle East and Asia 54, Industrial Development 53-54, Internal Problems 54, Politics 52-53, Revolution 51-52, Riots fanned by Communists 55, Two-Party System 53, Under Ataturk's Rule 52
Ulema 49-50
Understanding the Middle East 14-15, Developing of 14-15, History 14-15
Understanding the Twentieth Century Problem 19
UNESCO 162
United Jewish Appeal 250
United Nations 24, 63, 64, 69, 90, 145, 159, 165, 166, 168, 181, 205, 253, 266-67, Atomic Agency 235, Special Funds for Economic Development 252, Trusteeship Council 159, 165, 171
United Nations Relief Agency 62
United States 15, 17, 30, Attack on Pearl Harbor 105, 113, 125, Foreign Relations 190, Illegal Entry 184, Technical Assistance 166, 168, Treaty Rights 190, Treaty with Japan 126-27
Universal Conscription 122
Universal Suffrage 22-24
U Nu, Premier of Burma 28, 47, 153, 213, 214, 254

Western Ideas Introduced 165
World Bank (IBRD) 89, 250-51
U.S.S. *Missouri* 124
Western Influence 99-102, 132
World War I 34, 44, 51, 102, 104, 124, 195, 238
World War II 32, 40, 50, 54, 78, 82, 108, 109, 113, 118, 127, 128, 132, 145, 161, 166, 167, 184, 188

"Yankee Imperialism" 188, 194
Yat-sen, Sun 101-03, 109
Yugoslavia Created 51, Communist Ruled 52, "Democratic Socialism" 46

MENTOR Books You Will Enjoy

Mentor Religious Classics

THE SONG OF GOD: BHAGAVAD-GITA
Introduction by Aldous Huxley. The timeless epic of Hindu faith vividly translated for Western readers by Prabhavananda and Isherwood. (#M103—35c)

THE UPANISHADS: Breath of the Eternal
Translated by Swami Prabhavananda and Frederick Manchester. Concerned with the knowledge of God and the highest aspects of religious truth, these ancient Hindu scriptures are presented for the Western reader in a faithful and readable translation. (#MD194—50c)

THE TEACHINGS OF THE COMPASSIONATE BUDDHA
Edited, with commentary by E. A. Burtt. The best translations of the basic texts and scriptures, early discourses, The Dhammapada, and later writings of a great religion. (#MD131—50c)

THE WAY OF LIFE: Tao Tê Ching
Lao Tzu. A new translation by R. B. Blakney of a masterpiece of ancient Chinese wisdom, presenting the philosophy of Taoism, second only to Confucianism in its influence on Eastern thought and life. (#M129—35c)

THE SAYINGS OF CONFUCIUS
A new translation by James R. Ware. The sayings of the great wise man of ancient China, a classic which teaches such ageless virtues of civilized men as duty, devotion to family, tradition, and justice to all. (#M151—35c)

Economics and Political Science

IDEAS OF THE GREAT ECONOMISTS
George Soule. This stimulating volume examines the views, times and lives of more than 50 great economists from ancient days to the present. (#M143—35c)

THE THEORY OF THE LEISURE CLASS
Thorstein Veblen. A challenging analysis of social conduct that ironically probes conspicuous consumption and the misuse of wealth. With an introduction by C. Wright Mills. (#MD93—50c)

THE PUBLIC PHILOSOPHY
Walter Lippmann. A penetrating analysis of the changing state of Western democracies, by one of America's most influential political commentators. (#M174—35c)

THE PRINCE
Niccolo Machiavelli, with an introduction by Christian Gauss. The classic work on statesmanship and power, revealing, in advice to a Renaissance prince, the techniques and strategy of gaining and keeping political control. (#M69—35c)

THE MEANING OF THE GLORIOUS KORAN
An explanatory translation by Mohammed Marmaduke Pickthall. The complete sacred book of Mohammedanism, translated with reverence and scholarship by a British Moslem. Invaluable insight into one of the world's great religions. (#MD94—50c)

History and Biography

THE WORLD OF HISTORY

Advisory editors: Crane Brinton, Alfred Kazin and John D. Hicks. A stimulating journey through the living past, this brilliant selection of the best in contemporary historical writing, makes it meaningful and exciting for the reader of today. Introduction by Allan Nevins. (#M109—35c)

THE USES OF THE PAST

Herbert J. Muller. A vigorous inquiry into the civilizations of the past, how they flourished, why they fell, and the meaning they hold for the present crisis of civilization. (#MD112—50c)

THE SHAPING OF THE MODERN MIND

Crane Brinton. The concluding half of *Ideas and Man*—a self-contained history of Western thought since the Renaissance — an outstanding summation of our past, a realistic examination of our present and a hopeful look into our future. (#MD173—50c)

OUT OF MY LIFE AND THOUGHT

Albert Schweitzer. With Postscript 1932-1949 by Everett Skillings. The remarkable autobiography of one of the 20th century's greatest men, who renounced an extraordinary career as musician, philosopher and theologian to become a medical missionary in Africa. (#MD83—50c)

HEREDITY, RACE AND SOCIETY (revised)

L. C. Dunn and Th. Dobzhansky. A fascinating study of group differences, how they arise, the influences of heredity and environment, and the prospects of race improvement through eugenics. (#MD199—50c)

Archaeology and Anthropology

REALM OF THE INCAS

Victor W. Von Hagen. The history, culture, religion, art, and social and economic life of an enthralling Indian race that achieved a fabulous empire before Columbus discovered America. Copiously illustrated. (#MD192—50c)

GROWING UP IN NEW GUINEA

Margaret Mead. A famous anthropologist's study of primitive adolescence throws new light on many problems of life today. (#M91—35c)

COMING OF AGE IN SAMOA

Margaret Mead. An illuminating study of adolescence in the South Pacific by the renowned anthropologist. (#MD153—50c)

SEX AND TEMPERAMENT in Three Primitive Societies

Margaret Mead. Are personality differences between men and women linked to their sex? A famous anthropologist explores this intriguing question. (#MD133—50c)

PATTERNS OF CULTURE

Ruth Benedict. A highly lauded anthropologist analyzes our social structure in relation to those of primitive cultures. (#MD89—50c)

THE MEANING OF THE DEAD SEA SCROLLS

A. Powell Davies. A provocative interpretation of one of the most important archaeological discoveries of recent times, ancient documents which revolutionize religious teachings and beliefs. (Signet Key #Ks339—35c)